# The University of Hertfordshire

# The University of Hertfordshire
## Sixty Years of Innovation

University of Hertfordshire Press

First published in Great Britain in 2012 by

**University of Hertfordshire Press**
College Lane
Hatfield
Hertfordshire
AL10 9AB
UK
© University of Hertfordshire 2012

**British Library Cataloguing in Publication Data**
A catalogue record for this book is available from the British Library
ISBN 978-1-907396-83-0

Design by **Whiteing Design Partnership**, Redbourn, Herts AL3 7PB

Printed in Great Britain by **Charlesworth Press,** Wakefield, WF2 9LP

*This book is dedicated to the many thousands of staff and students who have passed through the College, Polytechnic and University. The few who have been mentioned within these pages are representative of the endeavour, enterprise and commitment of the many.*

*'Even for a vigorous and forward-looking institution, as we hope we are, an occasional backward glance is not necessarily out of place.'*

**Sir Norman Lindop, Director of Hatfield Polytechnic (1975)**

# The University of Hertfordshire: Sixty Years of Innovation

# Acknowledgements

Much of the content for this book was researched and written by Julie Moore, who gained her PhD in History at the University of Hertfordshire. The editor also owes a considerable debt to the authors of two meticulously researched but unpublished histories of the institution's college and polytechnic days, one by Peter Jeffreys (Secretary and Registrar at the Polytechnic for twenty-one years), and the other by Peter Kingsford, whose considerable contribution to the institution is acknowledged within these pages.

Other former and present members of staff also contributed text and information. My thanks to Philip Waters, Gordon Brand, Gabriel Newfield, Bill Boardman, Jane Housham, Peter Comben, Alix Green, Jon Easter, Steve Corbett, Tim Hitchcock, Rob Slater, Reza Sotudeh, Richard Price, Judy Glasman, Sean Ryan, Helen Boak, Pat Wheeler, Mimi Tessier, Guy Thomas, Bill Forster, Clare Cletheroe and Angela Holland.

The process of piecing together this history was aided by the oral history interviews with former and current staff and students by Verusca Calabria, Andrew Green and Rudi Newman. Some of those interviewed also provided photographs, written accounts and other archival materials. Thanks to those who agreed to be interviewed or provided written accounts: Sir Tim Wilson, Sir Norman Lindop, Ernest Mackenzie, Quentin Appleton, Sir Stuart Matthews, Pat Wheeler, John Chapman, Jane Singleton, Paula Sands, David Howell, Barry Cross, Peter Comben, Gobi Ranganathan, Celine Samarasinhe, Ferdinand Da Costa, Alan Thomson, Jim Hough, Bill Boardman, Adrian Stokes, Peter Lines, Mary Read, Mary Thornton, Betty Ward, Graham Lane, Rhea Martin, Del Singh, Gabriel Newfield, Howard Burrell, Gordon Brand and Jane Blacklock. The Students' Union and Alumni team helped get the oral history project up and running. Nazima Dace and Kelly Goldsworthy kindly donated photographs of their student days in response to an Alumni newsletter request.

Work on various archives and collections was aided by Kate Wakely, Annette Courtney, Rosemary Powell, Donald McLeod, Laura Buckman, Dave Pitt, Ann Bruno, Ed Layt, Simon Wesson of *Welwyn Hatfield Times*, and the staff at Hertfordshire Archives and Local Studies.

The book would not have come to fruition without the support of Andrew Clutterbuck, Philip Waters, Julie Newlan and Jeremy Ridgman. It was Andrew Clutterbuck's initiative and enthusiasm that enabled the project to get off the ground. The members of the project editorial board helped shape its content and style: Jane Housham, Sarah Elvins, Mimi Tessier, Philip Waters, Alix Green, Steve Corbett, Ross Renton, Jeremy Ridgman, Yasmin Bastow, Thom Palser, Julie Moore and Sarah Lloyd.

Gordon Brand and Gabriel Newfield kindly read through early drafts, providing valuable corrections and suggestions. Last but not least, my thanks to UH Press. Jane Housham and Sarah Elvins have been a pleasure to work with as usual, and have helped ensure the book was completed on time.

The book was devised and edited by Owen Davies.

# Foreword
## by the Chancellor of the University

The University of Hertfordshire is an exciting institution. Its beginnings as an engineering school for the aircraft industry are still evident: engineering is one of its many current strengths. Since then, as it has evolved into the large institution we know today, it has driven up its academic standards and has begun to occupy a niche of its own. It has become a university which has built a particularly strong two-way relationship with business, notably local business in Hertfordshire. It has also cemented a growing network of international relationships, which is reflected in the remarkable diversity of its student body.

Hertfordshire's university is important to our county. It is already our largest employer and it makes a key contribution to the skills and research base that make us such an attractive place to do business. That importance can only grow. Our future prosperity will increasingly depend on a highly skilled workforce producing advanced, high-value goods and services. Without its university, Hertfordshire would struggle to continue to offer those things. The University's success and our county's success are therefore inextricably intertwined.

We should also remember that business success does not depend on corporate financial statements alone. People will invest in a place which is friendly to business. However, nowadays, they will also seek somewhere that is agreeable to live and which has a sense of culture and community. The University is beginning to make an important contribution in this area as well.

It is a happy coincidence that the University's Diamond Jubilee coincides with the Queen's. It gives us a double cause for celebration and the chance to acknowledge our past and show confidence in our future.

**The Seventh Marquess of Salisbury**

# Foreword
## by the Vice-Chancellor of the University

The history of the University of Hertfordshire is in many ways the history of post-war higher education. It is a history founded on expanding technological innovation, industrial growth and civic aspiration, a history shaped by economic change and shifts in policy as higher education was opened up to greater numbers of students and new subjects introduced into the curriculum. It is a history with both continuities and transformations over sixty years of institutional life as college, polytechnic and university. As such, this history offers a timely and welcome opportunity to look back over this period and reflect on the development of the higher education sector, and on the contribution to that development of the technical colleges and institutions that became polytechnics and, later, universities.

I arrived as Vice-Chancellor at the University of Hertfordshire in 2011, aware of the contours of its history and of its roots in the aeronautical industry. Reading this history, however, has uncovered some fascinating details for me – such as just how early applied research and development work with local companies started, and how Humanities and Arts have long featured in the institution's portfolio. These discoveries only add to my pride and belief in the University. They also, importantly, strengthen my commitment to our mission and strategy, which are fundamentally informed by the institution's historical development. We call ourselves a business-facing university, but that is our description today for an ethos that has permeated this organisation from the outset.

I welcome this history as a celebration of a vibrant and dynamic past and as a reminder of the heritage and the achievements on which we now build.

**Professor Quintin McKellar CBE**

# Institutional Timeline

## Hatfield Technical College

**1949**     Dr W.A.J. Chapman is appointed first Principal of Hatfield Technical College.

**1952**     The official opening ceremony is performed by HRH Prince Philip, Duke of Edinburgh.

## Hatfield College of Technology

**1960**     Hatfield Technical College is renamed Hatfield College of Technology.

**1961**     The College is recognised as a Regional College.

**1966**     Norman Lindop joins the College as Principal.

**1967**     Bayfordbury Mansion is acquired as an additional teaching site.

## Hatfield Polytechnic

**1969**     Hatfield College of Technology is designated as Hatfield Polytechnic.

        Birklands Mansion is acquired as an additional teaching site.

**1970**     The first Fellowship of Hatfield Polytechnic is conferred upon Dr W.A.J. Chapman.

**1972**     Lord Snow is appointed the Polytechnic's first Visitor.

**1978**     Lord Todd, Nobel Laureate in Chemistry, is appointed the second Visitor to the Polytechnic.

        Balls Park Mansion is acquired as an additional teaching site.

**1982**     Dr John Illston PhD DSc (Eng) CEng FICE is appointed Director of the Polytechnic.

**1984**     Birklands Mansion is closed and the Management Centre is relocated to Balls Park.

        Bayfordbury Mansion is handed back to the County Council.

**1987**     Professor Neil Buxton is appointed Director of the Polytechnic.

        The Polytechnic merges with the Hertfordshire College of Higher Education. The Wall Hall Mansion becomes the new home of the Faculty of Humanities and Education.

**1989**     The Polytechnic is given corporate status, removing it from County Council control.

# University of Hertfordshire

**1992**    The Polytechnic becomes a university.

Sir Brian Corby is appointed the first Chancellor of the University.

Dr Mary Archer is appointed the first Visitor to the University.

The University merges with the St Albans-based Hertfordshire College of Art and Design.

**1993**    The University merges with the Hertfordshire College of Health Care and Nursing Studies, and the Barnet College of Nursing and Midwifery.

**1994**    The University is named 'Top New University' in *The Times Good University Guide*.

The School of Art and Design transfers to the former BAe Design Block, Hatfield.

**1996**    Sir Ian MacLaurin is appointed Chancellor of the University.

**2000**    The University joins with the Associate College Network to form the Hertfordshire Higher Education Consortium.

**2003**    Professor Tim Wilson is appointed Vice-Chancellor of the University.

HRH Prince Philip, Duke of Edinburgh, formally opens the de Havilland campus. The sites at Wall Hall and Balls Park are closed.

**2004**    The University receives the Queen's Award for Enterprise in International Trade.

**2005**    Lord Salisbury becomes Chancellor of the University.

**2010**    The University is named as the *THES* 'Entrepreneurial University of the Year'.

**2011**    Professor Quintin McKellar is appointed Vice-Chancellor of the University.

The St Albans campus is closed and the School of Law moves into a purpose-built building on the de Havilland campus.

# 1. Our place in history

*'It is the Garden of England for delight, and men commonly say, that such who buy a house in Hertfordshire pay two years' purchase for the air thereof.'*

**Thomas Fuller, The History of the Worthies of England (1662).**

## The birth of a college

Hatfield Technical College formally opened in December 1952, its existence shaped by regional and national concerns that emerged during the Second World War and its aftermath. Post-war Hertfordshire, like so many other parts of the country, had to deal with the problems of damaged and unsuitable housing stock. The county faced additional pressures on resources as the government sought to address the critical situation faced by Londoners, leading to the creation of New Towns to accommodate displaced and poorly housed families. The 1946 New Towns Act saw Hertfordshire chosen to host three such developments, at Hatfield, Hemel Hempstead and Stevenage, together with large London County Council estates at sites such as Borehamwood and Watford, and the continued expansion of Welwyn Garden City.

These initiatives saw the population of the county rise by more than 50 per cent in the twenty years after 1931, a trend which was set to continue. In 1953 the keys to the thousandth new home in Hatfield were handed over to Mr W.B. Edmonds, a de Havilland employee who had moved to the town from his previous home in North London just five months after the College's opening ceremony. Those who were moving into the area were for the most part families, and those families had children who needed educating. In 1952 it was projected that there would need to be an additional 6,000 school places in the coming year. It was not just the immediate provision of places for these children that was under the spotlight. The Labour government, which had come to power in 1945, was concerned that the type of education that children received as they moved into their teenage years and beyond should reflect the need in the country for a new generation of highly skilled workers. This concern was shared by the Conservative government that returned to power in 1951.

The Education Act of 1944 required county councils to draw up plans for further and technical education for those beyond the statutory school leaving age, which the Act raised to fifteen years of age, although this only came into effect in 1947. It was from this initiative that a technical school and a technical college were built on ninety acres of land generously offered in 1944 by Alan S. Butler, Chairman of the de Havilland Aircraft Company. The Technical School was to offer those aged eleven and upwards an education focussed much more on science, mathematics and modern languages.

Although it required success in the eleven-plus exam for admission, there were to be no classical languages on the curriculum and it was anticipated that the catchment area would extend to places such as Barnet, Hertford and even the Lea Valley, with pupils going on to do courses at the College. Hatfield Technical College was to form part of a chain of colleges focussing on technical education at Watford, Letchworth and St Albans, with other further education colleges, at sites to be selected, supporting them. The plan was for these other colleges to take on much of the first-year work, with students transferring to the better equipped laboratories and workshops of Hatfield as they entered the higher levels of their courses.

*Geoffrey de Havilland (centre), Alan S. Butler (right) and Hubert S. Broad (left). Broad was Chief Test Pilot for de Havilland when this photo was taken in the early 1930s. Image courtesy of BAe.*

## Alan Samuel Butler (1898–1987)

Alan Butler, a man of great wealth, was passionate about flying and in the inter-war years his adventures as the first owner-pilot of an aeroplane, often in the company of his wife, Lois, appeared regularly in the newspapers.

Amongst other ventures he operated a flying boat service between Palm Beach, the Bahamas and Cuba, carried the first airmail to Newfoundland, and in 1928 the couple set a world record for flying 100 km in a two-seater light aircraft at a speed of just under 193 km per hour. His passion extended beyond simply taking the plane aloft, and his enthusiasm for innovation and experimentation in aeroplane design led him to meet the designers at the de Havilland Aircraft Company, based at Stag Lane in North London. So impressed was he with their collaboration on the building of a plane that he had designed, that he invested in the company, enabling them to buy the Stag Lane premises and giving them enough financial security to expand their operation. In 1923 he was made Chairman of the company and in spite of spending much of his time in the air or at sea on his favourite yacht, the *Sylvia*, he was always keen to visit when tests were scheduled. Aware of the possibility of the next war being fought in the air, in 1925 he approached the Air Ministry

to set up a scheme to encourage boys from public schools to consider a career in aviation: a pilot would visit the school and give a series of lectures culminating in a demonstration flight in a modified de Havilland two-seater Gypsy Moth. His donation of the land at Roe Green was a reflection of his conviction that the future lay with enhancing technological expertise, and he could see the long-term benefits to the de Havilland Aircraft Company, of course. Butler continued to fly until he was seventy-five and in 1973 was awarded the Royal Aeronautical Society's Gold Medal for his contribution to the aeronautical industry.

The design and completion of the College and the Technical School buildings took place between 1947 and 1952 on a ninety-acre site alongside the Barnet by-pass. It was a collaborative effort involving the artist and architect Ralph Maynard Smith (1904–64), the architects John Murray Easton and Howard Morley Robertson, structural engineers Felix Samuely & Co., and contractors Gilbert Ash Ltd. Pooling the knowledge and experience of all those involved in the design under the auspices of Hertfordshire County Council enabled the development of an innovative pre-fabricated building that was swiftly erected and adaptable to any site.

Faced with the challenge of a national shortage of bricks, steel and labour, the design team innovated with the use of concrete, with as much of the work as was possible being completed off-site. Several five-ton crossbeams which supported the roof of the main hall were pre-cast in one piece and then raised into position by crane. This was a considerable feat at the time. In early 1952 the contractors found a tidy solution to the problem of what to do with all the excavated soil. Pits dug for the purpose were now full, but to cart the excess away would add a cost of around £13,365. Whilst investigating the area set aside for playing fields, however, the surveyor had discovered twelve previously unknown swallow holes – natural depressions formed in the underlying rock by dissolution. Killing two birds with one stone, the excess soil was placed in the swallow holes, thus levelling the playing fields and improving the drainage.

## The College Lane site: A brief history

In the aftermath of the First World War the response of many landowning families throughout England to a combination of long years of agricultural depression, high death duties and personal loss was to place part, if not all, of their estates on the market in the hope of selling to those who had made some profit out of the preceding years. It has been estimated by one historian that in the period 1918–21 'between six and eight million acres changed hands in England and Wales'. Many of the farms were bought by their tenants. With rents frozen during the war and high demand for their produce from a country suffering blockades, many farmers had seen a welcome return to profitability in the years after 1914. In addition, with a guarantee from the government of the maintenance of minimum prices, farmers across the county took the plunge and bought the freehold on their farms. They were wary of those rich in pocket but poor in understanding, who might be less sympathetic landlords should the bad times return.

In 1920 the Gape family, who had been resident at St Michael's Manor, near St Albans, since the seventeenth century, decided to realise some of their assets and advertised the sale of their farms in St Albans, Hatfield and North Mymms.

At Roe Green, Hatfield, Alexander Campbell Hill bought the freehold on his farm. Hill was one of a wave of Scottish farmers who had moved into Hertfordshire in the years preceding the war, attracted by low rents and the ease of transport into London, which offered a market for their favoured crops of potatoes and liquid milk. The profits of the war years were not maintained, however, as food imports resumed and the government was unable to fulfil its promise of a minimum price. Agricultural depression set in and many farmers, saddled with high mortgages, were unable to make their farms pay. One such was Alexander Campbell Hill, who sold his farm to Alan S. Butler. In the early 1930s de Havilland relocated its headquarters and much of its production from North London to Hatfield. In 1944, as the war drew to a close, the Board of Education alerted local authorities to the need for improved facilities and access to technical and further education. Butler, who had already overseen the establishment of a technical school for de Havilland apprentices, approached Hertfordshire County Council with the offer of the land at Roe Green as a site for the new Technical College and School. The site had many advantages, as it lay at the heart of the county with easy access to the A1.

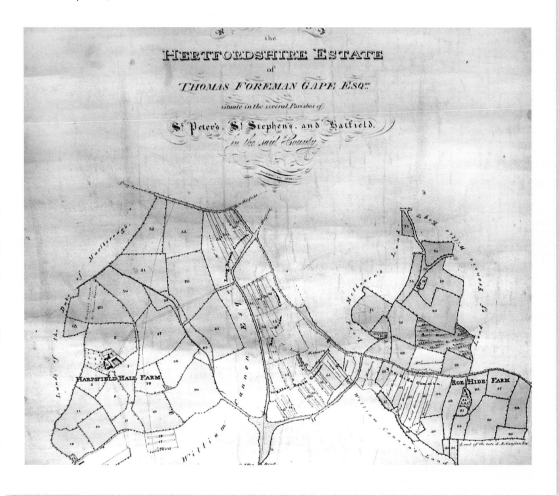

*Map of the Gape Estate showing Roe Hide Farm (1827). Harpsfield Hall was demolished in the 1930s to make way for the aerodrome. Image courtesy of Hertfordshire Archives and Library Service (HALS).*

The College's first Principal, Dr W.A.J. Chapman, recalled that the site was one of organised chaos when he settled in Hatfield on 1 January 1949:

> When I first arrived at the site there was a vast expanse of emptiness, a few contractors' huts and a large area covered with the reinforced concrete units which were to form the framework of the building. There was, however, a small protrusion in the centre of the site which on investigation proved to be the entrance steps – built prematurely, I always claimed, to serve as a landmark during the subsequent construction. Throughout the progress of the building I waited patiently to see whether the foyer floor, when it reached the steps, would be level with the top of their surface; but I need not have worried.

Whilst the design and execution of the buildings were grounded in a utilitarian need to accommodate the students quickly, they also reflected a sense that these were new buildings for a generation that would need to be much more technologically savvy than their parents if Britain was to prosper in the face of the new challenges of the post-war world. The choice of decoration reflected a confidence in that modern world, with the front wall carrying an abstract relief by Barbara Hepworth carved in Hoptonwood Stone entitled *Vertical Forms*. There were also two abstract paintings produced by her former husband, Ben Nicholson, which were sited in an upper corridor, and a carved plaque by Trevor Tennant based on the plan of the building and placed by the steps leading to the main entrance.

In the lower entrance hall stood a free-standing sculpture in bronze entitled *The Oracle*, which was created by Reg Butler, a Hertfordshire-born sculptor, whose work had appeared at the Festival of Britain in 1951.

*'One of the first reactions when coming to the new college was that it looked an act of faith. ... It was so strange when I first saw it, in the winter of 1951, to see a college out in the fields. I have never not wanted to come to work. There has never been a static feeling about the place. There have always been new projects and it is the same today.'*

**Ted Roberts, Academic Registrar 1952–72.**

*The University of Hertfordshire – 60 years of innovation*

*The Hatfield Technical College under construction in 1950.*

*The main hall (now the Prince Edward Hall) under construction.*

Then, as now, modern art was not always well received, Hepworth's relief, in particular, being the subject of significant criticism locally. In a single week in March 1953 Reg Butler suffered the indignity of not one, but two of his pieces being vandalised. His sculpture entitled *The Unknown Political Prisoner*, which had won an international competition to commemorate 'all those men and women who in our times have given their lives or their liberty to the cause of human freedom', was destroyed by a Hungarian refugee whilst on display at the Tate, and *The Oracle*, generally referred to as 'The Thing' by students, was daubed with blue distemper by an unknown critic whilst students were attending their evening classes. That such modern artists were represented within the College was due to the insistence of John Newsom, the county's forward-thinking Education Officer (knighted in 1964 for services to education), who believed in exposing children and young people to the best in original works of art. He pursued a policy of installing a mural or piece of sculpture in all of the new schools that were springing up across the county, a policy which was not always popular with councillors and the public at large. Still, this policy resulted in Hertfordshire accumulating a significant collection of paintings, sculptures and prints.

*(Right)*
*Ben Nicholson, 1934 (painted relief).*
*© Angela Verren Taunt 2012.*
*All rights reserved, DACS.*

*(Far right)*
*Barbara Hepworth, Vertical Forms, 1951 (part of the UH Art Collection).*

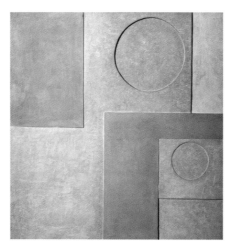

Throughout the early development stages of the Technical College there were problems in securing funding as both county and country adjusted to a time of austerity. In early 1952 the government withdrew funding for a promised second stage of building which would have seen the addition of a specialist science block. The council put together an appeal on the grounds that technical education should be seen as a special case with its benefits spreading beyond the confines of Hertfordshire, but the outcome of several meetings with the Ministry of Education was a dismissal of any possibility of additional funding from central government. Problems of space would plague teachers, students and administrators from the outset. Even before the first students enrolled, it became necessary to convert the cycle sheds beneath the classroom block for use as laboratories for physics and chemistry students, and the main hall was curtained off along its length so that the space could be used for teaching.

*(Above)*
*Reg Butler's* Oracle *displayed in the entrance hall.*
*(Below)*
*The relief plan of the College by Trevor Tennant.*

*'I remember the ground floor of the Main Building being built with wall to wall toilets. There were rows and rows of them. Gradually they reduced the numbers of these toilets to convert them to office space. Our maths office was born out of a ladies' loo!'*

*Graham Morris, interviewed in 1993. He was the longest serving member of staff on the University of Hertfordshire payroll at the time, being one of the original members of staff at the Technical College.*

The College was formally opened by Prince Philip, Duke of Edinburgh, on 16 December 1952. Chapman later recalled this day as one of the highlights of his career at Hatfield, saying of the Prince: 'A better choice could not have been made. Disregarding the timetable and hints from his distinguished followers, he insisted on seeing everything and conversing with students and staff alike. At the end of the tour, passing a closed door, he enquired, "What's in here?" On opening the door he found the room full of waitresses, and food, ready to serve the lunch!' The Prince, whose wife would be crowned Queen Elizabeth II six months later, spoke of the College very much in terms of its practical influence on young people in a world which was rebuilding itself

*The Duke of Edinburgh and Dr Chapman at the opening of the College, 1952.*

after the destruction of the Second World War, a world where Britain was re-negotiating its place within a commonwealth rather than an empire. He spoke of a second Elizabethan Age and a commitment to something other than the individual.

*'The characteristic of all the great periods of English history has been a nationwide sense of confidence and adventure which went at the same time with a feeling of personal service to the Sovereign. These islands are now at the centre of a vast family of nations. Let it never be said that Great Britain became the poor relation of the British Commonwealth in our time. No amount of talk will prevent this happening. Hard work and imagination is our only chance and I would ask the students to remember two things when they leave here to earn their living: first always look upon your work as your personal contribution to the welfare and prosperity of your country; secondly you will only do your best work if your heart is in it.'*

*From the Duke of Edinburgh's speech.*

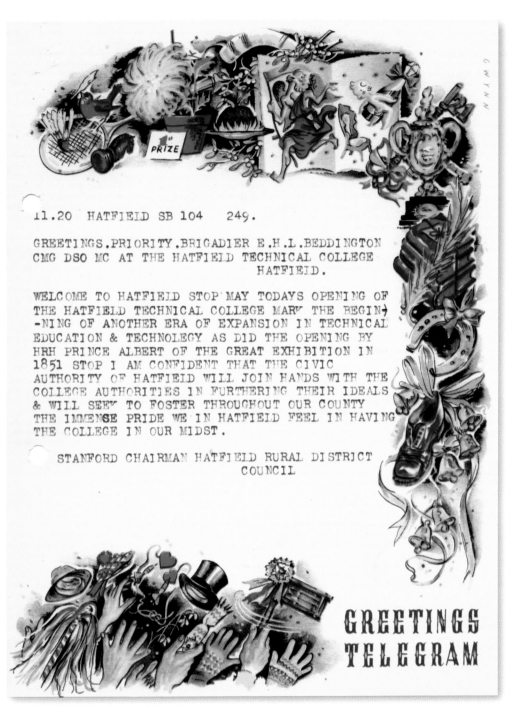

11.20  HATFIELD SB 104   249.

GREETINGS.PRIORITY.BRIGADIER E.H.L.BEDDINGTON
CMG DSO MC AT THE HATFIELD TECHNICAL COLLEGE
                        HATFIELD.

WELCOME TO HATFIELD STOP MAY TODAYS OPENING OF
THE HATFIELD TECHNICAL COLLEGE MARK THE BEGIN-
-NING OF ANOTHER ERA OF EXPANSION IN TECHNICAL
EDUCATION & TECHNOLEGY AS DID THE OPENING BY
HRH PRINCE ALBERT OF THE GREAT EXHIBITION IN
1851 STOP I AM CONFIDENT THAT THE CIVIC
AUTHORITY OF HATFIELD WILL JOIN HANDS WITH THE
COLLEGE AUTHORITIES IN FURTHERING THEIR IDEALS
& WILL SEEK TO FOSTER THROUGHOUT OUR COUNTY
THE IMMENSE PRIDE WE IN HATFIELD FEEL IN HAVING
THE COLLEGE IN OUR MIDST.

        STANFORD CHAIRMAN HATFIELD RURAL DISTRICT
                        COUNCIL

GREETINGS
TELEGRAM

*Congratulatory telegram from the Rural District Council, 1952.*

Those who also spoke on that opening day in December 1952 reflected the partnership that was foreseen between education and industry. Prince Philip's speech was followed by contributions from Alderman H.E. Fern, Chairman of the County Education Committee; Mr W.E. Nixon, a director of the de Havilland Aircraft Company; and Sir Vincent Tewson, General Secretary of the TUC. As Dr Chapman wrote in his first Annual Report as Principal: 'The College exists, to a great extent, for the education of the employees of Hertfordshire firms and the interest, co-operation, and goodwill of industry and commerce are essential factors in the success of the College.'

The sense of a new era dawning and reflection on the past inspired the first public exhibition hosted by the College in June 1953, which its organisers explained was 'designed to illustrate some contrast in economic and social aspects of life in the two Elizabethan reigns'. The exhibition was a strange mix of historical documents and modern technology, the latter reflecting the contribution the College would make to post-war rebuilding. The speeches at the opening of the exhibition reflected a sense of optimism and a drawing of comparisons between the national character of the people in both epochs, with the emphasis very much on the need to emulate those earlier Elizabethans. Dr Chapman was quoted as saying of the young people of the country that 'they were very much the same as they ever were. They may have different interests, but I think their character is just the same.'

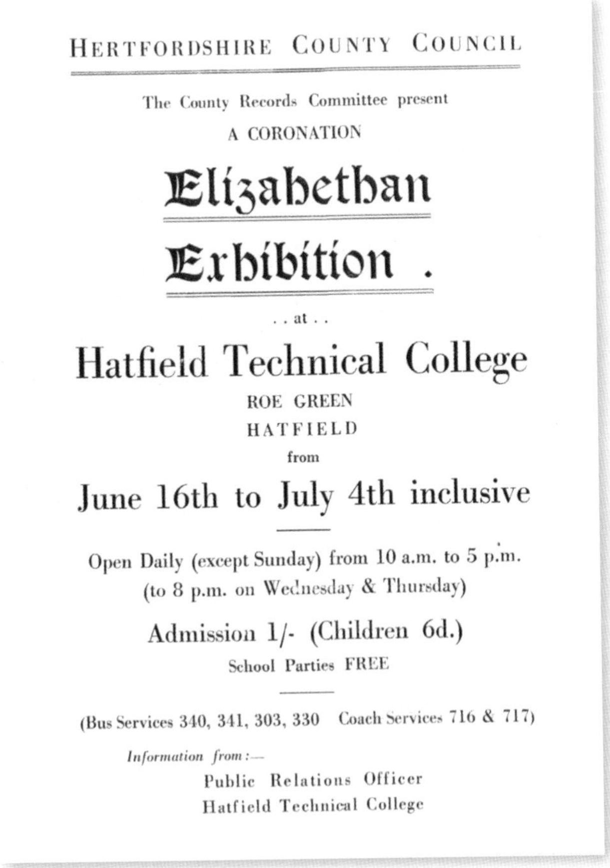

HERTFORDSHIRE COUNTY COUNCIL

The County Records Committee present

A CORONATION

# Elizabethan

# Exhibition .

. . at . .

# Hatfield Technical College

ROE GREEN
HATFIELD

from

## June 16th to July 4th inclusive

Open Daily (except Sunday) from 10 a.m. to 5 p.m.
(to 8 p.m. on Wednesday & Thursday)

Admission 1/- (Children 6d.)

School Parties FREE

(Bus Services 340, 341, 303, 330   Coach Services 716 & 717)

Information from :—

Public Relations Officer
Hatfield Technical College

# Dr W.A.J. Chapman MSc (Eng) PhD FIMechE HonFiProdE (1900–97),
## Founder Principal of Hatfield Technical College

William Arthur James Chapman was born in Weedon, Northamptonshire. After leaving school he trained for nine years in the tool room, drawing office and production shops of Daimler Co. Ltd, Coventry. He then spent four years designing tools and special machines for the Coventry Chain Co. Ltd.

Moving into education, he was appointed Lecturer in Engineering at a number of technical colleges in the Midlands, and produced several books which became required reading for students. In 1940 a copy of his handbook, *Workshop Calculations,* was given to every new entrant into the wartime industries, whilst his *Workshop Technology Part 1* and *Part 2*, which first appeared in 1943 and 1946 respectively, are still in print today, a fourth edition having been reprinted as recently as 2003. In 1973

a silk-bound copy of *Workshop Technology* was presented to Kenya's Minister of Education by Mr Richard Wood, Minister for Overseas Development, as the ten millionth book to be produced as part of Great Britain's low-price book scheme for developing countries.

*Dr Chapman in his office.*

At the end of the Second World War, Chapman was the Principal of the County Technical College, Stafford. It was at this time that he applied for the position of Principal to the proposed Hatfield Technical College, some three years before teaching began. He held this post until his retirement in 1967 when he took on the chairmanship of the Hatfield Local Committee of the Welwyn Hatfield New Towns Commission. He was also Chair of the Hatfield Rotary Club, a member of St John's Church, Hatfield, and was very involved in the work of the Air Training Corps 2203 (Hatfield and de Havilland) Squadron.

He and his wife, Hilda, lived in Hatfield from the time of his first appointment as Principal in 1948. One of the early students at Hatfield Technical College was his daughter, Susan, who took a secretarial course before finding employment at de Havilland, and subsequently moving on to Nottingham University to take a BA in Social Administration. In 1969 the Chapman Scholarship for students undertaking research was created. The local paper reported that the first recipient was off to study the ecological physiology of mammals in the Negev desert, southern Israel, and concluded with the following tribute to Dr Chapman:

*The Chapman Scholarship is a worthy memorial to the work of a college principal who was also something of a visionary. All he did was meaningful because of his special attitude to the young people who came under his influence and whose education was his responsibility. He tried to make them understand that, equipped with knowledge, the world was their oyster and the bounds of achievement vast and exciting. The young men and women who found inspiration in such leadership are now out and about in the world and some of them are already making names for themselves. The student who is now off to the Negev desert will find his time fully occupied with studies that may contribute to the marvels of a new century. He will also be a torch bearer for a man who knew that the disciplined use of knowledge is the stepping stone to a better world.*

In the first year of the College alone, 124 firms sponsored employees to attend day-release classes. The relationship between the Technical College and the nearby de Havilland Aircraft Company was particularly strong; both sat on land made available by the gift of the Chairman of de Havilland, Alan S. Butler, and the apprentices at de Havilland were amongst the first to take their technical classes at the College. In addition, representatives from de Havilland sat on the advisory committees of departments within the College, alongside members of the County Council, local industries and other experts, their role to offer guidance on syllabus development. Sir Vincent Tewson of the TUC sat on the Advisory Committee for the Social and Professional Studies Department. Offers of equipment from local companies proved invaluable in furnishing laboratories and workshops at a time when funding from mainstream sources was under severe pressure.

One priority for the College was to promote high-quality research, and with this in mind the structure of the academic year was based around four rather than the usual three terms. Each term lasted eleven weeks, with three terms devoted to teaching and the fourth to be of a sabbatical nature. In the fourth term staff were encouraged to visit manufacturing companies, commercial organisations and teaching establishments to view best practice and new developments, as well as taking part in their own research and improving their qualifications. This imposed a strain on the College's finances, however, and a three-term structure was introduced in the 1954–55 academic year in spite of Chapman's argument that staff were making good use of the extra term to improve the prestige of the College. 'The four-term year did not survive,' Chapman reflected years later. 'This was probably because it was in advance of its time and needed longer preparation than we were able to give it. One teacher, at least, used his term profitably, by travelling in Italy and bringing back an Italian wife!'

The first courses taught at the College fell within the remit of six departments: Building, Technical and Design Engineering, Works and Production Engineering, Science, Commerce and Retail Trades, and Social and Professional Studies.

*Students in the Building Department workshop, 1952.*

*Plumbing workshop, 1952.*

The Building Department concentrated at first on the basics of the building trade and worked hard to encourage the many trade and building companies engaged in the extensive projects across the county to allow their employees to attend for day-release courses. They had some success. By 1954–55 over 100 small businesses were sending students to classes, but, with pressure on space reaching critical levels, it was decided to relocate the Department to new premises at St Albans, where staff were joined by their counterparts at Watford Technical College, forming the new Hertfordshire College of Building.

Student numbers grew quickly, and it was a reflection of the focus on industry that the largest cohorts were to be found in the categories of part-time day and evening students, with engineering firms sending 634 of the 813 students enrolled on the day-release courses. The Technical and Design Engineering Department focussed on aeronautical design and electrical engineering, and from its inception the target was research that would have practical application within industry. One of the first pieces of equipment to be installed was a wind tunnel, and a postgraduate course in aeronautical sciences was introduced for engineering and science graduates who had no aeronautical experience, recruiting from amongst the employees of the de Havilland Aircraft Company and English Electric. It was this Department, together with the Works and Production Engineering Department, which first introduced both sandwich courses and block release schemes. The first sandwich course was introduced in Engineering in the College's second year of operations, with students spending a total of twenty-four weeks a year at the College and the remainder in industry. Responding to requests from de Havilland, a block release course was developed for second- and third-year students on the National Certificate in Aeronautics course; students attended the college for two periods of nine weeks each in the academic year. The idea of a sandwich course did not originate with the Technical College, but it fitted perfectly the College's mission to raise the standards, and respond to the particular needs, of a technical and commercial education. In his fourth Annual Report, Chapman mentioned with some pride the College's place at the forefront of this innovation.

With student numbers expanding, it was decided to reconstruct the Technical and Design Engineering Department in 1955–56, creating two distinct departments for Aeronautical and Mechanical Design, and Electrical Engineering. By 1959–60 new laboratories specifically designed for testing aerodynamics, aircraft structures and mechanical vibrations advanced the teaching and research potential.

The numbers studying aeronautical engineering remained fairly steady at around 750, with those who attended split fairly evenly between the part-time, block release students, and those attending in the evening. The numbers of full-time day students, including those on sandwich courses, remained small; the last available breakdown of figures, for the 1955–56 session, showed only twenty full-time day students on aeronautical courses. The newly established Electrical Engineering Department was the junior partner in the original, combined department, but numbers steadily increased and in the 1957–58 session its BSc degree course in Electrical Engineering was validated. These early degrees were all taken as part of the University of London's venerable external degree framework. In his Annual Report of 1958–59, Dr Chapman was able to report the College's first successful degree-level students: four in Aeronautical Engineering and two in Electrical Engineering. One student, a Mr D.H. Wilkinson, was the only external degree student in the country to receive First Class Honours, and even more successful in Chapman's view was a Mr I.J. Langley, who gained Second Class Honours in Electrical Engineering in spite of 'the presentation of a son to him on the eve of the examinations!'

The Works and Production Engineering Department was renamed the Department of Mechanical and Production Engineering in the fourth year of the College's existence, and was, from the start, very popular with both students and employers. In the second year of its existence, the large increase in enrolments made it necessary to double and even treble the number of classes on courses, and by 1955–56 streaming was introduced to enable more effective teaching. One of the areas covered by this Department was motor vehicle maintenance, and it was a reflection of the growing numbers of cars on the road that an evening course for the general public on 'the internal workings of the automobile' was oversubscribed, with four classes being held and a waiting list taken of prospective students. Even more successful was a course on 'Automation', which received over 270 enrolments for 10 lectures held during the bitterly cold winter of 1955–56. Each lecture was attended by an average of 250 people – no mean feat during a particularly harsh winter when travelling to the

College by public transport was itself quite an expedition. Dr Chapman recognised the implications of the drive towards automation: 'The full impact of automation may well lead to a revolution, not only in technical education, but also in the structure of industry and society, and we in this College are trying to keep abreast of the times in order that we may play our full part in whatever the future may hold.' A follow-up course in October 1956 on the 'Application of Computers to Automation' also proved popular and was the first course on computing to be held at Hatfield.

The College took pride in being open to approaches from industry and the wider public, arranging courses which met the needs of those seeking to adapt to new technologies in the post-war world. Requests from local companies were met with an intensive eleven-week course of two days per week on draughtsmanship entitled 'Designing for Production', a course which again was so popular that it became part of the annual programme.

The early days of the Science Department were very much constrained by the lack of space for laboratory work, although it should also be noted that in the first year of its existence it was also constrained by having only one member of staff, Mr D.I. Breese MSc, and no students enrolled. Student numbers did improve. The following academic year saw eighty-five part-time students at day classes and forty-six students attending evening classes. The focus was on the delivery of O and A Level courses for those whose schools could not provide adequate teaching in science subjects necessary for entry to higher education science courses. In 1955–56, 55 students took between them 120 papers at A Level and achieved good results across the board, but in particular in Physics, which saw a 100 per cent success rate. Although the Ministry of Education gave approval in 1953 to the teaching of HNC (Higher National Certificate) courses in Chemistry and the BSc General, Part 1, early reports from the Department stressed the difficulties of introducing higher-level courses, given the limitations of the existing laboratories. Finally, in the 1958–59 session, the Department was able to take possession of a new science wing and leave the space originally intended for use as a cycle shed. In the report for that year, the Science Department applauded the work of the Advisory Committee in supporting the large amount of research work undertaken by staff, but with a subtle reminder that such work could only be effective when facilities continued to be updated, since 'top quality staff will not come to a college where such facilities do not exist'. A consequence of the new building was that it allowed the removal of the curtains in the main hall, and the creation of more student social space.

The Commerce and Retail Trades Department was home to the largest group of full-time day students – the many young women enrolled on the one-year secretarial course. In his report on the 1957–58 session, the Head of the Department, Dr Peter Kingsford, highlighted the ambitions for this Department in raising standards and promoting female higher education. Kingsford noted with satisfaction that the course was attracting more and more girls of 'university calibre'. At a time when university education had yet to be considered a realistic alternative for bright working-class or lower-middle-class girls, the chance to develop a professional profile as a skilled secretary did offer some chance of self-improvement and a decent income. In 1958–59 the Department introduced a two-year course for secretaries. Alongside the secretarial courses, the Department introduced two courses in Management Development, which Kingsford noted were amongst the first in the country to tackle the skills required in managing people. This Department also responded to the needs of local companies, and in the same year took several courses on the subject of 'human relations in management' and 'industrial relations' out to the community, holding them in a factory – a reflection perhaps of Sir Vincent Tewson's presence on the Department's Advisory Committee.

The College saw its role as producing the next generation of engineers and technologists who would help the country face the particular challenges of the second half of the twentieth century and take up its opportunities. Yet it was not just by teaching men how to handle a slide rule, or even young women a typewriter, that the world would be best served. This was the rationale behind the commitment to a course of Liberal Studies for all students. It was intended that 10 per cent of their time in college would be allocated to the teaching of subjects such as history, economics, politics, geography and modern languages. When the College introduced its first sandwich course in Aeronautical Engineering in the 1955–56 academic year, it specified that, alongside the training in mechanical engineering, and the specialisation in aeronautical subjects, there should also be space for liberal studies, with the addition in the final year of a course in the fundamentals of management. Kingsford struggled to convince some of his colleagues that a broad education was necessary when resources were stretched and timetables congested. Yet, he explained, 'this role becomes more important as the technological work becomes more advanced and more specialised'. Chapman also recalled the early suspicion of the liberal studies content within a technological framework, but argued that, in this, Hatfield pioneered an approach which later became educational orthodoxy.

# Peter Kingsford

Peter Kingsford was born in 1908, in Battersea. He was employed as a clerk in the Superintendent's Office at Paddington station and was sent by his employers to evening courses at the Railway Department of the London School of Economics (LSE). So successful was he that he continued at the LSE, taking his BSc in Economics.

At the outbreak of the Second World War, Peter Kingsford was part of a unit that was sent out to ensure that there had been no bomb damage to the tracks. As a member of the Communist Party, he was opposed to the war and, when he was spotted at a Communist rally, he was reported to his superiors and moved to an office at Aldermaston, where he and three others sat day by day, with no work to do. With the invasion of the Soviet Union, the stance of the Communist Party shifted with regard to the war, and as Branch Chairman of the Paddington branch of the Railway Clerks' Association he campaigned for better meals for workers and better working hours. Called up into the forces, he served in the Army Educational Corps in India and Malaysia, and when peace returned he took a post as a lecturer in the Social Studies Department of the South-West Technical College and School of Art, Walthamstow. Whilst at Walthamstow he continued his studies with the LSE, receiving a PhD in 1952.

Kingsford was one of the first members of staff to join Dr Chapman at the newly built Hatfield Technical College. His first post was as Head of the Commerce and Retail Trades Department, although he also acted part-time in the capacity of Registrar before Ted Roberts was appointed as full-time Academic Registrar. In addition, Kingsford oversaw the development of the Liberal Studies content of the engineering and science courses. In April 2003, aged ninety-four, Kingsford was interviewed by *The Times* and asked for his memories of the early days of Hatfield Technical College:

> *We were an ambitious staff, and we were all terribly excited about the new, architecturally renowned buildings in which we were to teach . . . There were about 1,500 students; most of them were on day release from local companies, who paid their tuition fees. I remember being incredibly ambitious for the place. We thought the building was so impressive, and there was talk about it becoming a university even then.*

He told the reporter of the greater formality that existed in those days, with students wearing suits:

> *Students were not encouraged to question us, nor to enter into any form of discussion or response during lectures. It was all talk and chalk in those days. They studied from 9am to 5.15pm for one or two days a week because the rest of the time they were in employment locally.*

Kingsford retired from the Polytechnic in December 1973, and transferred his energies to chronicling the local history of his home village of Brookmans Park and the wider North Mymms area. He maintained his interest in matters political, campaigning for nuclear disarmament into his eighties. In 2008 Dr Kingsford was appointed a Fellow of the University of Hertfordshire. He died, aged 101, in June 2010.

*Peter Kingsford receiving his honorary doctorate from Professor Tim Wilson.*

The creation of the A.S. Butler Library, a 60ft by 30ft room located above the main entrance hall, was a vital constituent part of the College's commitment to inclusiveness. It had seating for forty readers at tables, with eight easy chairs in the periodicals section. It was open from 9am to 8pm. English college libraries had a poor reputation, but under the supervision of its first librarian, Michael Argles, formerly of Reigate and Surrey Public Libraries, the A.S. Butler Library became a model for demonstrating the centrality of the library to such institutions. Argles was at the centre of decision-making, being a member of the College Committee, Steering Committee of the Governing Body, and the Board of Studies. The library's stock almost doubled in size, from 4,405 books, pamphlets, reports and bound periodicals in 1953, to 8,774 items in 1956. Argles ensured that the collection policy was broad, with sections on history, geography, drama, art, languages and novels.

In 1956 Argles resigned and his position was taken by Gordon H. Wright, supported by two assistants. Wright developed a strategy to broaden the brief of the library, the intention being to integrate it within the County Library service as the central technical reference library – its stock to be accessible to local industries.

Innovations in identifying, cataloguing and micro-filming technical reports, books and articles led to increased demand from those outside the College seeking detailed technical information in an age when the digital revolution had yet to make such things commonplace. In just one academic year, 1959–60, the library loaned 2,270 books and 869 periodicals to other libraries, research organisations, colleges and industries. Requests included the ground-floor plans of the Rockefeller Centre and Grand Central Station in New York, use of infra-red in navigational aids, the corrosive effects of marine organisms on concrete foundations, and the oxidation catalyst for cold permanent-wave solutions based on thioglycollates and thioglycollic acid. In 1960 overcrowding in the library, which was thought to be contributing to poor student behaviour, led to the provision of a new library in the converted teaching block of the south wing.

*'The library should be a centre of information on all subjects taught in the college, as well as a valuable aid to the maintenance of that just balance between science and the humanities which is so much to be desired.'*
Michael Argles (1955).

As the 1950s gave way to the 1960s, lower-level courses were relocated to the network of further education colleges with which Hatfield had formed relationships of learning in order to concentrate on the higher levels of research and teaching. Whilst the College had been able to offer courses leading to degree-level qualifications, these had all been under the auspices of the University of London's external degrees programme. Of greater significance for the future was the recognition in 1959 by the National Council for Technological Awards (NCTA) of the College's right to award the Diploma in Technology courses for Aeronautical and Electrical Engineering, followed the year after by approval for the Diploma in Technology in Mechanical Engineering.

The award of Diploma in Technology was the equivalent of an Honours degree course, and marked an important milestone in the College's history as it meant that the College could set its own syllabuses and examination structure for the Dip. Tech., although still subject to external approval. Chapman recorded his pride in this achievement, which was 'an honour shared only by 23 other colleges'.

At the start of the 1959–60 academic year the Mathematics Department was created to deliver the mathematical content of courses across the College, but more significantly its inception heralded a profound new development: the introduction of computer technology across the College. At the end of May 1960 the Department organised a two-day conference on 'The Computing Laboratory in the Technical College', which was attended by 128 people from 62 colleges and 12 other institutions and firms. The conference included demonstrations of digital and analogue computers and desk machines by a range of companies including Elliott Bros who demonstrated their '803' digital computer, Ferranti Ltd, Standard Telephones & Cables Ltd and EMI. After the conference, the Advisory Committee took the decision that the Department should concentrate on digital rather than analogue computing, and announced its hope that it would soon be in a position to buy a high-speed digital computer.

## Into the sixties: The area in a state of flux

As the College grew, so too did Hatfield. Throughout the 1960s many residents of Hatfield, Welwyn Garden City and Stevenage might have been forgiven for wondering whether their towns would ever be completed as new homes continued to spring up across the county, and the problems of transport, shopping and leisure amenities were thrashed out in planning departments and the letters pages of local newspapers.

Hatfield was then in the throes of finalising a design for the town centre and the immediate surroundings, including the highly sensitive district of Old Hatfield. In 1963 the Development Corporation announced a £3.5 million plan to develop both the area around Old Hatfield and a pedestrian-only shopping precinct in South Hatfield. The first stage of the development was already under way and included the building of the 120ft-high, thirteen-storey residential 'skyscraper', Queensway House, which the local press welcomed as a 'focal point from many miles around and a signpost to Hatfield'. So significant was this new building that the opening ceremony was conducted by Sir Keith Joseph, then Minister for Housing and Local Government, who told onlookers, 'The eyes of the world are on Britain's new towns. Here are variety and vitality, a second generation of new towns and a fine example to those still being built.' Another landmark building was the new Church of St John's at the Hilltop, South Hatfield, its 'dramatic, triangular' design dominating the surrounding area. It attracted another high-profile visitor to the New Town, the foundation stone having being laid by Princess Alexandra in June 1958.

*Hatfield College of Technology
in 1966.*

*The University of Hertfordshire – 60 years of innovation*

Not all buildings were warmly welcomed. Proposals to build a swimming pool at a cost of around £200,000 were met with some anger from local residents who felt that the year-on-year increase in rates was out of control. One resident of Brookmans Park complained that Hertfordshire rate-payers were suffering 'the highest penal rate for education of any county' and that luxuries such as swimming pools should only be built after a referendum on the subject was taken. Expenditure on education received criticism too, with one St Albans resident asking 'whether all the expensive equipment in schools, technical colleges and art schools is really necessary'.

In those parts of the district that had longer histories, such as Brookmans Park, Welwyn, Northaw and Cuffley, the arrival of so many new families and the amenities to support them did take some getting used to. The 'variety and vitality' celebrated by Sir Keith Joseph were not necessarily welcomed by all. Romantic fiction author and Hertfordshire County Councillor Barbara Cartland was fiercely critical of much of the new building taking place. From her Camfield Place estate, on the road from Hatfield to Brookmans Park, she called on the authorities to do something to safeguard 'the few precious acres left' of the district, and said of the new houses being built close to the railway line at Oxlease that they were 'so appallingly ugly that it is difficult to conceive that reputable building authorities could have approved the design'. There were those who agreed with her, but others enjoyed being part of the New Town experience; Reverend Farnborough, vicar of St John's, argued that Oxlease, once the houses were 'peopled, the gardens cared for, the roads, shrubberies and green spaces laid out', would be one of the most pleasant parts of the New Town, a point of view echoed by one resident of Elm Drive, who was happy to announce that he had bought his house at Oxlease in preference to other parts of the county.

Those who were moving into the new homes of the Hatfield district were able to find employment in a number of engineering, pharmaceutical and manufacturing companies whose names were once locally familiar but whose presence is now long gone or sadly reduced: Hawker Siddeley Dynamics, British Aircraft Corporation, Marconi, Handley Page, Smith, Kline & French, Smith and Nephew, ICI and Nabisco. In the 1960s around 20 per cent of all aircraft workers were employed in Hertfordshire.

However, the mood was already somewhat cautious as the industry underwent some shrinkage in the post-war economy and, in a rather prophetic comment, James McDonald, the Works Convenor at de Havilland, warned that Hatfield should not be complacent about the threat of redundancies, which were occurring at sites in Portsmouth and Chester: 'People think Hatfield is synonymous with de Havilland's, but there are other towns where the major industry has gone and left a ghost town behind. There is no other major industry in this town, and if this redundancy spreads, it could happen here.'

The redundancies were a result of rationalisation by Hawker Siddeley, and whilst McDonald referred to de Havilland's, the aircraft company which was so much a part of the College's history had in fact been absorbed by the larger company of Hawker Siddeley, and two years later the company became only a smaller division of the larger, parent company. Yet, for now, redundancies in Hatfield were avoided and at Hatfield the College continued to attract those for whom an engineering, manufacturing or commercial future beckoned.

**Student numbers in 1961–62**

Full-time & Sandwich: 261
Block Release & Part-time Day: 1,266
Evening: 1,227

# 2. Coming together

*'Anyone who has been at the Hatfield College in Hertfordshire, England, during its comparatively brief yet hectic existence might be forgiven if, when asked 'what is going on, and where do you go from here?', he begs to be allowed to pass the question. So much has happened in less than twenty years' growth, and so much is still happening, that it is difficult to know how or where to begin to describe the College today.'*
**Norman Lindop, Director of Hatfield Polytechnic, writing in 1972.**

In 1960 the Hatfield Technical College became the Hatfield College of Technology – a reflection of its confidence in its role of preparing students for acknowledged degree-level qualifications under the auspices of the National Council for Technological Awards (NCTA). The first degree-level courses to be approved were the Diploma in Technology sandwich courses in Aeronautical and Electrical Engineering, whose first graduates would complete their studies in 1963. Further recognition of the College's standing came with its naming by the Ministry of Education in August 1962 as one of twenty-five Regional Colleges for England and Wales, ranking second only to the 'CATS' – the ten Colleges of Advanced Technology established in 1956 – in offering degree-equivalent courses outside the traditional university framework. Dr Chapman welcomed this as a 'great lift-up in status for the college' and a 'wonderful birthday present' as the College celebrated ten years of work. In acknowledging the award, Chapman also paid tribute to local support: 'the enlightened outlook on technical education in this area has been highly conducive to the success of the College'.

There were three designated engineering departments at the end of the 1950s: Aeronautical and Mechanical Design, Electrical Engineering, and Mechanical and Production Engineering. The growth in popularity of civil and industrial engineering courses saw these three departments restructured and, on the eve of acquiring Polytechnic status in 1969, they had been restyled as the departments of Mechanical, Aeronautical and Civil Engineering; Electrical Engineering and Physics; and Industrial Engineering. These departments continued to add higher levels of courses to their portfolio. By 1968 students could follow five pathways to Honours degrees in engineering subjects, as well as four leading to Ordinary degrees, which had a 'more distinctly "applied" flavour', together with three Higher National Diploma courses in Production and Mechanical Engineering. In 1963 Chapman applauded the achievements of the first graduates of the Diploma in Technology (Engineering) in words that made clear his conviction that a college of technology such as Hatfield could bring a new contribution to the training and education of the next generation, a contribution which might differ in nature but not in quality from that offered by the traditional universities:

> *This event is of outstanding importance, since it demonstrates the ability of the College to conduct, in its own right, academic work of university standard and justifies the enlightened policy pursued by the Governing Body and the Authority. The students who were instrumental in achieving for us this advance were fully worthy of the status they attained and in our opinion are equal academically, and superior professionally to the product of any university.*

This sense of the College department offering something both new and special in engineering was shown in the disappointment expressed by some students following the renaming of their Diploma in Technology as a 'Bachelor's degree' when the NCTA was redesignated as the Council for National Academic Awards (CNAA).

As part of the drive to raise standards and respond to modern developments, new ways of teaching that moved away from the traditional talk-and-chalk approach were introduced. The 1963–64 report from the Department of Mechanical, Aeronautical and Civil Engineering noted the greater use of subject tutorial periods, private study time and one-on-one supervision: 'These departures from the traditional technical college lecture situation produce more readily the habits of enquiry and enthusiasm in the student; this is particularly true in those aspects of study where the work is most individual.'

A particular feature of the courses run by these departments was the final-year project, which was worth around 25 per cent of that year's assessment. Introduced in the 1963–64 academic session, Chapman noted its potential to offer 'maturity and balance to the education of students', and in his report for the 1967–68 session, Norman Lindop applauded the high standard of work produced, which could often be compared without prejudice to that of research at postgraduate level. A further innovation was the introduction in 1967 by the Industrial Engineering Department of industrial placements for students in France and Germany. In this, the Department was proud to announce that it was 'blazing the trail', as students were required to study either French or German as part of their course and then spend three months in the relevant country, with the European experience complementing that built up with the sponsor company in the UK.

Alongside their teaching responsibilities, engineering staff continued to collaborate on
projects with industrial partners. In 1962–63 those projects included 'an ergonomic
approach to paint brush design, development of copy turning attachments, anti-scaling
coatings for the steel industry and the machining of alloy steels'. The Department of
Mechanical, Aeronautical and Civil Engineering introduced postgraduate short courses
and conferences, and through consulting industrial and research organisations were
able to ensure that the courses on offer were successful and well subscribed. The award
of a research grant into aircraft fatigue and approval for the installation of a 'supersonic
wind tunnel capable of operating at four times the speed of sound' were evidence of the
continuing high profile that the College had in the aircraft industry. At the start of the
1966–67 academic session the Geoffrey de Havilland Aeronautics Laboratories were
formally opened, timed to coincide with the first of the de Havilland Memorial Lectures.
The Memorial Lectures continue today under the auspices of the Hatfield branch of the
Royal Aeronautical Society.

In these years total student numbers fell somewhat, as lower-level courses were transferred to local further education colleges, but Chapman saw this as progress since 'a smaller body of more mature students' would offer staff an opportunity: 'No longer being pre-occupied in dealing with students in the mass, they are able to give more attention to academic and professional matters, and to the task of keeping abreast with scientific and industrial developments.' Whilst the overall number of students fell as a result of the policy of transferring lower-level work, the numbers of those studying full-time grew – a reflection of wider national trends as professional bodies such as the engineering institutions made membership less accessible to those who were studying part-time. Throughout the 1960s Chapman and his colleagues maintained their policy of strengthening contact with representatives from industry, technology and research, a policy which benefited all partners in expanding knowledge. As he noted in the Annual Report on the 1961–62 session, no modern organisation could expect to flourish in isolation and this was particularly true in education:

> *In this College, we have probably advanced further than most. This is probably due to our youthfulness and lack of unfavourable tradition, to our situation amongst industries having similar characteristics and to the character of the work we are doing. Even so, I feel we have yet a long way to go but we have the advantage of knowing this and striving accordingly.*

## Nearly a university...

In May 1961 Lord Robbins visited the College as part of a fact-finding tour looking at the future of higher education in the country, a visit which foreshadowed the Hatfield College of Technology becoming a polytechnic eight years later.

But Hertfordshire nearly had its own university even before Robbins had concluded his research. In 1960 residents of Stevenage attended a public inquiry into the Development Corporation's plans to further develop the town, plans which also included approaching Hertfordshire County Council to support a bid to build a new university for Hertfordshire on land adjoining the Fairlands Valley development. After deliberating for more than two years, the council's Education Committee decided instead to give its support for a new university to be formed from a merger between the Hatfield College of Technology and the Chelsea College of Science and Technology on a different site, the 240 acres formerly occupied by Hill End Hospital in St Albans. Early estimates of student numbers were of an initial intake of 1,500, rising to 3,000 in future years, and the estimated cost was upwards of £5 million.

## The Robbins Report and higher education

The Robbins Report was commissioned by the government and published in 1963. It recommended the swift expansion of the university sector, beginning with the transformation of the ten CATS into fully-fledged universities, and set in train the future creation of polytechnics. It also built on the recommendations of the 1960 Anderson Committee, which led in 1962 to the introduction of a national student finance system. Local authorities were to administer the system for students in their areas, dispensing a standard entitlement of payment of fees plus a maintenance grant. These reforms had the effect of consolidating the English model of the three-year, specialist undergraduate degree (in contrast to Scottish, European and American models), and – through making living away financially accessible to a greater proportion of students – of shifting the identity and sense of purpose of the civic universities away from their localities and towards national (and then international) status and ambition.

The 'Robbins principle', which states that places in higher education should be provided for 'all those who are qualified by ability or attainment to pursue them and wish to do so', is arguably the single element of the 1963 report that has caught and held in the consciousness of the sector. Robbins wanted to establish the principle – alongside that of equal access – of parity of esteem, with equal academic awards for institutions with different missions and functions within the system. He was concerned to avoid the 'freezing of institutions into established hierarchies' and to promote the 'recognition and encouragement of excellence wherever it exists and wherever it appears'. Twenty-first century debates suggest Robbins was prescient of some of the consequences of a mass system, where there are often tensions between the funding imperatives of the state, the demands of social equity and the diverse interests and priorities of the higher education sector. Robbins was not in accord with Crosland's plans for the binary system of polytechnics and universities, which he saw as introducing a more rigidly hierarchical 'caste system'.

The choice of the St Albans site raised some objections from the eastern part of the county, which was facing the loss of the John Innes Horticultural Institute at Bayfordbury, near Hertford. Residents, faced with the loss of this significant local employer, asked whether the Bayfordbury site would not be better suited to the new university for Hertfordshire. In addition, staff from the Chelsea College expressed reservations at the levels of noise at the St Albans site from aircraft testing by Hawker Siddeley at Hatfield, calling instead for an alternative site at Knebworth. This had the advantage of 'attractive landscaping' and easy access to Stevenage New Town with its industry, housing and recreational facilities. Hitchin MP Shirley Williams pressed her Labour colleagues within the Ministry of Education for a speedy response, the issue having dragged on into 1965. She called on them to consider seriously the Stevenage option as it was her view that the New Town could 'offer all the advantages of St Albans and more'. Finally, some five years after proposals for a new university in Hertfordshire were first mooted, the plan to merge the two colleges was rejected by Anthony Crosland, Minister for Education.

When questioned by local reporters on the failed bid, Dr Chapman sounded remarkably upbeat, stressing that the College could now go forward with plans that had been put on hold during the negotiations for university status. 'I feel there will be more cause for civic pride with us retaining the name of Hatfield and under the control of Hertfordshire than if we had become a university. Naturally some will be disappointed. But before us now is a challenge to prove that Hatfield can make it. In the long run Hatfield will make just as good a contribution developing in its own way.' In his Annual Report, Chapman was somewhat more frank: he expressed his relief at the 'conclusion of a frustrating period of waiting and conjecture as to developments over which we seemed to have little or no control'. Other colleagues were even more outspoken. The Head of the Industrial Engineering Department, Gerald Smith, complained that the previous year had been one of 'doubts, uncertainties and difficulties', which had 'taxed patience and morale to the limit; it will take a considerable time before equanimity is restored'.

Chapman noted, however, that as a result of the Robbins Report the ten Colleges of Advanced Technology had been removed from the public sector of education, joining the universities as autonomous institutions, thus leaving Hatfield as 'one of the leading colleges in this sector, so that it is evident, given favourable conditions, that a University of Hertfordshire may still emerge under a familiar name and having a rather different character'.

## Towards polytechnic status

Keeping the College on an even keel whilst the powers that be negotiated the merger with the Chelsea College of Science and Technology was Chapman's last gift to Hatfield College. He retired in 1966 and his successor was announced as Norman Lindop, formerly Principal of the South-West Essex Technical College and School of Art. The two men worked together for the first few months of the 1965–66 session and Lindop paid tribute to Chapman, who, he said, 'had created not only an effective institution, dedicated to high standards, and enjoying a national reputation, but also a friendly community'.

Lindop was immediately plunged into preparations to ensure that when the names of the new polytechnics were announced, Hatfield would be one of them. He and his colleagues drew up a development plan which aimed to face head-on the challenges and opportunities of the new structuring of higher education.

*We have taken a fresh look at many hallowed traditions and institutions in further education and have attempted to plan an academic community in which there will be the widest possible diffusion of responsibility and the maximum incentive for initiative. This will place on each and every member of that community the onus of accepting increased responsibility and developing the work of the Polytechnic.*

Norman Lindop (1921–). Principal of Hatfield College of Technology/Director of Hatfield Polytechnic (1966–82). Lindop graduated from Queen Mary College, London with a First Class Honours degree in Chemistry in 1942. He then spent four years in industry as a research chemist and chemical engineer, before returning to academia and Queen Mary College as a lecturer in chemistry. In 1973 he was awarded a knighthood, an honour which he attributed to 'recognition by the Government of the success of the polytechnics'. He was appointed Deputy Lieutenant of Hertfordshire in 1989 and represented the St Andrews ward of Hertford on the County Council from 1993 to 2001.

One hurdle which had to be faced if the College was to take its place as a polytechnic, with a projected student body of 2,000 full-time students, was the lack of suitable accommodation, both teaching and residential. This had been a problem since the College first opened its doors, and continued to exercise the imagination of both the Principal and his staff, with 'various unorthodox expediencies' being employed to cope with the problem of inadequate teaching space. Mobile classrooms and huts were brought onto the site to reduce pressure on laboratory space. The development of residential courses posed further logistical challenges. In 1962, the Electrical Engineering Department introduced a one-week residential course for first-year Diploma in Technology students. By 1967–68 there were seven such courses organised across the College. Norman Lindop recognised the value of these residential courses, as groups of forty or fifty students could mix with staff in a more informal setting, with talks and discussions planned around a theme that was not always simply technical in nature. 'It is a modest but significant attempt to broaden our courses and to overcome our lack of communal residential accommodation,' he said, 'and it has a beneficial effect which is out of all proportion to the scale on which we can operate it.'

In 1965 the local authority bought Fairshot Court, at Sandridge, near St Albans, to act as a hostel for thirty students, but Chapman noted that, whilst welcome, there still remained much to be done, for 'unless more hostel places can be obtained in the foreseeable future our development cannot take place at the rate we have planned'.

The following year, permission was given by the Department of Education and Science for the building of a new 200-bed student hostel, as well as a new library and additional teaching space. However, such funds were always subject to political whim in a changing economic environment, and shortly afterwards permission was withdrawn 'as part of the wider national review on spending due to the economic crisis'. Eventually some £750,000 was released by the government for building work. Lindop feared, nevertheless, that if the ongoing problems with the quality of residential, social and teaching accommodation were not rectified Hatfield would struggle in the post-Robbins environment: 'So long as this disparity exists the undoubtedly high quality of the education which we offer will only prompt the reflection that what is being attempted is higher education at cut price.'

Problems were eased somewhat with the acquisition of Bayfordbury as additional space in 1967. The College moved staff from the Department of Business and Social Studies into the recently vacated mansion, whilst the former John Innes laboratories improved the facilities available to the departments of Chemistry and Biology. Then, in 1969, the Department of Mechanical and Aeronautical Engineering's Design Centre and the newly established Occupational Research Centre were moved to Birklands, near St Albans. In 1970 the Department of Management Studies was also relocated from Bayfordbury to Birklands, occupying much of the upper floors and the lecture theatre of the former boarding school.

## Bayfordbury: A brief history

In 1757 William Baker, an Alderman of the City of London, bought the Bayfordbury estate, just a few miles to the south-west of the county town of Hertford. He was typical of many such men who bought estates in the county at this time, men who had grown rich in servicing an expanding empire. The son of a prosperous London draper, he amassed a large fortune by negotiating contracts to supply the army, becoming Governor of the Hudson's Bay Company in 1760, the year in which he was knighted. As Chairman of the East India Company he joined others in Hertfordshire who found it convenient for overseeing their London business whilst escaping to the cleaner air of the countryside.

William Baker followed a pattern of others who bought themselves an estate and he built a new and impressive house, which his son, also William, extended and improved when he succeeded to the estate upon his father's death in 1770. William also continued his father's ambitious planting scheme for an arboretum, which was a real vote of confidence in the family's future at Bayfordbury; the fourth-generation William also began work on a pinetum in 1837, with the planting of at least ninety-two specimens. The Baker family were able to maintain their estate through the difficult years of falling rents and agricultural depression at the end of the nineteenth century and the losses of the First World War. The cost of maintaining both estate and

*Bayfordbury Observatory.*

arboretum was becoming problematic, however, and with the death in 1939 of Admiral Sir Lewis Clinton Baker (the seventh-generation Baker to hold the estate), the house was left empty. During the Second World War the house was let to Barnardo's to house boys evacuated from other homes, but with the end of hostilities the estate was sold, the house and pinetum being bought to house the John Innes Horticultural Institute, which officially opened in 1950. They added additional greenhouses and laboratories for experiments in plant breeding and disease.

Then the company's directors felt that future development of its specialist genetics research laboratory must include closer links to a university, and a site at Norwich, close to the newly designated University of East Anglia, was selected. Bayfordbury was offered to Hertfordshire County Council, and so it became the first of the additional annexes attached to the Hatfield College of Technology on the eve of its transition to Polytechnic status.

*Field study group at Bayfordbury.*

# Birklands: A brief history

Whereas the history of Bayfordbury was representative of those men who had made their fortunes servicing the empire in the eighteenth century, the story of Birklands was more typical of the arrival in Hertfordshire, in the latter part of the nineteenth century, of those who had made their money from the growth in commercial and retail opportunities. Henry Jenkin Gotto was an Oxford Street stationer, who, in 1877, bought Newhouse Farm to the south-east of St Albans, with frontage onto the London Road, adding to the estate in 1886 when the neighbouring New Barnes estate came onto the market. Following a pattern adopted by many of those who moved into the county at this time, he set about building himself a much grander house on the site – a reflection of his newly acquired status – and named it Newhouse

Park. Upon his death in 1892, the estate was leased to yet another of those representatives of the expanding consumer society, Edmund Meredith Crosse, Chairman of the food manufacturers Crosse & Blackwell, and he was followed as tenant by Elizabeth Helen Cox, who arrived in 1905. Elizabeth Cox was Principal of Birklands School, Highgate – a district which by 1905 was being rapidly urbanised. St Albans offered a chance for more space and fresher air for the girls; a gymnasium was built and the girls had the opportunity to play lacrosse, tennis and golf. In 1923 Newhouse Park was renamed as Birklands and continued as a boarding school on the site until 1969, when declining numbers saw the school close and the lease taken over by Hertfordshire County Council.

## Now a polytechnic

In January 1969 the College was one of the first four to receive Polytechnic status, along with Leicester (now De Montfort University), Sunderland, and Sheffield (now Sheffield Hallam University). The following spring, Norman Lindop told the annual meeting of the Hatfield Chamber of Commerce that the Polytechnic was looking forward to a decade of expansion, which would see the creation of more teaching space, better communal social facilities and more residential accommodation for students. His optimism was based on the commitment to the polytechnic system announced by the newly elected Conservative government led by Edward Heath, an optimism which seemed fulfilled with the announcement by Education Secretary, Margaret Thatcher, in the winter of 1970, of a £7.3 million national investment in building projects for polytechnics.

Some building work did proceed at Hatfield. The first intake of students into Butler and Harold Fern Halls arrived in the autumn of 1970. These were the first Halls of Residence to be built on the Hatfield site and were named in honour of Alan S. Butler and Alderman Harold Fern, first Chairman of the Governing Body of Hatfield Technical College. Chapman Hall followed in April 1971. That year, the Polytechnic welcomed Lord Snow, who untied the ribbon marking the official opening of the new £204,000, four-storey library, which had begun operations the previous year. (Lord Snow was obliged to untie the ribbon as the necessary scissors had been misplaced.) This work was part of 'Phase 1' of a planned expansion that would bring the capacity of the Polytechnic to the equivalent of 2,000 full-time students. It was anticipated that 'Phase 2', due to begin in 1972, would see a growth in capacity to 3,500 full-time places. The government's Department of Education and Science gave its approval to a range of building projects, costing some £440,000 in total, which would see the addition of a Language Centre, an Engineering Design Centre, and further working space for staff and students. Plans were also being drawn up for two further Halls of Residence and better facilities for the Students' Union.

### Hatfield Polytechnic in 1971

- 1,800 full-time students, 6% of whom were from overseas
- 40 full-time and 10 part-time MPhil and PhD students
- 30% of full-time students came from Hertfordshire
- 1,000 part-time students, of whom 250 were preparing for Bachelor's or Master's degrees

The report of the newly knighted Sir Norman Lindop threw cold water on those ambitions: 'The economic blizzard of the winter of 1973–74 has set back the development of the Polytechnic by at least three years and probably more.' The fall-out from the Yom Kippur War and the subsequent oil embargo by OPEC in protest at Israel's military offensive had an immediate impact on the Polytechnic and its plans for growth, with all major construction programmes, other than those where building had already begun, postponed indefinitely. There was some cheer as the Language Centre and two new Halls of Residence were completed; Sidney Broad Hall (Broad was County Education Officer 1957–73) and John Coales Hall (named after Professor John F. Coales, a founder governor of Hatfield Technical College) were opened in 1974.

Meanwhile, a fundamental change had taken place in the way degrees were delivered at the Polytechnic. In 1973 the Common Modular Structure was introduced, whereby students were able to choose a range of credit-bearing modules, each designed according to the level of study within the programme. The system provided choice and flexibility for students, allowed

*'It was quite controversial because academics are a bit like cats, they don't like being herded too much, and I think all of us found something in the modular structure that we didn't like. ... Some of the things like common grading structures ... actually made people stop and think about what they were trying to assess and how they were going to assess it, and I think that was very beneficial to the institution.'*

**Peter Lines, Lecturer in Telecommunications in the 1970s and later Dean of Engineering, on the introduction of the modular structure.**

for the award of intermediate qualifications, and made the taking of combined programmes more manageable. The Open University was the first institution in British higher education to introduce such a credit-based modular framework. John Hall, who had arrived at the College in 1959 to head the new Department of Mathematics, and was by now Assistant Director (Academic) of the Polytechnic, engineered its introduction at Hatfield, making it one of only five higher education institutions in England to adopt the system. It enabled the Polytechnic and the University in its early years to promote foreign languages, for instance, as integral to the undergraduate experience. By 1995 nearly 90 per cent of universities were running modular courses, had a quasi-modular teaching structure, or were moving towards modularity.

*John Illston. Director of the Polytechnic 1982–87. Professor Illston was educated at Wallington County Grammar School, before moving on to study Engineering at King's College, University of London, from where he graduated with First Class Honours. He then went on to complete his National Service in the Royal Engineers before taking a job with a firm of consulting engineers. In 1959 he returned to King's College to take up a post as a lecturer in Civil Engineering and whilst there studied for a PhD in Concrete Technology and a DSc (Eng). He joined Hatfield Polytechnic in 1977 as Director of Studies, before becoming Dean of the School of Engineering in 1980.*

Any hopes that higher education funding might be boosted during the late 1970s were dashed by the reality of an economic downturn, which had implications beyond the halt to building programmes. Whilst large capital projects came within the remit of the Department of Education and Science, the Polytechnic's budget for normal running costs was submitted annually to the County Council for approval. The 1978–79 'Winter of Discontent' saw the election in May 1979 of Margaret Thatcher's Conservative government with its commitment to reductions in public spending. Hertfordshire County Council subsequently called on the Polytechnic to submit a new budget to take into account an expected reduction in expenditure of £100,000, and subsequent years confirmed there was to be no U-turn on this policy.

Cuts to the budget of £0.75 million in 1979–80 and of £1 million in 1980–81 left the Polytechnic with little alternative but to reduce overheads. This meant that for the first time it was forced to reduce staffing levels. An early retirement scheme was introduced which saw twenty-six members of staff leave the Polytechnic, many of them veterans of the College of Technology days. Sir Norman Lindop noted in his report of that year that 'it was not possible to pay the tribute they deserve to all those who left the Polytechnic in the great summer Exodus of 1981'. This was his final report as Director, as he left in April 1982, taking up a post as Principal of the British School of Osteopathy. Lindop was succeeded by Dr John Illston, his Deputy and former Dean of the School of Engineering.

# Wall Hall: A brief history

By the end of the nineteenth century the appeal of owning an English country estate lay much more in the opportunities it offered for gracious living in pleasant surroundings, with outdoor sports to hand, than in the establishment of a family seat that would bestow legitimacy and the potential for political power. This was exemplified in the renting and then buying of the Wall Hall estate at Aldenham by John Pierpont Morgan Jnr, third-generation member of the famous American banking family, in 1901. Wall Hall was typical of many properties within Hertfordshire: whilst Bayfordbury and Balls Park had been handed down within the same family for several generations, Wall Hall

had passed through several different hands during the nineteenth century. In 1799 the estate had been bought by George Woodford Thellusson, a director of the East India Company and one of those instrumental in the establishment of Haileybury School. It was he who employed Humphry Repton to landscape the gardens around his newly built gothic mansion, which he renamed Aldenham Abbey. At his death the house and estate were sold again, to a retired admiral, Sir Charles Morice Pole, but other than his grandson, who made some alterations to the house, no other members of the family who inherited chose to live in the house. The house stood empty until 1901 when Morgan Jnr was

Wall Hall, Hertfordshire College of Higher Education, 1978.

transferred to the London office; his delight in playing the English country squire, or at least as he understood it, with opportunities for shooting and visiting his herd of prize-winning pigs, saw him keep the house even when recalled to America in 1905. He bought the estate in 1910, changing the name back to its earlier title of Wall Hall, but only ever visited it for a few weeks every summer. At the outbreak of war in 1939, the house was used as an emergency maternity hospital and also as a Secret Service base. Morgan also lent it out to the American ambassador, Joseph Kennedy, as a weekend retreat. The Hertfordshire educationist John Newsom recalled, 'The first time I ever went there, it was being used as the headquarters of some branch of clandestine warfare in North East Europe. There were things like pistol ranges in the gardens and places where bombs and explosives could be tried out. It was very much James Bond in a way; big motor cars used to arrive in the middle of the night from airfields and people got out from Europe or people used to leave from an aerodrome not very far from here to be dropped in Europe.'

Morgan's death in 1943 gave Hertfordshire County Council the opportunity to exercise an option to buy the house, which then provided space for a teacher training college aimed in particular at demobilised service men and women.

*Wall Hall in 2011.*

The Polytechnic had a long tradition of supplying courses for teachers both during their training period and beyond. A part-time in-service BEd course operated in partnership with the teacher training colleges at Balls Park, Wall Hall and Putteridgebury.

A slow-down in the demand for places saw Hertfordshire County Council merge the Balls Park and Wall Hall colleges to become the Hertfordshire College of Higher Education. With this new beast based at Wall Hall, the County Council invited the Polytechnic to use the Balls Park Mansion, an invitation which saw the School of Social Sciences move from its split sites at Bayfordbury and Hatfield to a new home. The Polytechnic continued to maintain the Observatory and teaching classrooms at Bayfordbury, but gave up its tenancy of both the Bayfordbury and Birklands mansions in 1984.

*'When I was having the interview ... I just got that feeling when I looked around at the place ... the French doors were open and I could see onto the lawn and the lovely trees and the surrounds and I just had that feeling that, you know, I had a feeling I really wanted this job.'*

**Ernie Mackenzie, support staff member at Wall Hall, c.1995.**

The moving of departments to other sites was not without its critics. The Students' Union and Social Science students mounted a vociferous campaign against the move of their department to Balls Park. In February 1977 a group of around fifty students occupied the Administration Block, staging a twenty-four-hour sit-in, and followed up with a take-over of the telephone exchange, with bemused callers to the Polytechnic being told of their grievances. Georgie Scurfield, a fourth-year student and former Students' Union president, told the local press: 'We want to keep it as a one-site Poly. If we move, Balls Park will be just a second-class annexe. Any extension of the department should be made here on the Hatfield site.'

Hertfordshire College of Higher Education merged with Hatfield Polytechnic in the summer of 1987. The College, which had begun life as Wall Hall College of Education, occupied the sweeping mansion in the village of Aldenham, just on the outskirts of Watford. The mansion buildings which were situated at the end of a large drive from the village had been added to by a collection of teaching and residential blocks as the College grew in the post-war years.

# Balls Park: A brief history

In 1883, George Faudel Phillips, owner of warehouses in Newgate Street, London, and a future Mayor of the City of London, took a lease on the Balls Park estate, near Hertford. His arrival was a response to the downturn in the fortunes of the Townshend family, who had owned the estate since 1637, when John Harrison, a tax farmer and future MP for Lancaster, chose this district as ideal for fulfilling his ambitions to become a landowner and politician.

Faudel Phillips was heavily engaged in charitable work; his most high-profile campaign saw him raise £550,000 for famine relief in India, but at a more local level he and his wife, Helen, set up and contributed to a number of initiatives to help the poor on their own doorstep, from evening classes for young boys and girls to learn crafts, to workhouse treats and hot meals for the poor in the depths of winter. Many commentators on the changing nature of landownership at the end of the nineteenth century expressed concern that the new men and women who were moving into the country estates of the older gentry would fail to take on their local responsibilities, but this proved too pessimistic a view, as those who had made their money in the shops and warehouses of London and beyond proved, showing continuing commitment to an ideal of paternalistic support. George's son, Lionel, continued his father's work and it is perhaps appropriate that upon his death in 1941 Balls Park was used to house disabled children evacuated from London.

The house and one hundred acres were bought by Hertfordshire County Council as the war drew to a close, the intention being to adapt the site for a new teacher training college – part of that wider initiative by government and local authorities to improve educational opportunities for the post-war generation.

*The Balls Park mansion.*

*Aerial view of the Balls Park estate, 1970.*

In late 1987 the Polytechnic Director, Professor Neil Buxton, decided that the campus at Wall Hall was not sustainable in its current form. Education and humanities courses were delivered at Wall Hall, but at Hatfield there was also a small in-service Education Department and a large School of Humanities. He decided that these should merge to form a School of Humanities and Education and that the new School should be based at Wall Hall. Concerns were expressed that the loss of humanities subjects at the main Hatfield site would make the Polytechnic a less attractive proposition for potential students, as well as causing existing students difficulties of access and additional costs.

However, both Wall Hall and Balls Park grew to be appreciated by staff and students who were based there and, indeed, regrets were expressed when Humanities and Education were moved to Hatfield's new de Havilland campus in 2003.

*Dr Jane Singleton, retired Principal Lecturer in Philosophy, who began at Hatfield Polytechnic in the 1970s, reflecting on the move of the Humanities to Wall Hall:*

*'in philosophy we were a bit dubious about this because it did seem rather like an outpost, very isolating after having been right at the centre of College Lane…'*

*Hence the Philosophy Department stayed at College Lane and moved in with the Psychology Department, in the C.P. Snow Building for a while, before eventually being shipped out to join its Humanities colleagues.*

*Memories of Wall Hall days, Nazima Dace, BEd student 1990–4.*

Year-on-year restrictions on expenditure challenged the ambitions of the Polytechnic. In his report of 1983–84, Illston drew a comparison between the 20 per cent increase in the number of students in the five years since 1979 (from 3,635 to 4,364), and the 18 per cent decrease in staff numbers (from 1,000 to 824), concluding that 'looking to the future, it is impossible to perceive any lightening of the gloom'. In keeping with its tradition of strong links with industry, Illston noted that this was one source independent of the policies of central government that continued to bring in revenue: 'The Polytechnic soldiers on, raising funds from short courses and other activities not to put the jam on the bread but merely to provide the bread. It could have been worse – next year probably will be.' Yet alongside the very real difficulties faced by the Polytechnic in maintaining staffing levels, as Illston identified, the student population was steadily expanding, and whilst this put pressure on both teaching and residential space, it was a sign of the distance the Polytechnic had travelled from its early days as a technical college.

In its final days as a college of technology, the prospectus had offered potential students eleven CNAA-approved first-degree courses in a variety of formats including Ordinary and Honours, with full-time, sandwich, block release and part-time attendance. There was also a single MSc course in Control Engineering, as well as a range of

HND courses and others linked to the examination requirements of professional bodies such as the Association of Certified and Corporate Accountants. By 1992 the number of courses on offer had risen to fifty-five first-degree courses, nineteen taught Master's degrees, research higher degrees and an increased number of HND courses. In addition, the range of degrees had expanded beyond the original focus on Engineering and Applied Sciences to include such courses as Travel and Tourism, Nursing, Electronic Music and Combined Studies, which allowed students to design degrees reflecting their own expertise. Amidst all the gloom there were continuing signs of the growing reputation of the Polytechnic as both a research institution and a provider of first-class higher education. A 1985 *Sunday Times* survey of 500 employers of graduates reported: 'Hatfield is the favourite polytechnic for both arts and science', and in 1986 the Polytechnic was given the status of a CNAA-accredited institution, with the Polytechnic Academic Board assuming responsibility for the validation and review of all its taught schemes of study. Hatfield became one of only ten such institutions with this level of control over its own academic development. A committee set up by the Education Secretary, Sir Keith Joseph, and chaired by former Hatfield Polytechnic Director, Sir Norman Lindop, issued a report that argued that polytechnics should be allowed to direct their own affairs, as was the case with universities, and be freed from local authority control.

- **In 1970**, the Polytechnic was awarded 164 CNAA-approved first degrees, one MPhil (as an external student) and one PhD.

- **In 1986**, 941 first degrees, 99 Master's degrees, 3 MPhils and 16 PhDs were awarded

As a consequence of the Conservative government's Education Reform Act of 1988, in April 1989, Hatfield Polytechnic, like all other polytechnics, became a Higher Education Corporation. This took it out of County Council control, and made it responsible for its own finances. While some funding from central government would be available from the newly created Polytechnics and Colleges Funding Council, the government's intention, apart from further weakening the power of local authorities, was to give the commercial and industrial sector a greater role in higher education.

## And finally a university

In February 1992 the last complete aeroplane to be built at British Aerospace (BAe), Hatfield, rolled off the production line, and 'a proud era spanning nearly 60 years in Hatfield's history' came to an end with the transfer of final assembly to BAe's site at Woodford, near Manchester. In spite of a company spokesman confirming their 'commitment to the aircraft business at Hatfield', an initial loss of just over 2,000 jobs was followed in September of that year by the announcement that a further 2,000 would go with the closure of the Hatfield factory at the beginning of 1993. This was a devastating blow to the local economy, impacting on more workers than just those directly employed by BAe. The local authority estimated that over £15 million of goods were

*Hatfield Polytechnic signage coming down in 1992.*

purchased annually by BAe from suppliers around Hertfordshire. An estimated additional 1,300 jobs were at risk, together with a reduction in consumer spending power of £12 million a year. A further loss was the withdrawal of BAe from the newly completed £30 million office development at Bishop's Square, named in honour of aircraft designer Ronald E. Bishop, whose iconic Mosquito plane had been such a part of de Havilland's history. In February 1992, even before the announcement of the closure of the de Havilland site, Hatfield had the highest unemployment rate in the county at 16.3 per cent. In September The Galleria – Europe's largest shopping centre at the time of its opening in 1991 – celebrated its one-year anniversary by entering into receivership.

It was against this background that Hatfield Polytechnic Higher Education Corporation became the University of Hertfordshire, under the guidance of its first Vice-Chancellor, Neil Buxton. The award of University status had been made possible by the Further and Higher Education Act (1992), which increased the number of universities in the UK from forty-seven to eighty-eight. The CNAA was abolished and the new universities were now able to award their own undergraduate and postgraduate degrees.

The change in nomenclature was not without its critics locally. A representative from Hatfield Town Council was quoted as saying, 'We are delighted to see the polytechnic become a university but would be disappointed if it did not carry forward the name of Hatfield.' *Welwyn and Hatfield Times* columnist Charles Meynard, who continued to refer to the new university as 'Hatfield's University of Hertfordshire', sympathised with 'the punch drunk folk of Hatfield, [who] must be wondering what is going to hit them next. For now the proud name association of the town with an academic institution, like its plane-making past, is just a memory.' The change to University status offered a bold new future, but the funding realities of the time brought further job losses. Whilst the Polytechnic prepared for the official change in status in September 1992, it also sought to turn around an end-of-year deficit of £750,000. Most of the savings were achieved through an early retirement scheme.

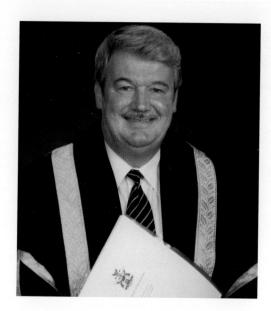

*Neil Keith Buxton (1940–). Director of Hatfield Polytechnic from 1987, and first Vice-Chancellor of the University until 2003. Buxton is an economic historian who was at one time a Senior Lecturer in Economics at Heriot-Watt University and is the author of* The Economic Development of the British Coal Industry *(1979). He was also a Scottish hockey international.*

Vice-Chancellor, Professor Neil Buxton, responded to local criticism with a letter to the press outlining the place of the University within its county:

'Members of the public, company representatives and various organisations have contacted us to wish the university well in the new era which began on Monday June 29. On that day we officially became the University of Hertfordshire and shed the name of Hatfield Polytechnic.

We were sensitive to the fact that there have been objections in some quarters to the disappearance of the word Hatfield from our title but we had to make the painful decision in order to identify the fact that we are now truly a Herts county university.

With campuses at Watford and Hertford as well as at Hatfield, the university spans the county, east to west; with the setting up of the exciting Associate College network with our colleagues in FE at Oaklands College, North Hertfordshire College, West Herts College and Hertford Regional College – plus our close links with

the Hertfordshire College of Art and Design – we have an education presence in every corner of Hertfordshire.

In addition to national and international recruitment, both staff and students of the University of Hertfordshire are drawn from many parts of the county. The organisation has hundreds of links with county firms through research, consultancy and student placement as well as by supply of short courses.

In some ways the rise and expansion of Hatfield Polytechnic since its post-war birth mirrored the progress of Hertfordshire. There were already in the county industries of great pedigree – including aircraft and aero-engine manufacturing, printing, brewing – some of which have been dealt harsh blows in recent years.

The post-war arrival of the New Towns of Hemel Hempstead, Stevenage and Hatfield brought a surge of new industry and laid the foundations for a prosperous county served by a rapidly growing network of roads and improved rail links with London.

The University's ancestor, Hatfield Technical College, also began in a small way and entered new avenues of work, all the time maintaining and expanding its influence locally and nationally, leading us to polytechnic status in 1969.

We who work and study at the newly-created University of Hertfordshire are fully aware of the trying times being experienced in many parts of our county – the university itself has not escaped financial rigours.

Our earnest hope is that Hertfordshire's commerce and institutions return to full health in the next few years and, like the University of Hertfordshire, head towards the millennium with keen anticipation and great expectations.Hertfordshire's own great writer E.M. Forster described his county 50 years ago as "England Meditative".

Perhaps it appears less contemplative today with all the industrial and social pressures of the late 20th century. But we, its university, have the greatest respect for Hertfordshire's modern qualities; in the coming years we hope that the county comes to know and respect the university for qualities which made it Britain's model polytechnic – an innovatory drive and an openness to change.'

# Ode to a New University by 'Ned Brown', Wall Hall Campus

We've done the work; we're all 'preferred',
Hatfield Poly has up-and-stirred
(The CNAA has got the bird)
'UH' is now our logo-word

Let all our Schools unite to be
In omnischolarly amity
One interactive polity
Where all might whinge equilaterally.

Let each, as well, improve its work,
Bring light where once was only murk
(As our Finals' students go berserk),
And chase each National Research Perk

So – Engineers who build the real
With metal, concrete, brain and 'feel'.
Electronics, blue-prints, jet and wheel:
Don't let your ideas (or sump) congeal.

Chemists, who con the elemental,
Compound your compounds (within 'rental');
Stay analytic – not sentimental,
And inter-disc – not compartmental

Biologists, who study life
In vivo, vitro (lust or strife),
Beware of cells with habits rife
And if in doubt, well – wield the knife.

Astronomers who scan the skies
And find that up there ain't no 'pies'
Yet see the strangest blobs – no lies;
Do check your screens for 'Green Men' spies.

O, Healthy Human Scientists seek
An 'oomph' for all – each last pip-squeak;
Translate your terms from Latin and Greek,
And 'salve' our problems when you speak.

Ye Information Scientists who
By byte not bark the world undo
Add Hypertext it as our NEW,
Remember those who question 'true'.

Philosophers who sift our thoughts,
Locke up our fancies, Mill fine 'oughts',
Made canny by Kant's (rather long) reports –
Pray, don't deride Derrida's textual sports.

Psychologists, you who probe the mind
And human 'bee-hive-iour', may you find
Despite the self's dreaded 'double-bind',
A prankish 'Soul' in human kind.

Literary theorists (long of word)
Let not your letters be deterred;
Dispute which 'Shakespeare' should be heard,
And invent new 'isms', freshly-spurred.

Linguists, historians, experts on religion:
Veracity guide you, that and precision
For placement of category, archives of region.
And if things go wrong – there's always revision

Musicians, artists – performing or passive,
May your energy mount to proportions massive,
Your creations never be found to be crass-ive
As you work in the playful world of 'as-if'.

Ye doctors of Business, Society, Law –
Succumb not to entropy, still produce more;
Let Smith be Adamic and Marx no bore
And make Justice more juste than ever before.

Mathematicians and physicists, rare of breed –
Multiply quarks and divide up Speed.
Keep Light enlightening (make that your creed)
And may the black hole of research-cuts recede.

Let Environment Scientists keep our earth pure,
For chronic pollution find some sort of cure,
Help preserve ice-caps, help the ibis endure –
Find friends in government (as well as the brewer).

Education's staff-members, O teach us to teach
(Especially those staff poor in reading or speech)
To those for whom classes are prime-time to retch,
'Special Needs' (all ages) – O help, we beseech.

Let all our 'Support Staff' receive our support
For opening locked doors or filing report,
Or filling our bellies with food (for thought),
Supporting both those who are teachers and taught.

To all who administrate, manage our 'Search' –
Don't knock our wild lecturers right off their perch,
Or leave student odd-balls quite in the lurch:
But guide all in peace (as they teach us in church).

Opportunities Equal – be herd and be seen!
May men be as women (and all of us Green);
Let's be open to all with ambitions keen
(And rake in more fees while becoming real 'clean').

Now God bless and succour our brand-new VC
Let his gown be of silk (not of PVC)
To preside over many an awarded degree –
And shore up our Corporate Identity.

So may hearts and minds unite now to cheer
Our outstanding new U of old Hertfordshire:
Farewell pretty Poly, you got us all here;
Let's not shed a tear – let's hoist a large beer!

Horizon. News of the University of Hertfordshire,
57 (October 1992)

The newly fledged University of Hertfordshire added to its profile when in September 1992 it completed a merger with the Hertfordshire College of Art and Design (formerly St Albans School of Art), to create the Faculty of Art and Design. The Pro-Vice-Chancellor at the time, Professor Tim Wilson, welcomed the merger 'as an extremely exciting event for the county', offering an expansion in arts provision at the University for both students and the public.

Established in the 1880s, the St Albans School of Art's original home was purpose-built by public subscription and sited in Victoria Street. In September 1974 it became the Hertfordshire College of Art and Design and spread over four sites in St Albans. At the time of the merger it had 1,253 students (345 full-time, 468 part-time, 440 evening only) plus more than 440 people attending courses run by the Short Course Unit. The move to transfer the School from St Albans to Hatfield required 2,000 packing crates, and 100 lorry loads of equipment were transferred from the St Albans sites to Hatfield, where the newly united School was based provisionally in the former British Aerospace Design Block at Hatfield aerodrome. This was built in 1952 and was home to the design of aeroplanes such as the Nimrod and Trident, but was demolished with the creation of a business park on the site. The move from St Albans to Hatfield also saw the transfer of more than 35,000 books and 70,000 slides. The former BAe buildings were in poor condition, and there was much relief amongst staff and students when the faculty finally moved into the purpose-built Art and Design building and converted Library building (Todd Building) on the College Lane campus in 1998. The new facilities provided a cutting-edge workshop environment for practical teaching, including a machine shop and specialist printmaking facilities.

*The University's student newspaper.*

The University's presence in St Albans was maintained by the School of Law, which occupied the greater part of the former College of Art and Design building on Hatfield Road from 1997 to 2011.

Meanwhile, the University was building strengths in other areas. In 1993 the Hertfordshire College of Health Care Studies and the Barnet College of Nursing and Midwifery merged with the University and were incorporated into the Faculty of Health and Human Sciences, joining the existing community nursing programmes. In the short term, new provisional accommodation had to be found for this team too, with a lease signed on Meridian House, The Common, Hatfield, to contain seven classrooms and a Learning Resource Centre, with larger classes to be taught in Hatfield's Forum Theatre.

In 1998, in his annual address to staff, Vice-Chancellor Neil Buxton announced that the University was exploring the possibility of developing part of the former British Aerospace site with a view to bringing the schools now housed at Wall Hall and Balls Park to a single Hatfield campus. In so doing, the University would be completing a story which began when Alan S. Butler, Chairman of the de Havilland Aircraft Company, had the factory relocated from its North London site to land just to the west of Hatfield.

*The de Havilland campus.*

Work began on the thirty-acre site in September 2001 when the University's then Chancellor, Lord MacLaurin, cut the first turf. Earlier that summer, in June, another turf was cut on the site, which heralded the building of a new clubhouse for the de Havilland Sports and Social Club, whose continued existence had been a matter of some concern to members as the former site of a thriving aircraft industry was dismantled. The partnership between the de Havilland members and the University secured not only the former's continued existence, but also, a bowling green and an all-weather pitch. When Lord MacLaurin returned in March 2002 to formally open the Sports and Social Club, Club Chairman Raymond Little applauded the commitment of the University to the town in which it sat: 'The building of this club and the assistance given shows the commitment the university has to the community of Hatfield. Hatfield is the home of the University of Hertfordshire; the university is now a very important part of our community.'

*The de Havilland Aircraft Company logo on the wall of Club de Havilland.*

The new de Havilland development was to be funded in part by the selling of the historic mansions of Wall Hall and Balls Park, both of which were expensive to maintain. The remainder of the £120 million costs were raised as a result of support from the Higher Education Funding Council for England (HEFCE), which gave £7 million to the project, and a partnership with Arlington Securities as a private finance initiative, the first of its kind in the UK. The bonds were all sold within half an hour and provided over half of the final costs. Tim Wilson, who, as Pro-Vice-Chancellor, had been Project Director for the build, was particularly proud of the fact that the building work came in on time and on budget.

As well as lecture theatres, teaching rooms, a Learning Resources Centre and administration offices, the new campus included a 460-seat auditorium, student accommodation in 1,600 study bedrooms, all with Internet connections, and a £15 million Sports Village. The latter housed an eight-lane swimming pool, a 100-station fitness centre, badminton courts, a cricket hall, floodlit outdoor and all-weather sports pitches and a 400 square metre climbing wall. In October the first students began to arrive and take up residence in the new Halls, each named after a Hertfordshire town or village. As part of their introduction to university living, they were encouraged to enter a *Ready, Steady, Cook* style competition, devising and preparing recipes on the theme of 'brain food' to showcase the kitchens of the new Halls of Residence. The winning recipe came from Deniece Francis, who produced a filo salmon pie on a bed of fresh spinach with cheese sauce.

October also saw the new auditorium perform its first official function when it hosted the inauguration of Tim Wilson as Vice-Chancellor of the University. A month later, on 3 November 2003, the new Vice-Chancellor welcomed HRH Prince Philip, Duke of Edinburgh, to the site and invited him to formally open the campus, fifty-one years after he had performed the same duty for Hatfield Technical College.

In 2011 the final piece of the University of Hertfordshire jigsaw came together when the School of Law moved from its home in the building previously occupied by the Hertfordshire College of Art and Design to the de Havilland campus, with the construction of the Law Court building at a cost of £10 million. The building provided new teaching rooms, an authentic Court Room, Mediation Centre and Law Clinic.

*(Above)*
*Deniece Francis with her winning dish.*

*(Left)*
*Professor Sir Tim Wilson and HRH Prince Philip, Duke of Edinburgh, 2003. Wilson was born in Leeds and educated in Yorkshire, before going on to study Mathematics and Computer Science at Reading University. His industrial career saw him working as an operational research analyst, employing mathematical and computer simulation techniques to model complexity. He then pursued an academic career at institutions which became Leeds Metropolitan, Cranfield and de Montfort universities before joining the University of Hertfordshire in 1991. Professor Wilson enjoyed an early sporting career in Rugby Union, first as a player at national league level, then in the 1980s as an England Staff Coach and into the 1990s as an England A-list referee.*

The new Law Court building, 2011.

# The University Mace

The University's Mace was created in 1997 by Martyn Pugh. Four feet long, the Mace has a silver head, rosewood haft and silver heel. The head's smooth streamlined silver skin, tipped with a titanium point, encloses a sphere that is visible through three openings set equally around the axis. The sphere is located by the blue titanium ribs that support the exterior silver skin and is pierced by a silver-gilt rod that forms the axis of the head. Each opening in the head displays a different view of the sphere – the protective outer ribbed casing, the internal layer of silver-gilt memory chips and finally the central axis of double helix DNA. The motto of the University is engraved around the head, close to the tip, the Coat of Arms being engraved three times at intervals around the base of the head.

All these elements represent both the University's connections and its specific areas of expertise. The streamlined silver head with its internal structure of titanium ribs was inspired by the **de Havilland** and **British Aerospace** connections. The ribbed casing of the sphere and engineered construction represents the **engineering sciences**, the secondary layer of gold memory chips – **information technology** – whilst the protected heart of the sphere containing the DNA helix represents the **biological** and **health sciences**.

The haft, turned in rosewood with an English oak band (legend has it that Elizabeth I learned of her accession to the throne while sitting under an oak in the grounds of Hatfield House) is encircled at its centre with four chased bands representing the four elements of earth, water, air and fire as found in the University's Coat of Arms and suggestive of the sciences of **Chemistry**. The 'air' band displays the particularly significant star constellation of Perseus (including the binary star Algol) that in the Coat of Arms represents the University's close links with the **computer, biological** and **pharmaceutical industries** and with the **health sciences**.

The heel of the Mace has the pierced and engraved Coat of Arms suspended above, and mirrored in, a polished silver-gilt concave dish that alludes to the polished shield used by Perseus in Greek mythology to slay Medusa – a reference to the **pharmaceutical industry's** use of certain harmful drugs that in a mirror form are curative. Finally, a quill decoration, representative of the **humanities** and **C.P. Snow's** associations, begins on the head and traverses the length of the Mace, linking all the elements together.

*Professor Sir Tim Wilson, Vice-Chancellor of the University from 2003 to 2010, holding the mace.*

# 3. Building success

In 1974 the subject areas taught by the Polytechnic had been restructured into five major schools of study: Engineering, Humanities, Information Sciences, Natural Sciences and Social Sciences (this became the School of Business and Social Sciences in a further change of name in 1981, reflecting the growing strength of Business Studies). More restructuring took place over the ensuing years with the creation of faculties and new schools, divisions, departments, units and subject groups. Departments merged, and schools split. Divisions disappeared. These shifts in language and structure occurred for various reasons: the expansion or reduction of student numbers, changing emphases in higher education provision, and the strategic visions of successive senior managers. Rather than trying to provide an account of these numerous internal structural changes (see the appendices for a general overview), this chapter explores how the institution's staff and students built on the growing reputation of the institution by developing and expanding the curriculum and its research profile in each subject area.

## Engineering

The School of Engineering, which included the departments of Civil Engineering and Construction, Electrical Engineering and Physics, Industrial Engineering, and Mechanical and Aeronautical Engineering, was particularly impacted by the economic difficulties of the early 1970s, which beset the industrial sectors of the country in general and of Hertfordshire in particular. Finding placements for students took an increasing proportion of tutors' time as companies struggled with short-time working, industrial action, redundancies and closures. However, placements were found and this was attributed to the strong links established with local industries in preceding years. Whilst applications to Engineering courses fell nationally in the early 1970s, Hatfield continued to attract high numbers of students, particularly in the field of civil engineering.

The budgetary restrictions imposed by the County Council hit the Engineering departments particularly hard. The early retirements which followed the budget cuts of 1980–81 saw fourteen full-time posts being lost across the School. Yet in spite of obvious difficulties, the School of Engineering continued to have its successes, maintaining its position as the largest of the schools. In 1978 a thousand applications were made for the 100 places on courses leading to a BSc or HND qualification in Electrical and Electronic Engineering. At the same time, there had been a reduction in the overall representation of the Engineering departments to 28 per cent of the student body – a reflection of the growth of other areas of the Polytechnic.

What was most commented upon in the Annual Reports was the shift from part-time and block release courses to a greater demand for full-time and sandwich courses in engineering. This was a reflection of both the economic constraints on industry, which saw companies less able to finance training for staff, and 'the School's continued and determined efforts to develop links with schools, including careers staff, subject specialists and sixth formers', and so influence the choices of those investigating the possibilities for higher education. Over the ensuing decades new strengths emerged, such as internationally recognised research in the detection of atmospheric pollution, optical communications, micro-engineered machines, biometrics, composite materials and alternative energy systems.

*Dick Horsfield and students repairing a Vampire jet, 1998.*

The university years saw Engineering staff and students working together on a diverse range of high-profile projects. One relatively modest but eye-catching project by a final-year Mechanical Engineering student was an investigation into the impact of 'rooftop accessories' (such as roof racks or signs) on cars' fuel consumption. His results, revealed in 1992, showed that by moving the 'For Hire' sign from the front to the back of a saloon car, a taxi driver could save up to £1,500 a year in fuel costs. Six years later, engineers from the University restored the mechanism that allowed the writing hut used by playwright George Bernard Shaw to turn to follow the sun. The hut was at Shaw's home at Ayot St Lawrence, now owned by the National Trust, with whom the School of Creative Art is now working on joint projects. Aerospace Engineering students helped former RAF pilot Dick Horsfield to restore the de Havilland Vampire jet he flew back in the 1950s. Around fifteen students gave their free time at weekends to help restore the plane, which was in a very poor condition; about ten birds' nests were cleared out of one wing. The plane had been discovered by Dick Horsfield in a builders' yard owned by Rodney Robinson, an aircraft enthusiast who had bought the aeroplane from the Air Training Corps at Welwyn Garden City with the hope of restoring it.

The UH Racing team is a long-running teaching and research project which has attracted a great deal of success and public interest. The Society of Automotive Engineers (SAE) in the United States began a student racing competition in 1981 to promote automotive innovations. Then in 1998 the British Institute of Mechanical Engineers held the first UK event involving two American cars and two British – one from the University of Hertfordshire. The UH Racing team has been a fixture at the event ever since and also competes in a similar German event. The 1998 team began well, with the final-year Automotive Engineering students winning the Best Presented Team prize at the UK Formula Student competition (held at the Motor Industry Research Association track near Coventry). By 2011 UH Racing had become the UK's Number 1 ranked Formula Student racing team, leading in the use of alternative fuel technology, producing the first hydrogen-powered Formula Student racing car and the first all-electric model to compete.

*The Formula Student racing team celebrating.*

# Mathematics and Computer Science

The School of Information Sciences was home to the departments of Mathematics and Statistics, and Computer Science. The Mathematics Department, as well as running its own courses, was also responsible for co-ordinating the teaching of mathematics on courses across the Polytechnic. The emphasis continued to be on offering a mathematical experience focussed on meeting very particular needs within the wider society. A restructuring of the sandwich course leading to an Honours degree in Mathematics, which took place in 1970, was undertaken with this focus very much in mind:

> *The new course, in addition to featuring modern topics, offers two alternative applications of Mathematics, namely to Physics and Engineering or to Industrial and Economic Systems. The course thus reflects strongly the newer applications of Mathematics and it can, therefore, be claimed to have a 'Polytechnic character' distinguishing it strongly from Pure Mathematics courses at many universities.*

John Hall, Head of the Mathematics Department, was a pioneer of computer science education in the UK. In 1963 approval was given for the NCTA Diploma in Technology in Mathematics, followed by an Honours degree in Computer Science (1965), making the institution one of only two colleges and one university in the UK providing Computer Science degrees, an Ordinary degree in Computer Science (1966) and a part-time Ordinary degree in Mathematics (1967). The part-time degree was particularly popular, attracting more than forty students in its first year, many of whom were teachers looking to improve their existing qualifications. In 1967 the Department made its first award of a First Class Honours degree in Mathematics.

The initial purchase of a National-Elliott 803B digital computer in 1963 at a cost of £24,010 (around £400,000 in today's money) was followed in 1967 by the purchase of a second computer. The Department was also expanded, which saw graduate staff within the Department increase from nine mathematicians to thirty-six mathematicians, computer scientists, astronomers, statisticians and logicians. The computer facilities were made available to local schools and in 1967 Hatfield School, which shared a site with the College, introduced an A Level in Computer Science. The School and College undertook research jointly into 'developing an online link between tape-editing equipment in the School and the 803B Computing System in the College'. In addition, the staff in the Computer Unit assisted the County Education Department with analyses of surveys and records relating to local schools, as well as advising local companies on modern computing techniques.

The Department continued to expand and in 1968 it was split into two new departments: Mathematics and Statistics, and Computer Science. By the beginning of 1969 plans for a multi-access computer system were ready to be put out to tender under a budget of £300,000, approved by the Department of Education and Science. In the summer of 1970 the new multi-access computer system, the Digital Equipment Company PDP-10, was installed – the first in any educational institution – at a cost of £256,500. It was the largest multi-access computer system in higher education in the UK, providing online access not only for the Polytechnic but also for colleges and schools across Hertfordshire. Dr R.W. Sharp, Head of the Computer Science Department, told the local press that the new computer system was 'a giant brain that many can pick at one time ... in the past the schools have had to either travel to the Polytechnic to get practical experience or had to forego practical work altogether. This will no longer be the case.' In the first year of operations, access to the computer system was via one of a number of 'teletype terminals': twenty-seven were set up within the Computer Centre itself, which was open Monday to Friday from 8.30am until midnight; there was one apiece on the other Polytechnic sites; five in colleges; and six in schools within the county. In addition, the Centre worked with other universities and industrial organisations, offering support for research programmes requiring complex programming and computer time.

The Computer Centre in the C.P. Snow Building, late 1970s.

Demand for the services offered by the Computer Centre was such that, with funding from the County Council, the numbers of schools and colleges making use of its services grew steadily. By 1980 almost half of the county's 108 secondary schools had installed terminals, a development made possible by the running of thirteen computers connected to a ring of computer stations, each supporting up to sixteen terminals. This 'Cambridge Ring' was designed and developed within the Polytechnic as there was no commercial system readily available, so rapidly was the computer landscape changing at this time. It was innovations such as these that led *The Times* to cite Hatfield as the creators of 'the best equipped computer centre in public sector education'. Students were able to store work on their personal online file area, and by 1974 all large lecture theatres were equipped with visual display units. As a consequence of demand, issues of space and computer time were a constant problem. In 1978 the Computer Centre moved into the C.P. Snow Building, and by 1984 the Centre was operating a three-shift system and opening over the weekend.

The growth of industrial and commercial interest in computer applications saw the Polytechnic develop a number of part-time and postgraduate courses for those whose first degree was outside the field. A part-time MSc in Computer Science was introduced in 1970, with the course attracting interest from a 'wide cross-section of industry'. In 1972 a part-time Polytechnic Diploma in Computer Science was approved, offering a postgraduate 'reorientation' course for those new to the subject, and this course proved very 'useful to local industry by providing new graduates with a firm grounding in the practice and theory of computing'. In addition, the Department of Computer Science organised a large number of short courses to keep local companies abreast of developments in the field.

*The Computer Centre, c. 1979*

There was also an awareness of the need to prepare the next generation for the rapidly changing world of information sciences. In 1974 a part-time two-year postgraduate Diploma in Computer Education, the first of its kind in the country, was introduced, with the intention of helping teachers to improve their own knowledge and skills base, which they could then take back to their colleagues and pupils. Another first for the Polytechnic was the development of a Braille computer terminal – a joint project with the Royal National Institute for the Blind – which also allowed students to produce Braille copies of hand-outs and other documents. In addition, research projects were undertaken with organisations such as the European Space Agency, the EEC/IT Task Force and Rolls Royce.

The Council for National Academic Awards (CNAA) visited the Polytechnic in 1984 to review and reapprove the Computer Science undergraduate and postgraduate degree courses. Its conclusions were noted with some pride in the Annual Report of that year: 'In the considered judgement of the visiting party the Polytechnic's work in Computer Science was at a remarkable standard of excellence. As such the Polytechnic must accept that it has a national responsibility in the field.'

Celebrating the fortieth anniversary of the BSc in Computer Science in 2006, the School looked forward to the new challenges of the dot.com age, and was busy developing online courses leading to the provision of complete Honours degrees in Computer Science and Information Science by distance learning. At the same time research on artificial intelligence moved apace, with the multidisciplinary Adaptive Systems Research Group looking at how robotics could be used in therapeutic treatment, for autism in particular. The Group's work has resulted in the creation of KASPAR, a child-sized human robot, as part of the European RobotCub Project, which aims to build an open-source robot platform for cognitive development research.

*KASPAR*

## Sciences

The growth of the Science Department very much reflected developments in the county of Hertfordshire. Just as the engineering departments had benefited from the physical proximity to de Havilland and its associated trades, the Science Department was able to take advantage of the growing number of post-war chemical and drug production companies that were attracted to the new sites and good transport links within the county. As Head of Department, Dr R.F. Robbins reflected that the Department had come a long way 'from the modest beginnings which included the teaching of elementary science in converted bicycle sheds'. The mutual benefit derived from working closely with the pharmaceutical and chemical industries was emphasised by Robbins in a later report, when he stressed the practical nature of research undertaken by the College: 'Ours is not an ivory tower existence. The contact we continually explore with industry will never make it so, and this we feel essential to both local and national needs.'

Space, as ever, was at a premium, but access to the laboratories at Bayfordbury made a real difference to the work of the Department, which in 1964 was renamed the Department of Chemistry and Biology, the Physics staff having been transferred to the Department of Electrical Engineering. In 1965 approval was given by the CNAA for an Honours degree in Biochemistry to join the existing Honours degrees in Applied Biology, Applied Chemistry and General Science. The departmental report of 1967–68 took particular pride in the results achieved that year: four students had received First Class Honours on the BSc Applied Chemistry course, 'an achievement made all the more remarkable as two of the students had previously been 11+ "failures" '. This pride in raising levels of expectation and achievement in students who might otherwise have found it difficult to access high-quality education was justified. In 1967 all three students who graduated with First Class Honours had entered the College with qualifications earned by part-time study at Ordinary National Certificate Level, a route which would have denied them a university education but which had now earned them the chance of a good post in industry or postgraduate research.

*A UH environmental scientist in the field, 1994.*

Research training in the Chemical Sciences continued to develop and in the academic year 1972–73 Hatfield Polytechnic had by far the largest number of candidates registered with the CNAA for research degrees in chemistry – no fewer than thirty-one. Research that year included work on potential anti-cancer and anti-viral agents, and was supported by the pharmaceutical industry in Hertfordshire. The naming of a Division of Biological and Environmental Sciences reflected a new area of growth for the Polytechnic, and in 1975 the first students enrolled on a four-year sandwich BSc/BSc Honours degree in Environmental Studies.

Over the last couple of decades, physics has grown to become one of the strongest research areas in the University, with two Centres: the Centre for Astrophysics Research (CAR) and the Centre for Atmospheric and Instrumentation Research (CAIR), with a total of eighty or so researchers. Unusual for a college, astronomy had begun back in the mid-1960s when some Engineering students were given the opportunity to study it – with the support of John Hall – as part of their wider syllabus. An Astronomy Unit was formed, and from May 1970 the Unit's work was centred on a newly established Observatory in the grounds of the Polytechnic's annexe at Bayfordbury. The Observatory soon had a radio telescope and a number of optical telescopes. Bayfordbury now provides one of the UK's finest teaching observatories, hosting eight domed telescopes, and the astronomers have attracted considerable public interest. In September 1992, Helen Sharman, Britain's first astronaut, performed the official opening of the International Library Technology Fair, held at the Hatfield campus. The fair itself was attended by representatives from over forty countries. Helen was given a tour of the Bayfordbury Observatory by research student Mike Inglis, who had himself applied to join the space programme, getting as far as the second round of the selection process. In October the same year, astronomer Patrick Moore, who had been awarded an honorary doctorate by the Polytechnic in 1989, attended a ceremony at the Bayfordbury Observatory to officially launch the introduction of two new degree courses: Astronomy, and Astrophysics and Applied Physics. Sixty students had already signed up for these courses and had the opportunity to meet Patrick Moore, who turned up in spite of being treated at Moorfield Eye Hospital in London for an injury sustained during a cricket match. Moore made his way to the University once again in 2000 to open the

*'Yes, I got the feeling this is a place where there is no pretension whatsoever, one gets down to the job it really is and ... a lot of the people we were teaching came from the local industry. There were a lot of day-release students we were teaching as well as full-time students. I always really liked that and of course we were doing the sandwich degrees so our students went out for their third year into industry.'*

*Quentin Appleton, who began lecturing in Chemistry at Hatfield Polytechnic in 1971. The Chemistry Department was closed down in 2001 on the basis of falling enrolments – according to those who took the decision. This situation mirrored the closure of other chemistry departments nationally at the time.*

*Patrick Moore (centre) attending a ceremony at the Bayfordbury Observatory.*

award-winning 'control building' named in his honour. University of Hertfordshire astrophysicists have also been part of a national team that built the UK's newest telescope, VISTA (Visible and Infrared Survey Telescope for Astronomy), which went into operation in 2009.

## Business

At the start of the 1970–71 academic year, the departments of Psychological and Social Studies, Administrative and Business Studies, and Management Studies had a total enrolment of 522 students (298 full-time, 224 part-time); of these the largest portion belonged to the Administrative and Business Studies Department, with 257 full-time and sandwich students, and 141 part-time and block release students. Student numbers in business subjects grew rapidly over the next decade, so that in 1982–83 – by which time they were taught in the School of Business and Social Sciences – there were 1,163 students (757 full-time, 338 part-time, 68 evening). This growth also helped redress the gender balance amongst the Polytechnic's student body with, for example, 493 female students enrolled in the 1982–83 academic year.

Where the engineering and chemical sectors of industry were quick to form a working relationship with the College, other areas of the commercial world were less clear-sighted in recognising the opportunities that collaboration might bring. In 1963 Dr Chapman commented on the 'lukewarm support' which the Business and Management staff had received in spite of much 'hard and painstaking work'. Whilst there were signs that those whose interests were focussed on 'the "business" and "office" activities of the professions and industry, [were] becoming more aware of the needs of organised technical education', it was a matter of some regret that the College had yet to establish a degree-level course in Business Studies, a failure Dr Chapman ascribed to the tardiness of the business world in seeing how much such a course would benefit not just their own interests but also those of the wider nation.

Whilst slow progress was being made in this area, the Department of Business and Social Studies continued to run short courses for industry on 'special aspects of management and business', drawing on the disciplines of sociology, psychology, English, accountancy and industrial and human relations, and aimed at those who already had some experience of the world of management. The Diploma in Management Studies, introduced in 1968, was welcomed by those companies sponsoring students as particularly effective in helping develop staff, and was applauded for 'its relevance to the managers' real problems as contrasted with the excessively academic approach of the university business schools'. In addition, this course 'proved successful as a resettlement course for officers about to retire from the armed services and the police. The service personnel derive great benefit from mixing with industrial course members in the Department and from small familiarisation projects carried out in industry.'

Although commercial organisations had been slow to see the benefits of continuing professional development, the 1970s saw a change in approach and the demand for management courses increased. In 1975 Hatfield joined with Middlesex Polytechnic and eight other colleges in London and the Home Counties to set up the North West Metropolitan Association for Management Development at the Birklands site, its goal to co-ordinate specialist areas of work and raise standards generally.

Again, there was an emphasis on continuing education and personal and professional development for those already in work, offering part-time and evening courses for those studying towards qualifications in subjects such as accountancy, banking and marketing. There was an emphasis on modern languages, particularly French and German, as British involvement in the European markets was promoted as part of the new economic future. Both the HND in Business Studies (1969) and the BA and BA (Hons) degrees in Business Studies (1973) included specialist options in modern languages. In addition, students on the Business Studies degree course were called upon to think creatively and be entrepreneurial – like students Catherine Rumbelow and Simon Smith who, in 1989, got through to the finals of the national Innovation for Business Awards with their idea of a moulded rubber handle for plastic carrier bags – an idea that had its origins in their own struggles with heavy shopping bags.

## Social Sciences

In 1969 the first students enrolled on the BA in Applied Social Studies, which was a four-year sandwich course with professional qualifications in Social Work or Social Administration. The part-time BSc degree in Sociology was introduced two years later, attracting over a hundred students in its first five years. Run predominantly as an evening course, and with most students being self-financed, those who enrolled were drawn from a cross-section of teachers, policemen, local government employees, housewives and those employed in commerce and industry.

A full-time BA (Hons) in Social Sciences was introduced in 1977. The Head of the Psychological and Social Studies Department, Gabriel Newfield, recalls the considerable challenges faced in getting the full-time BA up and running. The Polytechnic Academic Board twice rejected the proposal, and it took three attempts to gain CNAA approval. Years passed. The experience shows how the successful expansion of the institution's curriculum was not always plain sailing, and faced internal as well as external obstacles. Also in 1977 the first Hatfield student received a CNAA MPhil research degree for his work in the social sciences: 'The student, who holds a senior position in the careers service of a neighbouring authority, carried out his research entirely on a part-time basis. His success illustrates the opportunities which the Polytechnic can increasingly offer to persons living or working within travelling distance who would like to obtain the MPhil or PhD by part-time study.'

In 1970 Psychology began to build its reputation, becoming part of the new Department of Psychological and Social Studies. Just prior to this, staff had begun offering the academic element to the postgraduate programme leading to the MRCPsych award

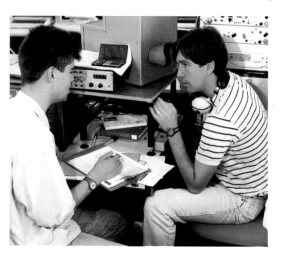

*A UH psychologist conducting tests, 1989.*

required for entry into the psychiatrist profession; it was the institution's first contribution to postgraduate medical provision. Driven by a new Head of Psychology, a full-time BSc (Hons) degree course in Psychology was approved in 1971. In the first year, 24 students enrolled; by 2011 the intake was 170 students. Research Council research studentships followed. Within a few years it was regarded as one of the top three polytechnic psychology units. A part-time MSc in Occupational Psychology began in 1979. Most of the full-time teaching staff hired to support these developments were research active, with particular strengths developing in the areas of infra-human sensory processes, human cognition and language development. With the restructuring of the Polytechnic in 1974, the psychologists chose to join the new School of Natural Sciences, which gave them more opportunity to apply for the larger pot of Natural Sciences research funding.

One of the numerous practical research initiatives carried out by the psychologists was the Linden Clinic, which ran a Nocturnal Enuresis Research Programme and supported local children and their families. In the university era, Psychology would develop to become one of the larger schools in the University, and its staff were early adopters of email and the Internet, with the School's first departmental website appearing in 1995. The National Centre for Tactile Diagrams (NCTD) was based at the School in 1999, designing and producing tactile diagrams, maps and pictures, and providing a variety of training and consultancy services to improve university expertise in supporting blind and visually impaired students.

## Humanities

The Department of Humanities was created on the eve of the shift to Polytechnic status, providing courses in English, history, modern languages and philosophy, which were taught as part of the General Studies programme, still a requirement for students at the College on a range of technical courses. History and philosophy were required elements of the BSc (Economics) external London degree, whilst modern languages became a compulsory element of the BSc in Industrial Engineering. This emphasis on the place of modern languages was an important component in the thinking behind broadening the education of students. In 1964 the College adapted a classroom to become a language laboratory able to accommodate sixteen students – an addition welcomed by Chapman: '[T]he potentialities of this as a contribution to the national welfare might well be as valuable as the contribution of the computer or any other equipment we possess.'

One of the Humanities lecturers, Ian McLuckie, attracted the attention of the international press in 1966 when he was quoted at a welfare workers' conference as stating that in the twenty-first century the country would have to face the possibility of introducing polyandry, or the practice of allowing women to have more than one husband. He predicted that by 2020 there would be in excess of 4.5 million more

*National Centre for Tactile Diagrams, 1999.*

women than men in the 16–40 age range. The notion of allowing polyandry was greeted by the General Secretary of the Marriage Guidance Council with the terse response: 'We do not think this would work.'

The College never lost sight of the need for a broad education. So in 1967 the first Drama lecturer was appointed. Meanwhile, Peter Kingsford, whose own background was in economics, gave more prominence in General Studies courses to the history of science and technology, reflecting his own conviction that 'the past has a bearing on the present'.

The Department of Humanities entered the new era of the Polytechnic very much with its prime function 'as a service unit' providing teaching across disciplines in English, modern languages, history and philosophy, and organising the various residential courses which ran throughout the year. In 1969 the CNAA carried out a validation exercise and approved the Polytechnic's first humanities degree, a part-time Ordinary degree in English, and this was followed by the launch, in time for the 1973–74 academic year, of a full-time BA degree in Studies in the Humanities. The structure of the degree followed a major/minor format, with the first major subjects on offer being English Literature and Linguistics, with minors in English Literature, Linguistics, and History of Ideas (along with Sociology and Computer Studies elsewhere). These were followed by majors in Philosophy and History, and minors in French and German, with Spanish added in 1980.

Just as science students were encouraged to engage with the Arts and Humanities, there was also an emphasis on non-humanities subject teaching for arts and humanities students, with numeracy seen as a crucial element of any education. This raised some anxieties for students wary of subjects outside their arts comfort zone, as Sir Norman Lindop noted in his 1975 report:

> *The policy of requiring all students on the Studies in the Humanities Degree course to take a subject requiring some degree of numeracy seems to be working well, despite some initial alarm on the part of the students. The non-humanities Minor study in Mathematics and Logic, which students may take throughout the three years of the course and on which they can spend up to 40% of their final year, is particularly interesting. Many arts students believe themselves incapable of studying anything remotely mathematical. This new course has been designed with these prejudices in mind and carries no special A or O level prerequisites. In its first year it attracted 35 out of 80 students – a considerable achievement.*

The School of Humanities was responsible for running the BA in Contemporary Studies, which was specifically aimed at those, mostly women, who were looking to return to studying. It had a family-friendly, intensive part-time attendance structure. Many of those enrolled had little in the way of formal qualifications but, as was noted in the Annual Report of 1977–78, 'The performance of the students is extremely high and there is little to distinguish the achievement of those who come in with normal entry qualifications and those who enter by interview and essay.' Courses such as these encouraged many to consider higher education during the 1970s and 1980s and were responsible for seeing the School of Humanities increase its student numbers from 27 part-time students in 1970–71 to 583 students in 1982–83 (310 full-time, 197 part-time, 76 evening students).

*There was a certain antagonism towards Humanities from some of the scientists in the polytechnic years, with the following joke about Humanities staff circulating widely:*

*'It's a pity they have to come into work on a Wednesday because it spoils the weekend.'*

The gender representation on Humanities courses was heavily in favour of women at this time – a profile it shared with Education, with only 161 of the 583 students enrolled in 1982–83 being men. The gender ratio amongst staff was also improving, helping to vanquish the traces of the paternalistic and condescending atmosphere that lingered in businesses and institutions of the era with regard to women in positions of responsibility. Philosophy lecturer Dr Jane Singleton, who joined the Polytechnic in 1975, recalls, for example, how, after her interview, her husband was contacted to check whether he was aware of her application and intentions.

History had contributed to the curriculum in a service capacity since the early days of the College and was a part of the teaching programme at the Hertfordshire Colleges of Education at Balls Park and Wall Hall. During the late 1970s and early 1980s, History lecturers also taught on the part-time study programmes in Sociology, Social Work and Contemporary Studies, as well as providing 'Polyprep' Access courses for those desiring to enter higher education. In the latter years of the Polytechnic, the History Group pioneered a community-participation research initiative, the Hatfield Historical Research Resources Project, which was cutting edge in its use of computers to collect and analyse historical data. Through 'forging links between the Polytechnic's non-technological areas and the business community', in 1990 donations from Royal Insurance (UK) Ltd, Mitsubishi and Marks & Spencer facilitated the development of the project. Over the next two decades the History Group expanded, developing further research and teaching expertise in social history, digital history, and political and business history.

In the 1970s English Literature at Hatfield Polytechnic was deemed to be one of the most innovative courses in the country, teaching a broad range of issues and leading the way in the development of the subject. At that time, the Essex Conferences on the Sociology of Literature were a forum at which polytechnic academics dedicated to reforming the Humanities featured on an equal basis with universities. Lecturers from the Literature Group were represented on two occasions, elevating the reputation of Hatfield on each occasion and contributing to the reforms in the teaching of literature across the country.

*The Hatfield Historical Research Resources Project in action, 1991.*

In 1982 members of the Literature Group were invited to participate in discussions with Oxford English Limited – a group devoted to curriculum reform in English, at Oxford University, during which they outlined to them what was being taught at Hatfield Polytechnic. What was new was that the Literature Group devised courses building 'critical theory' into their teaching. The Group was also one of the first in polytechnics to be CNAA-validated for an MA in English Literature. Entitled 'Literature in Crisis 1890–1930', and beginning in 1981, the degree was born out of the Group's objective at that time of putting into practice the developments in critical theory. The awarding of University status coincided with the decision taken at this time to name the body 'Literature Group' rather than 'English Group', as part of an attempt to signal a more international and non-canonical understanding of literature in English.

Philosophy began to expand in the mid-1970s. At first the teaching was centred narrowly on seventeenth-century philosophy to complement the broader History of Ideas content being provided for the Humanities degree. But from 1975 onwards the course content began to expand, beginning with a concentration on the teaching of metaphysics, then political and moral philosophy, and, as more Philosophy staff were recruited, ancient and modern elements were introduced to the curriculum. Philosophy was taught as part of the Combined Studies degree and also contributed to the Cognitive Science curriculum, working with Psychology. The moral philosophers played a significant role in shaping the remit of the institutional Ethics Committee set up to ensure good conduct in empirical research.

By the early 1990s the School of Humanities and Education consisted of four departments, including a new European Languages Centre. Then it was decided to have just two departments – Humanities and Education – with Languages separating as it had a cross-university servicing role (and staff based on three campuses). English as a Foreign Language (EFL) then joined Languages. At this time many degrees had compulsory languages modules, including Law, Engineering and Business, whilst other degree programmes offered a language option. With the reduction in the number of modules students had to take (twelve a year in 1991) and the removal of EFL to the Faculty of Interdisciplinary Studies, which had set up Foundation degrees for overseas students, the Department of Languages was no longer considered viable and so it was merged with the School of Humanities with effect from the year 2001–02. It was around this time that Humanities became a major player in the University's research profile, with History and Philosophy building on the earlier success of English.

*Philosophy staff celebrating their successful QAA inspection outside the front entrance of Wall Hall, 2001.*

In the late 1990s, but particularly after the move to the de Havilland campus in 2003, Humanities expanded its provision in teaching and research. Mass communications developed, introducing undergraduate pathways in the burgeoning areas of film and journalism and forging a strong international profile, with franchises with TMC Singapore (2010) and with IACT Malaysia (2011). Postgraduate courses were validated in 2011 – an MA in Journalism and Media Communications, and an MA in Film and TV Aesthetics, and in 2012, the Mass Media Communications Group established an accredited exam centre for the National Council for the Training of Journalists (NCTJ). It was also in this more vocationally oriented area of humanities provision that work placements began to develop, with students located in institutions ranging from the *Sunday Times* to local museums to the British Film Institute (BFI). Gradually the commitment to ensuring the employability of humanities graduates would lead to a spreading of work placement opportunities across the School's subject portfolio.

Another new discipline that was to grow under the umbrella of the Humanities was creative writing. It began in 2002 with the development of two stand-alone modules on the Literature degree. In 2003, as a result of the success of this provision, a further module was added and in the following year the English Literature Group introduced 'Creative Writing' as a named subject area within the provision. Since then it has become one of the most successful of the minor subject areas, drawing in increasing numbers of students. In 2011 the Group developed an MA in Creative Writing that will run for the first time in 2012–13. With the demise of the Faculty of Interdisciplinary Studies in 2009, the English Language Teaching Unit was relocated to Humanities, enabling the School to play a significant and often rewarding role in working with the growing number of overseas students enrolling on the University's programmes.

## Education

For Education staff, the merger of the Hertfordshire College of Higher Education with the Polytechnic brought new working practices and concern over redundancies. There were also innovations for those ensconced at Wall Hall. Phones appeared on their desks for the first time, and photocopiers arrived to replace the Banda machines with the distinctive odour of their reprographic sheets, so familiar to staff and former students of a certain age. New options opened up for students too. Students at the former Hertfordshire College of Higher Education who failed their teaching qualification failed their degree – three years wasted – but after the merger students in this situation could convert some of their studies to a Humanities degree or the Polytechnic's BA in Education Studies.

The year of the merger saw the Education team participate in a major initiative of national significance. They began a partnership with Hertfordshire's Local Education Authority, with financial support from British Petroleum, to operate the Hertfordshire Action on Teacher Supply (HATS), which aimed to attract those seeking a career change into teaching – potential Mathematics and Physics teachers in particular. It provided 'learning on the job' training in schools – a scheme that was watched very closely by other education authorities, the government's Department of Education, and the teaching unions – and provided the template for the government's Licensed Teacher Scheme. Whilst such 'on the job' training has attracted criticism, the Hertfordshire experiment was considered a success, with 127 trainees recruited in three years.

The old College of Higher Education had welcomed many groups of overseas visitors and organised international exchanges over the years. But once part of the University, the Education team met the challenge set for all subject areas to increase international student recruitment. In the mid-1990s a two-year BEd was created to enable overseas students who already had a teaching qualification in their home countries (but that was not recognised in the UK) to convert to UK-qualified teacher status. Around the same time a very successful inspection of the School of Education's provision by Ofsted, the government's Office for Standards in Education, helped to boost the University's commitment to teacher training, enabling the School to build its research culture and develop new programmes. In 2000, for instance, it introduced a BA/BA (Hons) degree in Early Childhood Studies. This was a part-time course aimed at those already working as nursery nurses, classroom assistants and childcare assistants, and offered the chance to acquire skills and a professional qualification for a group previously untargeted. The School also developed a suite of Continuing Professional Development initiatives, including a Professional Doctorate.

*Student teachers working for their BEd teacher training degree in Malaysia, 2006.*

# Law

The teaching of law began in the mid-1960s as part of the Department of Business and Social Studies. It was another 'service' subject taught to Engineering, Business and Social Sciences students – in other words, to students who had no intention of becoming lawyers but who would benefit from some knowledge of employment or commercial law. It gained a more significant place when a Social Sciences degree was created in the early polytechnic days that consisted of four component subjects – economics, sociology, social policy and law.

The law component was very much developed under the guidance of Rhea Martin, who became a lecturer at the College in 1967, soon becoming head of a Law Group consisting of three or four lecturers. She recalled many years later that relations between the Law lecturers and those of the other three subjects teaching the degree were none too good at first. One of the Group's first achievements in the 1970s was to have the law component of the Social Sciences degree recognised by the Law Society. Another advance for the subject was the creation early on of the Student Law Society – one of the longest continuously running student societies in the University.

By the late 1990s, in the words of the Vice-Chancellor at the time, Neil Buxton, the Law School had 'grown to become the premier provider of legal education in the northern home counties, running courses for undergraduates and postgraduates as well as practising solicitors'. In 1998 the interior of Hatfield Magistrates' Court No. 1, which dated to the 1930s, was loaned to the School of Law to allow students to take part in mock trials in authentic surroundings. The courtroom included the press bench, which had carved into the wood the doodled names and graffiti of national and local reporters. In recent years the School has developed a national reputation for its mooting prowess, a 'moot' being a mock Appeals Court hearing in which students take on the roles of the advocates, representing an appellant or a respondent and submitting arguments as to points of law. The School enters three national competitions each year and also takes part in the London University Mooting Shield. In 2008 its students won the English-Speaking Union/Essex Court Chambers National Mooting Competition, beating teams from Oxford Brookes, Birkbeck, Glasgow University and the London School of Economics.

## Medicine

The year 1993 saw a big step forward for the University in its contribution to research and teaching in the field of medicine. The merger with Hertfordshire College of Health Care and Nursing Studies and the Barnet College of Nursing and Midwifery brought an important new dimension and over 160 new staff. But before this, the Polytechnic had been building its healthcare provision. In 1988 nursing was established as a subject when Stevenage College merged its programmes with the Polytechnic's School of Health and Human Sciences, providing comprehensive coverage in training health visitors, district nurses and social workers. Then, in 1990, a competitive tender was won from the North-West Thames Regional Health Authority to provide degrees in Diagnostic Radiography and Radiotherapy. New staff and the first cohort of students commenced in September 1991. The following year another competitive tender was won from the North-West Thames Regional Health Authority to provide a BSc (Hons) programme in Physiotherapy. With the merger, a multi-million pound grant to become a major centre for training nurses and midwives soon followed, as well as a five-year agreement with the North-West Thames Regional Health Authority to train more than 1,000 student hospital staff. In the same year a Radiography Suite was opened in the Division of Chemical Sciences. The University had won the bid to train and educate radiographers and physiotherapists funded by the health authority. Also, in the mid-1990s, the University's Cellular Toxicology Unit obtained a research grant of £137,000 from the Biotechnology and Biological Sciences Research Council to investigate mast cells in the brain with a view to developing treatments for Alzheimer's, multiple sclerosis and migraine.

New and innovative teaching programmes were developed. In 1994 the BSc (Hons) Learning Disability (Nursing and Social Work) became one of the first degrees in the UK to combine both professions. The following year another ground-breaking BSc (Hons) in Specialist Community Nursing Practice was validated. In 1999 the first cohort of twenty-nine students on the full-time BSc (Hons) Paramedic Science degree course completed their first period with the London Ambulance Service. This degree, launched in 1998, was the first of its kind in the UK. By the year 2000 the University was also running the only Infection Control degree course of its kind in the country, with the Department of Post-Registration Nursing running a related programme of research investigating psychological factors to improve hand hygiene practice.

*The first cohort of Paramedic students, 1998.*

Long-standing links between the institution and the pharmaceutical industry continued. In 1996, for instance, a new postgraduate course was designed in Pharmacovigilance – 'the study of adverse reactions at all stages in the development and marketing of medicines'. The course was aimed at drug safety scientists, medical information scientists, pharmaceutical physicians, clinical research scientists and drug information scientists. The first thirty-five students to attend came from the UK, Denmark, Germany, Norway and the United States. Then, in 2005, the University launched the Bedfordshire and Hertfordshire Postgraduate Medical School and the School of Pharmacy to enhance medical education, training and research in the region. The first students were recruited to its MPharm degree that year.

# Art and Design

The Hertfordshire College of Art and Design had pioneered a range of innovative programmes of study in the Arts. It was the first to run an Access course and to offer a free-standing part-time BA course in Fine Arts. It was also the only college in Europe to offer postgraduate courses in Arts Therapies, and the first to offer a BA (Hons) Design in Representation in the UK. With the merger, some of the national diplomas that they offered passed down to the further education colleges, but they held on to the Foundation courses in Art and Design. At the Polytechnic, meanwhile, a thriving Music Department had developed, and, even before its existence, music courses had been offered on the modular programme since the late 1970s. In 1987 the first polytechnic Electronic Music degree was devised, and the same year Music joined the School of Information Sciences, rather than Humanities, to enhance future developments in using technology in research and teaching.

*'I remember going to bed one night in 1987 and saying to my partner before I went to sleep, "Computers. It's got to be in computers. That's where we've got to go."'*

**Howard Burrell, Professor of Music, who began at the Polytechnic in 1972.**

Further cross-disciplinary relations were forged, with an innovative BA in Music and Entertainment Industry Management being developed in collaboration with the School of Law and the Business School. In December 1992 the University launched its first Master's degree in Music Studies, with John Cox of the Royal Opera House and Mark Elder from English National Opera asked to be patrons of the programme. It was designed to extend the training of singers leaving college, with one requirement of the course being that students should study the French, German and Italian languages.

After 2000, the portfolio of design courses was greatly strengthened with the launch of the BA Fashion course in September 2006 and the BA in Interior and Spatial Design in 2008, examining notions of the 'consumer' and, in the case of Fashion, the importance of design to the high-street shopper. The School of Art and Design embraced digital technology with gusto, founding one of the first of the new generation of courses in collaboration with Computer Science: the BSc Software Systems for the Arts and Media, in the early 1990s. The Art and Design curriculum expanded further and developed in new directions in 2005, with the opening of a £10.5 million Film, Music and Media building, providing 4,500 square metres of work space. The film provision within the portfolio of the current School of Creative Arts has been a major focus for investment and development, bringing together existing disciplines as a platform to exploit current links and emphasise the importance of the regional film industry. The BA Digital Animation course launched pathways in 2D Animation, 3D Animation, Games Art and Visual Effects, and the new BA in Film and TV was launched in September 2007.

## The Technical Library and Information Service

The Technical Library and Information Service was central to the development of the curriculum and research across the institution. Its brief was not only to ensure a well-stocked library but to develop innovations in how information was disseminated and could be used. The attention the Information Service attracted from both national and international observers was a matter of some pride for Gordon H. Wright, the County Technical Librarian. He noted in his Annual Report for 1963–64, 'No other authority in this country has yet succeeded in developing the comprehensive service we offer, and there are only a few similar examples to be found overseas.' By 1967, 117 organisations were subscribing to the Information Service; it answered 866 major enquiries in just one year. In addition, the staff had overseen the establishment of library space at the new campus at Bayfordbury. Expansion of the Information Service continued alongside the expansion of higher-level courses, which all required new books. A large number of foreign language technical dictionaries were purchased in 1963 to cater for the demand from the Industrial Engineering students, and Wright urged those with their hands on the purse to recognise that if Hatfield College was to compete with the best technical colleges both in Europe and in the United States the stock held by the Library must be up to date and comprehensive.

Space, or the lack thereof, was a constant theme of Wright's reports in these years. In February 1961 he took possession of a new, larger library, but within two years Wright was complaining of the lack of suitable study facilities and working space for staff. The twin functions of a technical information service and an academic library working under the same roof did create certain difficulties, which Wright noted in his report of 1965–66: 'Traditionally, the Library provides an atmosphere where the individual can browse or study in quiet comfort; an information service, however, forms the hub of an intricate communication network, which, if functioning perfectly, will be in a constant state of movement.' Accommodating the one with the other called for more space and more staff than Wright already had at his disposal. In 1967, however, he welcomed the inclusion within the budget for the building of a new, purpose-built library. At the end of 1969, Wright left to take up a post as Director of the College Bibliocentre in Toronto, Ontario, just three months before the new Library was open for business. Thus it was that in April 1971 Gordon Wright's successor, David E. Bagley, welcomed Lord Snow to the official opening of the new £204,000 four-storey Library.

## Charles Percy Snow, Baron Snow of the City of Leicester CBE (1905–80)

Snow came from a modest middle-class background and attended grammar school, becoming a successful novelist and physicist. He was a Cambridge academic but was vocal in his criticism of the old educational elite. In 1959 Snow delivered a powerful and influential lecture at the Senate House in Cambridge on the topic of 'The Two Cultures and the Scientific Revolution', in which he explored the dangers of the chasm that he saw had opened up between scientists and 'literary intellectuals'. When published, his argument that the Sciences and the Arts and Humanities should resume their historic embrace for mutual enlightenment attracted huge debate.

In 1972 Lord Snow accepted the invitation to become the first of the Polytechnic's esteemed 'Visitors', an honorary position described as 'an office to some extent like that of a Rector of a Scottish university; an eminent personality who could act as the friend, adviser and advocate of the institution'. At the ceremony to mark his installation as Visitor, Lord Snow referred to Hatfield as 'the prototype' for all polytechnics, and argued that the Polytechnic was 'in the best position to adapt and introduce new ways of teaching, unlike universities which are often strangled by tradition'.

*C.P. Snow opening the new library, 1971.*

As Norman Lindop noted:

> *In order to mark the special significance of the occasion as the first major piece of new building on the Hatfield site for many years, and the first stage of the Polytechnic's physical expansion, the choice of the official guest was a decision of some importance. Lord Snow's distinguished career as a scientist, politician and author, symbolising all that polytechnics strive for in achieving the close educational integration of sciences and arts, was a particularly happy choice.*

Considerable interest was generated in this first Library, planned around the particular needs of polytechnics. A team from the government's Central Office of Information visited shortly after the opening to make a film, designed for an overseas audience, 'emphasising the many novel features incorporated to assist users'. So popular was the Library that David Bagley noted: 'at one stage the student readers began to wonder whether the library had been built for their benefit or for the constant stream of visitors.'

Space continued to be an issue, and within a few years the complaint was being heard that there was not enough room to adequately meet all needs. This was an inevitable accompaniment to the increasing range of courses offered by the Polytechnic, set against a background of high inflation, which impacted on budgets for buying books and periodicals. As David Bagley noted, 'Libraries are a bottomless pit as far as resource requirements are concerned. Every new course brings demands for reading material in support, every extra student is another demand made upon bookstocks and changes in teaching methods all seem to favour student-centred learning and hence greater reliance upon library services.' As befitted a library serving a polytechnic that spearheaded the wider utilisation of computers, the introduction of new technologies continued. In August 1973, Hatfield, together with four other university and national institutions, was selected to take part in a trial into the use of computers and online information retrieval, and in 1978, after three years' work by staff, library users were greeted by the arrival of new microfiche machine readers in place of the existing card catalogue – causing some 'initial shock' amongst staff and students.

The National Centre for Reprographic Documentation was established at the end of 1966, thanks to a £32,691 grant from the Office of Scientific and Technical Information, part of the Department of Education and Science. Its initial brief was to collect, evaluate and disseminate information regarding developments in reprographics, organise courses and lectures, test equipment, and sponsor research projects. The aim was to find solutions to 'the problems arising from the exploitation of non-conventional recording systems within an information communication network'. Over the years, it built up an impressive list of clients. By the end of the 1982–83 session there were 823 organisations signed up, 40 per cent of which came from overseas. This involved a range of work including support for copyright development, the design of microform viewing equipment, production of duplicate microfiche resources, comparisons of systems for file updating, and the various print reproduction and life expectancy qualities of different forms of printing mediums. In 1983–84 the name of the Centre was changed to CIMTECH, the National Centre for Information Media and Technology – a reflection of its expansion into the areas of electronic information storage and retrieval. The Centre had a number of homes during the polytechnic years, moving from its original site at Endymion Road, Hatfield, to Bayfordbury Mansion, before returning to Hatfield and the main campus site in September 1984.

In 1997 a new Library and Information Services Department was formed to deliver integrated computing, library and media services, and was housed in the largest new Learning Resource Centre in the UK, sited on the College Lane campus.

## Fostering international links

From the early years the institution sought to build its international profile. For sheer numbers of visitors, it was the Technical Library and Information Service which received the most attention, with visitors from around the world including Brazil, Canada, India, Japan, Libya, Sudan, Australia, Venezuela and the United States. Particular mention was given in the report of 1961–62 to a large party of Russian librarians – a noteworthy event at a time when the Cold War was at its height. Indeed, the Library's Information Service seems to have operated across the increasingly hostile lines of East–West diplomatic relations, with requests for information from universities in Sofia and Prague being answered in 1961. In May 1968 librarian Gordon H. Wright accepted an invitation from the Czechoslovakian government to visit their various scientific and technical library services, with arrangements being made for future exchange visits. Unfortunately, as Wright noted in his report, 'the regrettable events of August have seriously disrupted these arrangements'. These regrettable events were the occupation of the country by Warsaw Pact troops as part of a Russian response to the 'Prague Spring' and the attempts by the Czech government to introduce a range of liberal reforms.

In the early 1960s the College played host to students from Bingen am Rhein in Germany, who came to learn about aeronautical engineering. Large international conferences were held on such diverse subjects as the 'Development of the Blue Streak Satellite Launcher', 'Chemistry and the Mode of Action of Fungicides', 'Teaching Machines and Further Education', 'Space Technology' and 'Nitrogen Heterocyclic Chemistry'. The latter, held in collaboration with the Chemical Society, drew an audience of more than 200 chemists, many from abroad at a time when international travel was both more costly and less convenient than today. Dr R.F. Robbins, Head of the Science Department, noted in his Annual Report that this was quite an honour as this was the first time the Chemical Society had held such an event outside a university.

Over the ensuing decades all parts of the University promoted international co-operation in research and teaching. Taking a snapshot of the transition year of 1992, the Business School signed a franchise agreement with the Independent Science and Technology Studies Institution in Athens, which saw the introduction there of a BA degree in Business Administration. Student exchanges were arranged between the School of Engineering and West Virginia University's College of Engineering. The prime minister of Romania and the British ambassador to Romania attended the opening of a Centre for the Improvement of Management Performance on the campus of Bucharest Polytechnic – the result of a collaboration with the University of Hertfordshire's Organisational Development Centre – with staff training organised by the University's psychologists. The Polytechnic played host to a group of Russian students and environmental scientists from the Department of Industrial Ecology at the Mendeleev Institute of Chemical Technologies, near Moscow. The previous year a party of Hatfield students and staff had visited Moscow and, on this return visit, both groups toured the country looking at sites of environmental importance, including a visit to an acid lake, Loch Grannoch, near New Galloway, to assess the role of atmospheric pollution caused by power stations in the acidification of rivers and lakes. Dr Derek Clark, from the Polytechnic's Civil Emergency Management Centre, flew to the former Yugoslavia to help in the sad task of identifying the bodies of the victims of the wars following the break-up of the country. The Polytechnic was the only institution in the world running courses on the management of civil emergencies. In July 1992 the University's Business School agreed to franchise its Master's of Business Administration to the Swedish Växjö *högskola* (college), which itself became a university in 1999. It was the first time the University's MBA was taught on a franchise basis, with Business School staff involved in the validation and ongoing support but Växjö lecturers doing the teaching. It was the first MBA to be taught in Sweden.

Other European collaborations in the next few years included courses in biosciences, business, social work and education in Holland with an Inter-University Co-operation Pact with the Hogeschool Gelderland, Arnhem; specialist courses for daycare surgery nurses with the Institute of Mikkeli in Finland; and in-service training courses for teachers in independent schools in Turkey. Extending its vision even further, the University looked to expand its operations into the growing markets of the Far East. In June 1995 a franchise was agreed with Tuas Polytech, Kuala Lumpur, to offer the University's HND Medical Electronics course, with the possibility of transferring onto the final year of the BSc (Hons) Medical Electronics course for successful students. This was shortly followed by the formal recognition of links with the INTI College in Malaysia, which allowed the Malaysian college to provide accredited University of Hertfordshire courses for its 4,000 students.

Further courses in Malaysia, Hong Kong and Singapore followed before attention turned to opportunities for expansion in the Chinese mainland. In 1998 the Asia-Pacific Business Unit was set up within the Business School to encourage stronger links with China. In collaboration with the Beijing INTI Management College, the University was able to offer a BA (Hons) Business Administration degree. This was followed in 2004 by the announcement of the establishment of the new Fuzhou University–Hertfordshire College in Fujian Province, China. A partnership between the University, the China University Training Center for Science-Technology (CUTC) and Fuzhou University enabled students to study for an initial Foundation Certificate in English for Academic Purposes, validated by the University of Hertfordshire, before then choosing from a range of undergraduate programmes. Announcing the arrangement, Vice-Chancellor Tim Wilson said, 'The level of intellectual understanding this is going to open up has got to be a win-win situation for all concerned.'

The University's links across the continents continue and in 2012 the University has partnerships with educational institutions in Canada, China, Cyprus, Ghana, Greece, Hong Kong, Hungary, Malaysia, Malta, Mauritius, Russia, Singapore, Sri Lanka, Trinidad and Ukraine, delivering support and degree programmes to students in courses across the educational spectrum.

# Research: Integral to the institution

The University's current research culture was built on a long history of research development and support involving staff and students. As already noted, the College's innovative four-term academic year was intended to free up time for staff to engage in research and work with industry. It was an admirable if ultimately unfeasible policy for the time. Still, research was seen as an important pathway to obtaining Regional College status, even though it was not a requirement. To this end, a Research Sub-Committee of the Governing Body was created, and, in 1957, under the chairmanship of Dr John Flavell Coales, a Head of Engineering Research at Cambridge University, principles and procedures for supporting research projects were approved. The Sub-Committee recommended that those staff engaged in research be given three hours per week teaching relief, although this was not fully implemented. At its 1957 meeting, the Sub-Committee considered thirteen project applications – seven in Engineering, five in Science and one in Social Sciences – and supported nine of them.

*'The Sub-Committee is of the opinion that the general standard of research being carried out is very much higher than could be expected in a young college and it is suggested that it would bear favourable comparison with that being carried out in any other technical college. The Sub-Committee is of the opinion that it is vital for the future of the College that this research being carried out or proposed in collaboration with industry and the universities cannot fail in the long run to attract even better staff to Hatfield.'*

*Research Sub-Committee (1957–58).*

By 1960 the first research assistants had been hired in the Science Department, and staff across the College had published thirty or so academic publications. Several lecturers had gained doctorates, one had won an MIT research scholarship and another a Fulbright travel grant.

**Number of research projects undertaken at the College in 1967–68 by subject:**

- Chemistry 31
- Mechanical, Aeronautical and Civil 13
- Mathematics 8
- Biology 7
- Industrial Engineering 7
- Psychology 7
- Humanities 6
- Electrical Engineering 2
- Social Sciences 1

In the early 1970s Norman Lindop set out the philosophy which governed research at the new polytechnic:

*Research workers in the Polytechnic are encouraged to develop 'action-orientated research' which is intended to lead to a definitive benefit such as the improvement of standards of life, services or goods, the conservation of natural resources or the solution of human problems. It is believed that in this way the educational objectives of research and also the aim to provide a service to society can best be combined.*

This commitment to making its research relevant to wider society was highlighted by an editorial in the local paper which appeared in 1969, applauding the spirit behind the award of a grant to a Hatfield student to study the lives of mammals in the harsh conditions of the Negev desert. This project was seen as offering a very real chance of adding to the knowledge and progress of under-developed countries. Research expanded considerably during the polytechnic years, both in terms of the number of research-active staff and the range of subjects contributing to the research culture. In 1971, for example, the Numerical Optimisation Centre became a fully-fledged research and consultancy centre of the Polytechnic, its function to use computer-based mathematical modelling to help students, staff and commercial interests develop solutions to practical problems. In that first year alone the issues considered were: best practice in buying and selling stock to maximise efficiency on an African cattle farm; the most effective shape and density for protective material designed for transporting fragile items; and the most cost-efficient settings on machine-cutting tools.

Lindop noted in his Annual Report of 1971–72 that whilst the majority of research projects within the Polytechnic continued to be found in the areas of engineering and science, both the Humanities and Social Sciences departments were experiencing real growth in this area. He called for the research to reflect the contribution that such projects could bring to the society around them: 'It is right, for example, that members of the Polytechnic should concern themselves with such social problems as that of the subculture of the homeless alcoholic, and one hopes that something of practical value will result from such concern.' Funding that year was received from such organisations as The Runnymede Trust for work into the problems of homeless immigrants and Harlow Council for support for a project into counselling services for one-parent families.

Elsewhere across the Polytechnic the award of external grant funding multiplied. In 1974–75, for instance, a contract worth £12,380 was obtained from the Ministry of Defence for work on 'Digital processing methods applied to facsimile transmission'; another award came from the Agricultural Research Council to research 'the interaction between herbicides, straw decay and over-watering of cereal pathogens'. The Economic and Social Research Council awarded the largest grant given to any public sector institution in 1984 to 'support research into language maintenance and viability in the Scottish Gaelic speech community'. The Biological Sciences also saw an increase in the levels of postgraduate and research work, at a time when funding for projects was increasingly difficult to obtain. Hatfield was one of only three institutions in the 1984–85 academic year to receive funding for research into biotechnology in collaboration with the Rothamsted Agricultural Experimental Station at Harpenden. In that same year, the newly formed Division of Biological and Environmental Sciences won research grants of £40,000 and £90,000 to support the financing of staff and equipment for teaching and research in the areas of plant biochemistry, molecular biology and genetics.

In 1983 the Polytechnic was one of a limited number of institutions invited to bid for funding to run courses on information technology and received the largest grant awarded in the maintained sector of higher education. The same year, again in response to a limited invitation, the School of Engineering was one of only four institutions selected to introduce an extended degree, the BEng in Mechanical Engineering, specifically aimed at the brightest students to prepare them for a career at the highest levels of the engineering profession. The Polytechnic won a contract in 1985 worth £500,000 to design a research programme regarding VLSI (Very Large Scale Integration) systems, fatigue in aircraft structures, and composite materials for BAe. In the last few months of the Polytechnic, more than £700,000 was awarded to carry out research projects in engineering and science for application to healthcare.

Some of the research had a more light-hearted spin. Andrew Lewis and Vic Marshall, described as two 'top University of Herts boffins', from the Department of Mechanical and Aeronautical Engineering featured in the local and national press when they announced a year-long research project into a pressing concern for all (English) cricket fans: just how were Pakistan bowlers Waqar Younis and Wasim Akram able to swing the ball so cleverly and defeat the England test team?

With the use of a wind tunnel, a bowling machine and cricket balls in various states of wear, they were hoping to answer the question of how a ball bowled in one direction could take a completely different direction once released from the bowler's hand.

Consultancy continued to be an important part of the institution's mission, with the School of Engineering playing a leading role. In 1977 stands were taken at both the Farnborough Air Show and the International Engineering Design Exhibition mounted at Olympia, helping to present the School's services to a larger audience. In 1978 four members of the Industrial Engineering team were consulted by ITT Corporation regarding engineering aspects of the trimphone. By 1985–86 the School of Engineering was receiving almost £2 million in external grants and awards, one of which was the maximum grant under the Department of Trade and Industry's 'Poly Cad' initiative, which saw the installation of nine computer-aided design workstations.

From the mid-1980s onwards the research strategies of universities were shaped to a considerable extent by the introduction of the government's Research Assessment Exercises (RAEs) to determine the allocation of public research funds across the sector. The first RAE, although not yet called that, was undertaken in 1986 under the auspices of the University Grants Committee – predecessor of the Higher Education Funding Councils. Further exercises took place in 1989, 1992, 1996, 2001 and 2008, becoming more complex and comprehensive over time.

It was the 1992 audit, named the 'research selectivity exercise', that gave the new University of Hertfordshire an opportunity to showcase its research credentials, with Psychology, English Language and Literature, and Computer Science performing well in national comparisons with other more venerable universities. The *Independent* included a feature on the University's first mixed experience of the research exercise. 'Older universities have played this game once and know how to score on presentation,' the Vice-Chancellor, Neil Buxton, told the paper. 'Any score we get over one is a bonus. We will learn a few lessons this time round.' The top grade was 5*. The newspaper reported that 'at the psychology division, Professor Ben Fletcher, an expert on stress, was a touch put out by the Department's grade three. "We have done well, but we expected a higher rating, actually."' This was understandable considering that the division had won grants totalling £1.1 million over the period of the exercise from charities, government agencies and industry to study disease, schizophrenia, Down's syndrome and children's sleeping difficulties.

Seventeen subject areas were submitted to the 1996 exercise, the results showing how the University was developing its broad-based excellence across the Arts, Humanities, Sciences and Social Sciences. The 2001 exercise saw continued high ratings for Psychology, Computer Science and Physics, and demonstrated the enduring contribution of English Literature. It also highlighted the growing research prowess of Nursing and Midwifery, History and Philosophy – again showing how, in the intervening years, the University had supported a broad research profile, and demonstrating that it was a university in the truest sense. The RAEs influenced not only the external perception of the University but also how the University's senior managers viewed the strategic value of certain subjects.

*'Because we were starting to do very well in that [the RAE 2001], I think the University suddenly felt, "Oh, okay, maybe these people are fairly good, we should give them support," and it is through doing well in that RAE that really the opportunity to build the staff [arose].'*

**Astronomy Professor Jim Hough, who began as a lecturer at the Polytechnic in 1972.**

In the years following the 2001 RAE, the University created three research institutes: the Health and Human Sciences Research Institute, the Science and Technology Research Institute, and the Social Sciences, Arts and Humanities Research Institute. They were designed to focus and foster research development and multidisciplinary collaboration between staff and research students – with future Research Assessment Exercises in mind. An open-access Research Archive of staff publications was also created with external funding to meet the growing calls for publicly funded research to be made freely available to the global academic community and the general public. The outcome of the 2008 RAE confirmed History as the best performing research unit of the University's second decade, proving that the Arts and Humanities could punch their weight when it came to contributing to the University's research income and profile.

# 4. Working with communities

During the late 1960s Hatfield continued to expand with the development of both the Old and New Towns, in particular around the Queensway area. Much of this was overseen by former Principal of the College, Dr W.A.J. Chapman, who had been invited to take on the chairmanship of the Hatfield Local Committee in 1966. In 1970 the new Tesco superstore was opened by radio and television personality David Jacobs, and Tesco's Chairman and future Chancellor of the University Ian MacLaurin announced that within two years the store would double in size. The continuing problems of traffic negotiating the A1 on its way through Hatfield saw the building of a 1,150 metre cut-and-cover tunnel to enable traffic to pass more safely through the Roe Green–Stanborough portion of the road. It was at this time that College Lane was closed to through traffic in an attempt to avoid congestion in the town centre.

The original plans for the tunnel, with three lanes each way, were revealed at a public inquiry in 1981. Space was allocated above for light industry, a garage, a hotel, a sports complex, car parking, a garden centre and a public open space. This would see the removal of Hatfield landmarks the Stonehouse Public House – a watering hole for students – and four large blocks of flats: Cumberland, Altham, Haddon and Rodney Courts. A compulsory purchase order on these blocks of flats by the Department of Transport meant that for several years they were allowed to stand empty – a tempting target for squatters – and their condition severely deteriorated. With its annual problem of finding homes for its expanding student body, the Polytechnic was able to take short-term leases on some of the flats in Cumberland Court to house students who then had to deal with poor conditions and the occasional burst pipe during severe winter weather. The site above the tunnel eventually took shape as The Galleria, Europe's largest shopping centre at the time of its opening in 1991.

In the town of Hatfield itself, plans were drawn up in the early 1970s for a large leisure centre complex next to the town's swimming pool, to include a theatre, multi-purpose hall and meeting room; this multi-purpose building opened under the name 'The Forum'. Facilities were sorely needed in the town, with residents calling for alternatives to the pub and bingo for recreation. One teenager put it more bluntly, describing the town as 'one big dump. There is absolutely nothing for teenagers to do', and doubting whether anything would change. Residents of South Hatfield complained of being 'the forgotten part of town', as the local bus service was unreliable, with no local buses on a Sunday, only one bus an hour to and from the QEII Hospital at Welwyn Garden City, and no connections with the train service.

A complaint that to catch the last bus to South Hatfield meant leaving the cinema fifteen minutes before the end of the film became redundant when the cinema was turned into a bingo hall in early 1972.

Many of those who had moved into the district in the early days of the development of the New Town were now families with teenage children. In 1969 a committee of local churches, led by the Polytechnic's chaplain, Reverend Michael West, met to consider the challenges faced by youngsters in the town, after some scuffles at dances held at the Polytechnic. Their conclusion was that the friction was the result of the lack of facilities in the town for local teenagers and young people; the fights that had broken out during those events at the Polytechnic, which had been open to non-students, led to students confining these events to their own student body and this, in turn, fuelled the jealousy of local youngsters. The church committee concluded that the Polytechnic students should be encouraged to interact more with the people of Hatfield, perhaps by setting up babysitting services, whilst local groups should be made aware of the range of facilities that the Polytechnic offered. They also proposed that sporting competitions be set up between the two groups.

Town and gown relationships were always a live issue in the years that followed, in part due to the continuing shortage of resources within the town and the pressures resulting from the growth in the numbers of students from beyond the immediate area who required accommodation. Some of the problems faced by the Polytechnic can be glimpsed in an item which appeared in the local paper in 1972:

> Hatfield Polytechnic is to clamp down on people who use the grounds of the college without authority because of vandalism and abuse. Members of the public will still have access to its playing fields and woodland, but horses, dogs, motor-cycles and other vehicles will be banned. Also banned will be the lighting of fires and camping, the cutting of timber and the removal of plants and turf.

Academic Registrar Edward Roberts said that the Polytechnic was happy to allow local people to use the grounds, but recent vandalism had seen destruction of the environment to such an extent that something had to be done.

> It goes without saying that those people who have taken pleasure from walking in the grounds with their children will be very welcome to go on doing so. What we are not prepared to do is to allow the grounds to be turned into a race track or a sports arena or to permit the normal college activities to be hampered in any way and I rather think the general public would support us in this.

A conference held at the Polytechnic in that same year heard a plea from an NUS representative for students to make more of an effort to 'bridge the gap' between themselves and the local residents, calling on students 'to go out into Hatfield and the surrounding area, instead of remaining cloistered in an academic setting, and get to know the problems of the people living in the town'. Norman Lindop warned, however, that this might seem 'condescending to the community', and suggested instead that a stronger sense of connection might be forged by students living in the town alongside their non-academic neighbours. Yet the growing numbers of students living in accommodation within the town brought its own problems, most notably the perennial issue of car parking, with frequent complaints from residents about poorly parked cars causing problems of access and visibility for pedestrians; students, in turn, complained of cars being vandalised when parked overnight.

Students were not unaware of the problems which their presence might cause in the local community and attempts were made to foster better relations. Each Rag Week included an 'Olde Tyme Music Hall' show, free to local pensioners, and there was an annual Christmas party organised by the Halls of Residence, again for local pensioners, with transport arranged for those unable to make it under their own steam. During the prolonged electricity black-outs of the early 1970s, students visited local pensioners to make sure they were coping. Students even offered their services as gardeners and decorators. These initiatives, however, were geared to an older generation, and difficulties remained in relation to the local youngsters at a time when the economic crisis was impacting on both employment and leisure. Still, the Polytechnic was an important rock music venue in the area. The Police performed there in 1979, for instance, with the concert filmed by the BBC for the music programme *Rock Goes to College*.

The Students' Union alternated between a policy of open and restricted access for local youngsters, but difficulties remained. In March 1977, during the Rag Week Ball, a fight broke out and the planned all-night event was curtailed on the advice of police. This followed on from an incident only two weeks earlier that had seen two Hatfield students stabbed by a local man during the 'Jazz and Beer' night. Events such as these were far from common, nor were they unique to Hatfield, but they were a reminder of the difficulties faced by any higher education institution in co-existing with its neighbours, especially in times of economic uncertainty.

The Polytechnic continued to see itself as very much part of the local community, and whilst there were some sites of conflict there were also points of contact. Open evenings at the Bayfordbury Observatory to observe the night sky drew large audiences, and continue to this day; the passing of Halley's Comet saw 15,000 people enter a ballot for one of the eight public open nights, although, sadly, poor weather meant that five of these nights were a somewhat frustrating experience. Public lectures by such luminaries as Nobel Laureate Professor Anthony Hewish and Sir Bernard Lovell attracted large audiences, and, in 1982, 500 people attended Patrick Moore's lecture on '25 Years of the Space Age'.

The Polytechnic also developed an excellent reputation locally for its contribution to the Arts. In 1970 the Hatfield Philharmonic Orchestra and

*Open evening at Bayfordbury Observatory.*

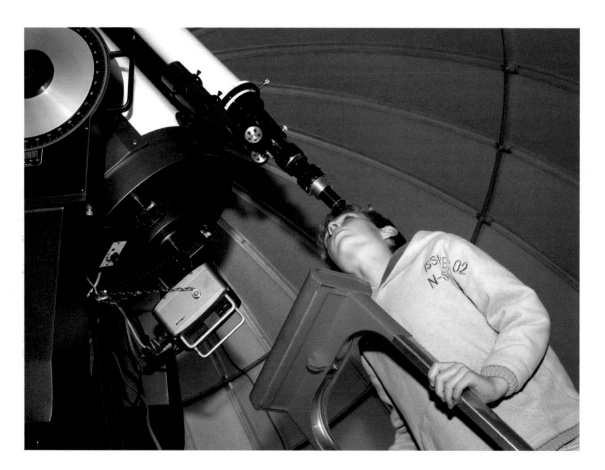

Chorus gave their first performances under the musical directorship of Frank Shipway; the programme for that year included Brahms's *Requiem*, Holst's *The Planets* and Mozart's *Jupiter Symphony*. Membership of the hundred-strong choir was largely drawn from the Polytechnic and the local area, whilst those in the orchestra came from all parts of the county. The music profile of the Polytechnic was strengthened by the creation of an Early Music Ensemble, a Chamber Orchestra, a Brass Ensemble and 'The Klangers' – a handbell-ringing team coached by Dr Mike Cox, a chemistry lecturer. The Polytechnic was also home to a succession of resident quartets. The Amphion String Quartet gave a series of evening and lunchtime recitals in 1973–74. The quality of music performed at the Polytechnic was high and the *Welwyn and Hatfield Times* welcomed the 1980 debut of the Locrian Quartet with the comment, 'there cannot be the slightest doubt that they are designed for success'.

UH Arts presents... The Beethoven Gala

John Lill & The Philharmonic at UH

ethoven

8 June 1997
The Prince
Edward Hall

In 1973 the Polytechnic hosted its first 'Polyfestival', which ran for 14 days, attracting 3,500 visitors. Its programme included performances from actors David Kossoff and Michael Gough, Scottish singer and accordionist Ronnie Ross, and singer Sandy Denny, formerly of The Strawbs and Fairport Convention, as well as a production of Harold Pinter's *The Caretaker* by the Polytechnic's own Drama Group, Dramatek. Highlights of the festivals which followed included performances by soprano Norma Burrowes, the Phillip Jones Brass Ensemble, flamenco guitarist Pepe Martínez, the BBC singers, and Valerie Masterson, principal soprano with English National Opera, as well as celebrity lectures from guests such as Raymond Baxter and stage productions including *Oh What A Lovely War*, Alan Bennett's *Forty Years On*, and T.S. Eliot's *Murder in the Cathedral*.

One of the most popular of the Polytechnic's cultural forays was the annual pantomime put on by the Drama Group, which toured local schools and old folks' homes. In 1975 Dramatek took two productions to the Edinburgh Festival Fringe, 'but the most ecstatic audiences they had were probably the six primary schools they toured in December 1975 with a Commedia dell'Arte style pantomime'. This was followed a year later by 'An improvisation exercise on "Robin Hood" with rock band, custard pies and hoary jokes, which toured local schools, an old people's home and then knocked 'em dead at the Polytechnic'. A particularly memorable tour was undertaken by the Drama Group during the extremely poor spring and summer of 1978. A performance of John Barton's *The Hollow Crown* at Camden Borough Council's open air theatre was carried out in particularly trying circumstances, as recalled in the Annual Report for that year:

> *still vivid in the memory are the joys of changing in the backstage bushes before the show –*
> *in the teeth of a brisk north-easter and before the puzzled gaze of a family of ducks, who,*
> *from their expressions, were obviously recalling a line they'd heard in the previous week's*
> *production* [A Midsummer Night's Dream], *'Lord, what fools these mortals be!'*

In 1987 a more sombre piece was a performance by students of a play written by Cuffley playwright Mary Rensten to mark the International Year of Shelter for the Homeless. Entitled *No Fixed Abode*, it was based on the lives of homeless people in Hatfield. The students gave three performances at the Polytechnic, followed by one for the public and guests at Campus West theatre in Welwyn Garden City.

More recently the University has been involved in fostering sports as well, with events such as the UH Sports Football in the Community Scheme in 2000, which saw students run sessions during class time and afterschool clubs for pupils in several local schools. Bryan Clark, the organiser, said, 'It gives the students a chance to gain some experience and put something back into the community where they live.' Furthermore, the new £15 million Sports Village on the de Havilland campus was designed not simply to enhance the studies of Sports Science students, nor purely to give students and staff somewhere to have a swim, play games, get fit or test their nerves negotiating overhangs on the climbing wall. At a time when the town of Hatfield in particular was still coming to terms with the loss of the economic heart of its community, the new state-of-the-art facilities offered local schools and the public a valuable resource. It has also been used for training by the likes of the Arsenal FC Ladies team, the British Swimming squad, the men's National Badminton squad, the England Women's rugby team and Saracens rugby team.

To help with the challenges and problems that arose for local residents living in a campus town, the University created a Community Partnerships Office, funded in part by a grant from the Higher Education Active Community Fund, with the aim of fostering community links through working with local residents' associations. This became particularly important with the development of the de Havilland campus and the adjacent Salisbury Village, where many students rent properties. But, as we have already seen, all areas of the institution have a history of working with and for local residents. In 2005, for instance, the School of Law introduced a 'pro-bono' clinic for members of the public seeking legal advice, with numerous cases being referred to it each year from local Citizens Advice Bureaux. To mark Hatfield New Town's fiftieth anniversary in 1998 an adult outreach project run by the University's Lifelong Learning Centre in the former Faculty of Interdisciplinary Studies worked with local Hatfield residents to collect oral histories and memories of the experience of being part of the development of the New Town. The project led to an exhibition entitled 'Boom Time: Hatfield in the 1950s and 1960s' and a book, *Hatfield Voices* (1999). In recent years the Creative Writing Group has run a successful community outreach programme which has spread to other humanities subjects. Through its many outreach projects, often involving Journalism and Film students, the School of Humanities has built strong relationships with local community groups, also providing a wide range of evening classes as well as workshops for schoolchildren.

*The restored Hatfield beacon at the entrance to the de Havilland campus.*

The value of working with the local community was amply demonstrated by the Heritage Lottery-funded Hatfield Aerodrome Community Heritage Project (2009–11), which worked with ex-employees at the aerodrome, local residents, primary schools, Hertfordshire Archives and Local Studies and Digswell Arts Trust, to generate a series of activities celebrating the engineering innovations of those who once worked at the site.

This led to the creation of a heritage trail and the restoration and re-siting of the last surviving pre-Second World War guidance beacon, which was brought to the aerodrome in the 1930s and remained there until it was removed to North Weald Airfield Museum in the 1980s. As a result of this project, in 2009 a Heritage Hub was created with the aim of pooling expertise across the University, working with communities in the region to explore and promote their heritage.

## Working with businesses

In July 1955 Hatfield Technical College played host to the Hatfield Industrial Trades Fair. Held over one week, the fair, which was officially opened by Lord Salisbury, 6th Marquess, attracted around 4,000 visitors on its first day and continued to pull in crowds of 2,000–3,000 daily during the week. Lord Salisbury gave a speech which drew on the history of Hatfield, from an agricultural economy to its present situation as an attractive site for commerce and industry. He then opened the fair with a silver key, made especially for that purpose. The fair was a joint collaboration between the Hatfield Chamber of Commerce, led by the fair's Director, Sidney Rumbelow, and the Technical College. Dr Chapman was the Chair of the Executive Committee. There were over sixty stands, with exhibitors representing a wide range of interests, both commercial and industrial, as well as civic groups such as Hertfordshire Constabulary and the Church. Displays were laid on to entertain the crowds, including a fashion show, confectionery and cake-making by local bakers, Simmons, and Scottish country dancing.

In his report on the 1979–80 academic year, whilst celebrating the Polytechnic's growing national profile, Norman Lindop emphasised its close connection with the people and industries of Hertfordshire:

*Of our total enrolments of all kinds more than half are of Hertfordshire residents. The national pattern is for most full-time higher education students to leave home when they embark on their studies, but it is an interesting fact that since the college was first mentioned as a polytechnic-designate in 1966, although the total number of full-time and sandwich students has almost quadrupled, the proportion of Hertfordshire residents has remained constant at just below 25%. A high proportion of these students follow sandwich courses and are placed in employment for the professional parts of their courses; many of these placements are, of course, local, and constitute an important link between the Polytechnic and employers in the county.*

A particular strength of the Polytechnic was its ability to respond to requests made by companies for training programmes designed around specific needs. In some cases this involved short courses such as a three-week introductory course in computing for graduate entrant employees of Hawker Siddeley. Other companies that approached the Polytechnic for training courses included Hertfordshire County Council, Nabisco, Rank Xerox, ICI and the British Road Research Association. In the 1983–84 academic year, the School of Information Sciences alone designed thirty 'tailor-made' courses for local industry. The Polytechnic also undertook much more extensive courses in response to very particular requests. In 1971 an Ordinary degree course in Motor Vehicle Engineering was instituted after an approach by a working party from the motor industry, whilst in the same year a part-time, day-release Polytechnic Diploma in Community Work was designed following a request from the county's Youth Agency. Moving beyond the immediate locality, in 1976 the Polytechnic received a request from the Arab Organisation for Industrialisation to design postgraduate management courses for its Egyptian employees, based in Cairo; this involved a stay in England, tours of local industries and intensive coaching in the English language.

Research and consultancy were crucial ways of raising funds, standards and reputations, and in difficult economic times the winning of awards and contracts was of even greater importance. This led to the setting up of the first of the Polytechnic's companies, Polyfield Services, which was a collaboration with the County Council and designed to exploit the very good industrial and commercial links already in place, with the aim of promoting closer co-operation and improving revenue sources. It was not just large organisations such as BAe, Rolls Royce and ICI that benefited from the Polytechnic's expertise. A scheme developed in 1985 was specifically targeted at firms within a forty-mile radius with a workforce of under 300. In practice, most of those who responded employed fewer than 100 people. The idea behind the Small Manufacturing Industries Development Association (SMIDA), based in the Industrial Engineering Centre, was to make available to small businesses the advanced computing, robotic and design services which were usually beyond their budgets. Students supported by staff were able to assist companies in implementing new ideas whilst at the same time gaining some practical commercial experience.

A 1996 study produced by the UH Employment Studies Unit entitled *The Impact of the University of Hertfordshire on the Local Economy* calculated that the University directly employed 1,882 people and indirectly supported another 1,801 jobs in Hertfordshire through spending by staff, students and the institution itself, contributing £64.5 million to the local economy. The University as an institution bought £17 million worth of goods and services annually, of which £6 million went to Hertfordshire companies, including £1 million to Welwyn and Hatfield companies.

Net spending by students was £8.17 million, of which £3.15 million was spent in Welwyn and Hatfield. The staff spend was £4.2 million.

In 1993 the University was a founding partner with the Hertfordshire Training and Enterprise Council, Hertfordshire Chambers of Commerce and Industry, and Hertfordshire County Council in the county's new business help and advice centre in St Albans called Business Link. This eventually morphed into Exemplas, which was acquired by the University in 2005 as part of Vice-Chancellor Tim Wilson's 'business-facing' vision of the modern university. Working closely with the Business School, Exemplas provides courses and training to managers and employees, particularly of government departments and small- to medium-sized enterprises.

## Working with the region's schools

The School of Education has, of course, made a major contribution to the development of teaching in the county and beyond, and in recent times has trained more than 500 teachers every year. But engagement with schools dates back to the days of the technical college and stretches across all subjects. The College, for example, organised an annual series of Mathematics conferences for sixth-formers and their teachers from the grammar school sector, on 'the role of mathematics in modern industry and business'. These proved very popular, with numbers attending growing from an initial 300 pupils and their teachers (from around twenty-three schools) in the session 1961–62, to over 600 by 1963–64 – numbers which were sustained in subsequent years. One project which sparked a great deal of enthusiasm was a two-day seminar held in autumn 1969. Invitations were sent to ten schools for groups of four boys, plus a teacher, to attend a seminar on the subject of 'Technology and Design'. At the end of the event the different groups presented their design for a pedal go-kart, which they took back to their schools to build. Polytechnic staff made visits to keep an eye on progress and then, in July, the six schools which had completed the project returned to be assessed on a number of aspects of their work, including design, manufacturing technology and cost. The assessment culminated in the racing of the go-karts on a 180-yard track. Bourne Valley Secondary School carried the day and was awarded the Hipgrave Trophy for Project Technology, a rose bowl donated by staff in memory of Harry Hipgrave, a long-time member of the Technical Services Staff.

*'I was in the first [1964] cohort of [Hatfield] school kids to be allowed access to the 803 and it was a great experience that remains with me as one of my most rewarding encounters with computing.'*

Professor Peter Excell, Dean of the Institute for Arts, Science and Technology, Glyndwr University.

The commencement of a digital computing service in the College from 1964 saw the start of a long period of provision of courses and facilities for schools. Throughout the 1970s and 1980s a series of courses and conferences was organised to encourage schoolchildren to consider their potential for personal development and future careers through a range of subjects in particular mathematics, computing, natural sciences and engineering. In 1975–76 alone, a total of twenty-seven courses were arranged by departments across the Polytechnic for local sixth-formers; these included a three-day programme of lectures aimed at those showing a particular talent for mathematics. A symposium on 'Science, Society and the Future', which drew an audience of over 600 sixth-formers, was the first event organised by the Polytechnic's Science Teachers' Centre. In addition, the School of Natural Sciences produced a newsletter highlighting the research activities it carried out, which were 'primarily aimed at prospective students and schools to give them a flavour of the School and its interests in all fields of science'.

In 1969 Chorleywood College (a grammar school for blind and partially sighted girls) was provided with an online link to the computer at Hatfield, and one girl, Julia Schofield, subsequently enrolled on the BSc (Hons) in Computer Science, becoming, in 1975, the first blind Computer Science graduate in the UK. Julia received an honorary degree of Doctor of Science from the University in 2007 for her outstanding contribution to the development of computing.

The University continued this tradition of inspiring schoolchildren of all ages with the wonders of science. In 1993 the University won an award under the Young Engineers Scheme for encouraging schoolchildren into engineering. Twenty-four Engineering students were placed in schools in Hatfield, Welwyn Garden City, St Albans and Hertford for a minimum of six weeks to raise the children's awareness

*Mark Riggimonti with schoolchildren at Wall Hall Sculpture Park.*

of engineering opportunities. Professor Peter Lines, Dean of the School of Engineering, commented, 'This is making a significant contribution to the development of engineering interest in young people'. Two years later, the University and the Hertfordshire Science and Technology Regional Organisation (SATRO) staged a week-long event designed to demonstrate to the wider public that science can be fun. Called 'Discovery '95', it involved talks and experiments from guests such as astronomer Heather Couper, TV presenter Johnny Ball, Professor Heinz Wolff and Ian Russell ('of exploding custard fame'). There was also a programme of events designed for local primary schools, and in all around 180,000 visitors attended. University of Hertfordshire lecturer Steve Ford took a telescope on a tour of primary schools as part of the Stars for Schools project. The original project had been to take a telescope to senior schools, but a £3,000 grant from the Particle Physics and Astronomy Council had made it possible to extend the project to primary schools for day visits. The same year, 1997, budding engineers from thirty-six schools met at the University's Hatfield campus to compete in a contest to build a bridge out of spaghetti. The prize was £300 and a computer for their school.

The University also promoted the Arts and culture amongst schoolchildren. In 2002, Head of Music Howard Burrell, and former Senior Lecturer in Drama, Sean Williams, wrote the score for a musical production based on the story of Sir Gawain and the Green Knight, to be produced by children from schools in Stevenage. Students from the Music Department also helped with providing musical accompaniments and behind-the-scenes support. In addition, a summer programme was put on for children entitled *Artscool!*, which gave local children the chance to sample the full range of facilities offered by the School of Art and Design.

The University of Hertfordshire has long supported the AIM Higher scheme to encourage schoolchildren from lower socio-economic groups and disadvantaged backgrounds, who live in areas of relative deprivation, to participate in higher education. One of numerous activities in 2005, for instance, was a Summer School for Year 11 students from sixty schools, who were given taster courses and careers advice in subjects such as journalism, music, physics and astronomy. Meanwhile, the English Literature Group was one of the first university groups to support the Institute of Ideas in its national competition for sixth-form students, Debating Matters, which encourages students to hone their debating skills – rewarding content and substance over rhetoric and style. When the competition was starting out, the English Literature Group regularly hosted the regional heats of the competition on the new de Havilland campus, with members of the Group acting as judges. Since then, the competition has gone from strength to strength, with national recognition and heats across the UK and in India.

## Widening access

The Polytechnic also continued the College's endeavours to promote widening access to higher education for adults. Considerable thought was given to part-time programmes of degree-level study designed with the mature student in mind. Norman Lindop commented in particular on both the high quality and dedication of these students. In his review of the twenty-five years since the opening of the Technical College, he commented, 'it is an indication of the motivation and fortitude of part-time students that under these arrangements, in which they are effectively competing with full-time students, they have frequently attained the highest honours'. The 1978–79 Annual Report praised the School of Humanities for its part-time BA degree in English: 'Clearly there are a large number of very able people, some of whom lack the usual formal entry qualifications, who welcome and are able to benefit from the opportunity to undertake degree-level studies even while they are doing full-time jobs. This type of part-time degree responds to an educational need that is likely to increase rather than decrease in the future.'

Access to education was also widened with the introduction of the 'Associate Student' policy, whereby mature students could opt to study particular modules from those on offer to degree-level students across all the schools of study, without signing up for a complete programme; examinations were optional and any credits acquired could be transferred at a later date to a degree programme. In September 1976 the first intake of thirty Associate Students included housewives, the self-employed and representatives from a range of commercial and industrial organisations, with previous qualifications spanning the entire range from O Levels to Honours degrees. The most popular courses were in computer science.

A further development of this commitment to mature students, and a unique format for the time, was a scheme begun in the mid-1970s which allowed students to design their own degree, drawing on courses already running within departments such as Chemistry, Engineering, Computing, Astronomy and Business Studies, to achieve a Combined Studies degree. In each of the first two years of the scheme's operation, the annual prize for the best performance was awarded to a mature student who had left school with little in the way of qualifications. As the 1980–81 report for the Combined Studies Department concluded, 'the two winners of the first year prize will themselves benefit greatly from their time on an undergraduate course, but, perhaps more importantly, will return to jobs more suited to their true ability benefiting society thereby.' In 1983 Dr Illston reported on a former student who had studied for a combination degree built around a major in Chemistry and a minor in Astronomy. Following his graduation, he had taken a PGCE course at Sussex University and had just found his first teaching post at a school which had specifically advertised for a chemistry teacher able to take courses in astronomy.

As well as those whose focus was on new or improved career prospects, the Polytechnic also catered to those who were simply interested in spending an informative evening considering something new. In 1971, the Humanities Department ran a literary evening class entitled 'Reason and Romance', whilst those interested in mathematics could join the 'Recreational Mathematics' course, which offered 'a variety of mathematical and statistical topics set in interesting or amusing contexts'. In 1981 a course entitled 'Learning in Later Life' attracted thirty-two students, mainly in their sixties and seventies, who followed a full academic programme. Many of them expressed an intention to continue with their studies as Associate Students. The 1980s brought many challenges, but throughout there remained that sense of the

Polytechnic as very much an institution for all people, including those who might be excluded by a more narrow definition of the role of education. As Illston wrote in 1984, 'We are conscious that, if the Polytechnic is to serve its community well, it is important that its work should be known and understood by as wide a section of the community as possible.' Increasingly, however, that commitment to reaching out to the community became a valuable means of withstanding the economic restraints of the 1970s and 1980s. The revenue from short courses and consultancy was, more than ever, a factor in securing the future of the Polytechnic.

In the university years, the School of Law offered a 'LawPrep' Access course for those interested in studying law but lacking A Level qualifications, or for those wishing to change career, whilst the School of Art and Design offered Access courses again aimed at those thinking of a change of career. In 2000 a bus equipped with Internet technology visited five Hertfordshire towns to publicise the support available to those considering returning to work or changing career.

Enabling women to get into the workplace and develop career paths was a key objective. One of the most successful and long-running schemes was NOW – New Opportunities for Women courses. Begun in 1971, these short courses run by Ruth Michaels were widely praised in the sector and by some in the women's liberation movement. Many of those who took the courses went on to study for a degree. In 1976 a conference was held at the Polytechnic on 'Continuing Education for Women', at which another recent Hatfield initiative, 'Polyprep' Access courses, were commended for giving further routes to higher education for those from working-class backgrounds who had left school at the minimum age. A BA in Contemporary Studies was also designed specifically for mature students who had come through from NOW and Access courses.

During a House of Lords debate in 1984 on barriers to women returning to work, Baroness Beatrice Seear, an influential social scientist, applauded Hatfield Polytechnic for introducing its two-year course for women who had been out of the workplace, which enabled them to re-train as accountants. It was the only such course that she was aware of, and one that adjusted its hours to fit around the particular needs of raising a family. In February 1992 the Polytechnic re-launched its free eight-week 'Promoting Women' course, which aimed to encourage more women into management via a series of lectures, seminars and workshops. Later that year the newly named University of Hertfordshire advertised a free nine-week short course entitled 'Professional Updating for Women', built around the school day and sponsored by the Hertfordshire Training and Enterprise Council. The course included a similar programme of lectures, seminars and workshops, but with the added bonus of one day each week and one full week of the course being spent working in a local company.

## Attitudes towards 'career mums' in 1973:

'In an age when everyone is supposed to have more leisure time it is remarkable that, at 35, women with children and all the responsibilities of domestic life are itching to prove themselves worthy of a chance of a new career. What they say they are up against is the prejudice of a "sick society" which puts obstacles in the way of the mums who want to work. They examined their predicament at a conference at Hatfield Polytechnic, where they are taking a course on new opportunities for women. Because they feel that opportunities for retraining married women are limited, they will ask the polytechnic to set up an education centre to cater specifically for them. If this is agreed, the authorities will be engaged in a fairly formidable undertaking, for the mothers want them to provide a crèche and nursery facilities while they attend courses.

In the meantime they intend to let professional societies and firms in the area know that they take a poor view of the shortage of part-time work for women. Unfeeling ones might say that these career mums should not expect to be able to have their cake and eat it. And a great many employers have discovered that having mums on your pay roll is not without its problems – especially young mums with a great deal of domestic involvement. Good luck to the women who are fighting for what they consider to be the need for a better deal. But they must remember that it is also an employer's right to expect a fair deal. It works both ways.'

*Hatfield and Welwyn Advertiser,* **2 February 1973**

In 2000 a successful course aimed at encouraging women to set up their own businesses was run again by popular demand. It was attended by 187 women, with the ideas proposed ranging from children's fashion to IT consultancy. In the same year, six-month 'Return to Nursing' courses were introduced, which saw over one hundred former nurses retrain in the first six years. Widening access was further enhanced when, shortly after becoming a university, UH established an Associate College Network allowing students at Hertford Regional College, Oaklands College, North Hertfordshire College and West Herts College to take Access courses as part of their preparation for enrolment on university degrees. This became an important route for mature students to enter higher education.

# From Vice-Chancellor Professor Sir Tim Wilson's 2010 Annual Lecture, 'Hertfordshire and its University: Past, Present and Future'

'Twenty years ago, almost to the day, we formed a partnership with the four further education colleges in this County, and that partnership continues to thrive. It is a partnership that enables students to enter higher education within one of those four colleges and transfer to the University if they attain the required standards. This gives them the opportunity to graduate, perhaps progress into postgraduate study. There are many stories of students who have benefited from the partnerships that we have with Hertfordshire's colleges.

We would be here all night if I shared them all with you. But there is one story that has a special meaning for me. A few years ago, I was receiving graduates in the Cathedral Abbey of St Alban. It is the highlight of the year – our graduates celebrating their achievements, their hard work and their dedication, and sharing that celebration with their tutors and their families. Amongst the graduates, there was a lady who was clearly very nervous walking across the stage towards me.

She was a mature student, probably in her late thirties; I guessed she had taken a great deal of care selecting her graduation outfit. As she walked slowly towards me she clearly wanted to say something.

She stopped and spoke softly. In less than thirty seconds she told me her story. She had left school at sixteen pregnant with her first child and without any qualifications. But later in life she started at a college with an access programme and progressed to the University – eventually attaining a degree in Midwifery with its licence to practice. Her whole family was in the Abbey, including her grandchildren, watching the first person in their family to study beyond the age of sixteen graduate. I could only imagine the determination, dedication and commitment that that woman had displayed to achieve what she had. It was one of those moments when you feel immensely proud of our university and its role in our society. I was about to congratulate her with enthusiastic words, when she held my eyes in hers and said, "Vice-Chancellor, thank you for the opportunity." Thank you for the opportunity. The humility of that graduate was overwhelming. There was no sense of entitlement, no belief that this was her right, no triumphant statement that she had overcome the obstacles that life had thrown at her.

Just that humble statement, "thank you for the opportunity". That moment will live with me for the rest of my life.'

## The media

The social, cultural and economic value of higher education can be transmitted in many ways, and this institution's students have long played a valuable role in promoting it through the media. Back in the college days, the student Pram Race team, long-distance mower drivers and cross-Channel bed sailors (see next chapter) were all reported in the national news. The Polytechnic students' spirit of protest and their Rag adventures were well covered by the press and news channels. The nature of television programming has changed hugely since the 1980s, of course, and the University's students have consequently found themselves engaged in a wide range of screen genres.

In 1998 students from the University's Midwifery degree course featured in a Channel 5 television series called *Baby School*. This was a fly-on-the-wall documentary which shadowed undergraduates as they trained at Watford General Hospital and Hemel Hempstead Hospital. The BBC reported on five postgraduate students at the University of Hertfordshire who, as their entry in a 1999 biotechnology competition, proposed genetically creating a Christmas tree whose needles glowed naturally. Neurophysiology student Katy Presland explained, 'We're talking about a green luminescent Christmas tree that glows in the dark and produces a noticeable light during the day.' The stumbling block was cost, she said. 'We calculate that the initial trees would cost about £200, which means going for the upper end of the market. But I'm sure a lot of people would love them, especially the Americans.'

The following year, a team from the University of Hertfordshire entered a robot named Behemoth in the popular BBC2 programme *Robot Wars*. The model was built by two students, Kane Ashton, a computer scientist, and Anthony Pritchard, a model maker. Anthony designed a robot in the shape of the BBC2 symbol as part of his academic course in model-making. Then, in 2005, a student team from the University had an impressive run on BBC2's long-running *University Challenge*. They came from behind in the first round to beat Lucy

Cavendish College, Cambridge, 160 to 110, then in the second round again came from behind to beat the University of Wales, Lampeter, 145 to 140 after trailing by 55 points at one moment. They finally lost in the quarter finals to the University of Liverpool 195 to 140.

Long before the 'Impact agenda' focussed the minds of university researchers as to the need to explain and explore the social, cultural and cultural value of their work, members of the Polytechnic and University were making their presence felt on screen and radio. In 1993 a BBC film crew spent two days at the University of Hertfordshire

*The University of Hertfordshire's University Challenge team, 2005.*

filming and interviewing staff for an item on its training programme *Careering Ahead*, which focussed on the opportunities for re-training after redundancy. The same year, research being done by the University's Electronics Research and Development Centre into monitoring the flow of red blood cells through capillaries was featured on BBC1's *Tomorrow's World Live* programme.

Psychology Professor Richard Wiseman began a successful media career in the 1990s, leading to the creation of a chair for the Public Understanding of Psychology at the University. In 1994 the BBC's *Big Science* programme filmed Wiseman and his research assistant Matthew Smith conducting an experiment in a BBC television studio. The research was to check if there was any truth in 'that niggling feeling' we sometimes have that somebody is watching us. This was one of numerous research projects over the years in which, through media participation, he was able to engage the general public in accessible psychological research: 'This is a new way of carrying out science – instead of bringing people to the lab we are taking the lab to them,' Wiseman explained. His 2002 project LaughLab, a year-long project in collaboration with the British Science Association, invited the international public to send in contenders for the funniest joke ever. The 40,000 jokes submitted were then analysed to explore why they were funny and to identify gender and cultural differences in humour.

Professor Wiseman has also appeared on numerous television and radio programmes investigating psychic phenomena and hauntings. But long before he arrived at the University, the Polytechnic students had attracted media attention for their ghost investigations. In 1977 the local press reported:

*The spirit of adventure is not yet dead, at least in Hatfield Polytechnic. A group of first year students are determined to find the ghastly truth about things that go bump in the night. Under the chairmanship of history student Bill Brown they have formed the Hatfield Polytechnic Psychic Research Association. Bill said this week: 'We have no preconceived ideas. None of us has actually seen a ghost, we just want to find out the truth.' Now he is asking anyone who knows of a ghost to tell him about it. 'We want to carry out a proper investigation,' he said.*

The University's 'Dancing Doctor', Peter Lovatt, has both entertained and instructed the international public with his work on the psychology of dance, through his appearances on television, radio and the stage. For those who like their science to go with more of a bang, there are the University's engineers, with their long-standing expertise in rocketry dating back to the de Havilland days, and who in recent years have been called upon many times by television companies. Dr Ray Wilkinson appeared on CBBC's *Blast Lab*, when he lashed a teddy bear and a slice of pizza to a rocket-powered sled that reached speeds of around 838 mph. In February 2012 engineers from the School of Engineering and Technology made their fourth appearance on the BBC television programme *Bang Goes the Theory*, when they fitted a Vauxhall VX220 car with a rocket motor capable of producing over half a tonne of thrust for three seconds. Previous appearances have involved a rocket-powered bicycle fuelled by toffee, a rocket-powered railway car and a tug of war between a rocket motor and a jet engine.

Making research relevant also involves exploring how it can influence policy and change public understanding. An excellent example of the latter is the successful BBC1 legal drama *Garrow's Law*, which began in 2009 and has won a Royal Television Society award. Its creator, Tony Marchant, was inspired to write a drama about the eighteenth-century barrister William Garrow after exploring the Old Bailey Online digital archive, which was a project directed jointly by UH History professor, Tim

Hitchcock, and Professor Bob Shoemaker at Sheffield University. This free, fully searchable archive of the largest body of texts detailing the lives of common people ever published contains 197,745 criminal trials held at London's central criminal court. As Marchant explained, 'There's an immediacy about the Old Bailey online records, with transcripts of the actual trials which makes it a fantastic oral and written history of those who went through the criminal justice system, a riveting insight into the lives of ordinary people who were caught up in it and, of course, a revelation about the way that law was conducted then.'

## Arts and culture

As has already been seen, from its earliest inception as a college, the institution that became the University of Hertfordshire had made a commitment to supporting the Arts. The current UH Art Collection originates from 1952, when John Newsom championed the inclusion of artworks from leading British artists within the construction budget, his wider aim being to bring 'all the arts into the education of ordinary children, and to widen their horizons'. The collection was further developed after the merger with Hertfordshire College of Art and Design, and now has some 500 artworks in the portfolio, ranging from photography, textile and ceramics to sculpture and mixed media, some by former students.

*An attendee at a vampire conference organised by English Literature in 2010, which attracted international media attention.*

As we have already seen, and will explore further in the next chapter, the College and Polytechnic were also active in community drama. The institution's contribution to musical performance was boosted in the early 1970s when Howard Burrell, a music lecturer who had arrived in 1972 to join the Culture and Recreation Unit, started up a theatre and opera company, Operabout, which became the fully professional Opera East in 1984, owned and funded by the Polytechnic. It consisted of a community orchestra made up of teachers and professionals who mentored student members, and it played concerts all over the country. The Polytechnic was responsible for the rehearsals, whilst the orchestra took care of the organisation and handling of concert fees.

A popular staff–student 'big band' called Tuesday Night was also set up, which grew to twenty-five members and played in local venues as well as at the Polytechnic.

Over at Wall Hall, in June 1992, Sean Williams of the School of Humanities and Education organised an 'International Festival of Theatre and the Arts', held over five days, as a celebration of closer ties to Europe. Drama students from Belgium, France, Germany and Hatfield each performed two productions in their own languages, with performances in the morning and afternoon for schoolchildren studying foreign languages and a further performance in the evening for the general public. One of the plays chosen by the Hatfield students was Stephen Berkoff's interpretation of Franz Kafka's *Metamorphosis*. Additionally, there was a programme of lectures and debates, including contributions from French poet Jacques Darras, who had delivered the 1989 BBC Reith Lecture; Phil Redmond, creator of *Grange Hill* and *Brookside*; composer Professor Nigel Osborne; BBC presenter Sarah Dunant; and the then Director of Studies of Humanities at Wall Hall, Professor Graham Holderness, author of *The Shakespeare Myth*.

*'Le Jazz' performing in 1994 at a UHArts event.*

UH*Arts* was set up in 1994, with generous support from the University's director of finance to co-ordinate and promote the University's programme of arts and cultural events. Hatfield Philharmonic (now the de Havilland Philharmonic), which has been going since 1969, was brought under its umbrella, whilst the first classical performance under its auspices was a concert by the Symphony Orchestra of Bohemia of works by Dvorak and Smetana as part of their UK tour. The concert took place in the Prince Edward Hall. Over the years, UH*Arts* has also staged exhibitions of national significance such as an exhibition of Picasso's *Late Etchings*, which 'offered a remarkable opportunity for people who live outside London to view works by one of the great masters of twentieth-century Modernism'. Local artists such as Graham Bond were also showcased. Bond's works reflected his travels around the world as well as his impressions of his home in Hertfordshire. In 2005 UH Recordings was set up as another branch of UH*Arts* to record and release interesting and contemporary classical recordings and pieces by new and upcoming contemporary artists.

## UH Press and HEDS

The University of Hertfordshire Press also celebrates its twentieth anniversary in 2012. Indeed, there is a pleasing neatness in the fact that the very first book published under the UH Press imprint was put together in 1992 in order to celebrate the institution's change of status from polytechnic to university. *Our Heritage* was a short history of the various campuses of the new university written by Tony Gardner, a member of staff in what was then known as the Library and Media Services Department.

The Press was propagated in the fertile soil of the technical library services. The prime mover behind it was Bill Forster, who worked for HERTIS, the Hertfordshire Technical Information Service, and who was based at the College Lane campus of the Polytechnic. HERTIS was a county-wide information service for industry and the brainchild of Gordon Wright. Wright saw the value of sharing the knowledge held in each of the specialist technical libraries of Hertfordshire not only with each other but also with local companies in order to encourage innovation. Bill Forster was heavily involved in Libtech International, an annual trade fair held at College Lane to bring together innovators in library technology. So much new information was pouring out of HERTIS that Bill started to publish collected papers under a HERTIS imprint. The first was *Getting in Print; Staying in Print* in 1990.

From this initiative, UH Press was born. Books in this vein continued after the imprint changed its name, most notably the pioneering *Bibliographic Software and the Electronic Library* in 1995.

Forster enjoyed his forays into book publishing and, gradually, books on new topics began to appear on his list. It was in 1995 that the imprint really took off. Amongst the new titles published was a short volume entitled *Guidelines for Testing Psychic Claimants*, the first book by Richard Wiseman, who would go on to publish bestselling titles including *The Luck Factor*, *Quirkology* and *59 Seconds* (although not with UH Press). This year, 1995, also saw the first publication in a subject area that would become UH Press's most distinctive specialism. The Press was invited to join Interface, a Europe-wide consortium of publishers that aimed to disseminate scholarly studies of Romany Gypsy life, culture and history. *English Gypsies and State Policies* and *On the Verge: The Gypsies of England* were the first Gypsy-related titles to be published by UH Press. The Romani Studies list has developed to include not only books by respected experts but also books by Gypsies and Travellers themselves. Maggie Smith-Bendell's autobiographical memoir of growing up as an English Traveller, *Our Forgotten Years*, became a *Sunday Times* bestseller when paperback rights were licensed to Abacus in 2010. In 2004 the writer Louise Doughty wrote in the *Independent on Sunday*, 'You could do a lot worse than buying the entire back catalogue of the University of Hertfordshire Press, a tiny but valiant publishing house which is the main source of Romany Studies in this country'.

*Historian Lady Antonia Fraser (centre) and, to her right, actor Timothy West, with UH Press Manager Bill Forster (far left) at the launch of UH Press's anthology* The Roads of the Roma *(1998) on National Poetry Day.*

Tiny, yes. With just one full-time member of staff until 2003, and then two subsequently, the Press is almost certainly the smallest academic publisher in the UK. But it has been included in a list of the 'leading UK University publishing houses' (*Times Higher Education Supplement*, 2004), and punches above its weight in terms of the quality of the scholarship it publishes and the high production values it espouses.

From the early years, a number of members of University staff supported the Press in practical ways, editing series or offering their own books for publication. Professor Nigel Goose's series *Studies in Regional and Local History* has now reached Volume 11 (with Philip Slavin's *Bread and Ale for the Brethren: The provisioning of Norwich Cathedral Priory, 1260–1536*, published in 2012) and enjoys a reputation for excellence in the field of academic local history. Professor Graham Holderness generously gave the Press his Shakespeare trilogy, beginning with *Visual Shakespeare* in 2001. A landmark for the Press's drama-related publishing was winning the Theatre Book Prize in 2001 for *Reflecting the Audience* by Jim Davis and Victor Emeljanow. The Press now regularly publishes theatre history books in association with the Society for Theatre Research.

The next year saw the Press forging an agreement with the Hertfordshire Association for Local History to take over the distribution of books they had already published and to publish fresh Hertfordshire local history titles under a new imprint – Hertfordshire Publications. The first of these was *Cinemas of Hertfordshire*, launched in great style at the art deco Rex Cinema, Berkhamsted. As well as bringing out new commercial titles each year (sold worldwide through distributors in London and Chicago), UH Press also works frequently with different University departments to produce books for them. In recent years these have included *Scope of Radiographic Practice 2008* (for the School of Health and Emergency Professions), *Learning together through international collaboration in teacher education in Malaysia* (for the School of Education) and *The de Havilland Legacy* (for the School of Humanities).

The Higher Education Digitisation Service (HEDS) was another outgrowth from the innovative information sciences heritage of the University. It was established as a national service in 1996, funded by the Joint Information Systems Committee (JISC) to provide expert consultancy for higher education. The HEDS team provided advice on and managed the digitisation of archives old and new. Amongst its first consultancy jobs was to help organise a pilot study of the proposed digitisation of the

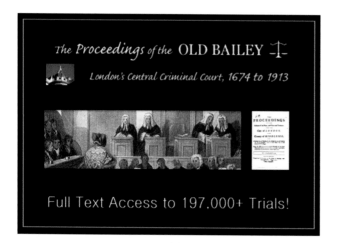

journal *Nature* (1869–1992), and it also advised on the digitisation of meteorological observatory data between 1881 and 1975, and the Transactions of the Institute of British Geographers. Closer to home, it provided a hugely valuable service for a series of projects emerging from the History Group at Hertfordshire, including the Old Bailey Online (www.oldbaileyonline. org) and London Lives (www.londonlives. org). HEDS both advised on the process of digital capture – specifying standards and formats – and undertook the arduous task of creating digital images and transcriptions of hundreds of thousands of pages of historical texts and manuscripts. Together HEDS and the History Group established a new standard of digital capture for historical materials, and in combination made the University the natural national centre for digital history. HEDS was closed down in 2009 unfortunately, at a moment when the digitisation agenda was developing in new and exciting ways.

## Keeping the community moving

As early as 1953, Chapman highlighted the problems posed for students by an infrequent bus service that stopped more than half a mile away from the College, and persuaded the governors of the necessity of a shuttle bus to bring in students from Potters Bar, Borehamwood and Barnet. It was agreed by the Further Education Sub-Committee that, subject to approval from the Ministry of Education, coaches would be hired to transport students to the College from New Barnet, Borehamwood and the Stonehouse pub, Hatfield. The initial cost would be £2,279, to be paid to Highway Coaches. Fares for those over the age of eighteen were expected to produce a return of £745 from New Barnet, £373 from Borehamwood and £143 from the Stonehouse, leaving a net estimated cost of £1,018 per session. It was argued that an estimated annual saving of £1,800 could be made by laying on more coaches to bring students to Hatfield who currently went outside the county for their education and for whom fees consequently had to be paid.

The various campus moves during the polytechnic years created further problems that needed to be solved. The move to Balls Park saw the introduction of the first free inter-campus shuttle, although pressure on overheads meant that in September 1980 it reverted to a fare-paying service. The move of Humanities to Wall Hall and the integration of the College of Education into the Polytechnic raised the stakes. Wall Hall was relatively isolated, being nearly a mile from the village of Aldenham, at the end of a long drive. The village was not well served by public transport in any case. It had only one bus route, the 311, which connected Aldenham village to Watford town centre in one direction and in the other connected the village to Radlett and then out to Shenley and London Colney. The route was only hourly in either direction.

As a teacher training college, Wall Hall arranged teacher training placements across Hertfordshire. As many of the students lived in residential halls on campus, a way had to be found to get the students to and from their placements. The County Council took a decision to base a small fleet of coaches at the college, operated by a small team of drivers led by a transport manager, Peter Ward. This self-contained existence continued until the merger with the Polytechnic in early 1987. Late that year the Polytechnic Director, Neil Buxton, decided that the campus at Wall Hall was not sustainable in its current form and that a new School of Humanities and Education should be based at Wall Hall. There was considerable opposition to the move by the School

of Humanities, not least due to concern about how staff and students would get to and from the campus, and how contact would be maintained with other departments and other students at Hatfield. This concern was understandable, and, to meet this, Buxton promised that a frequent bus service would be in place from when the move was effected. The newly merged School took residence in September 1989

*Actor Stephen Lewis who played Blakey in the 1970s comedy series* On the Buses, *and Roger Duke, Estates Services Manager.*

and the Polytechnic provided services which connected the Wall Hall site to the Polytechnic site at Hatfield, whilst a service connected Wall Hall to Watford. The first timetable was a photocopied affair that gave not only the services (which were basically hourly in frequency) but public transport connections and service timetables.

Wall Hall may have been attended to but the main Polytechnic site at Hatfield was still poorly served. By the late 1980s the College Lane campus contained about 3,000 students and several hundred staff.

Furthermore, just under 1,000 students studied at Balls Park, several hundred living in Halls off Mangrove Road and in accommodation in the grounds, whilst the rest commuted from the town and surrounding areas. Even at this time the Polytechnic was already becoming heavily reliant upon the motor car.

In looking to provide improved bus services not only for Wall Hall but for Hatfield, as well as for the Polytechnic, the climate was problematic. The two major operators, London Country North East and London Country North West, were in difficulty and service innovation was not uppermost in their minds. When the Polytechnic Director decided to ensure that those newly moved would have a good transport service, he asked the recently arrived Deputy Secretary and Academic Registrar, Philip Waters, to make arrangements. Waters worked with one of the senior Estates staff, Roger Duke, and together they assembled a main route connecting Hatfield and Wall Hall. The service started in September 1989 and was lightly used in the first instance. Subsequently the service was hourly in both directions, with the journeys in the morning peak focussed on Wall Hall. An infrequent route into Watford was also started. In the 1990–91 academic year, the route between Wall Hall and Hatfield was adjusted to take on more stopping places, and a route to the Hertford campus was added. Thus in September 1990 the true beginnings of the Uno operation began. Students and staff were asked for a small charge but the service remained private.

Whilst efficient, the route network could not be expanded further without more resources. Student demand was growing but how could capacity be increased? These factors led to the decision to commercialise the whole operation. Commercial routes were launched in September 1991, first as a division of UH Ventures, and then in November 1992 University Bus Ltd was formed as a separate University company. Waters emphasised the wider value of the service: '[W]e hope that in future the quality and range of services will be such that it encourages people in mid-Herts out of their cars and on to the buses. This will of course help the University's own environment which is suffering already from major parking problems and traffic congestion.' In 2005 University*bus* changed its name to Uno to reflect the fact that it provides a service to the whole community and not just staff and students.

Increased student car ownership in the 2000s has created new challenges for the University's Estates Department, and made Uno all the more important in getting students and staff to work. Since 2006 a park-and-ride scheme has been in place to encourage the use of public transport and reduce local traffic congestion.

**The University of Hertfordshire in 2003:**

- 20,000 students
- Turnover of £120 million
- 300 teachers and 750 healthcare professionals found jobs within the county
- An estimated £275 million generated for the Hertfordshire economy annually
- A provider of 4,000 jobs in the area

# 5. Student life and learning

*'[T]hey are the life-blood of the institution, and without them we should not exist. In the nature of things it is their contribution, in work and play, in study and recreation, which determines our success. It is a particular pleasure for me, in congratulating them on their achievements and thanking them for their co-operation, to report my conviction that, in their hands, the present and future reputation of this College is safe.'*
**Norman Lindop, Director of Hatfield Polytechnic (1968).**

During the early years of the College the student body ranged from fifteen-year-olds receiving training in the Building Department to those in their twenties taking advanced qualifications, those who went home at the end of the day and those who lived independent lives in digs and hostels. The mix between junior and senior students was not always harmonious. When, in 1954, a sixteen-year-old Machine Shop student was attending a social studies session and was encouraged to make nominations for Students' Union elections, he replied, 'No, we're not smart enough to be on that committee, they only want posh blokes like B–. But those chaps do look good about the college, give it a sort of air. Do you think you could help us to be posh blokes like those committee chaps?'

Many students found lodgings with local families, but Norman Lindop noted that the students of the late 1960s were showing signs of being a different breed from their predecessors:

> *All who are concerned with student living accommodation in the universities and colleges are finding that young people are showing signs of increasing independence and are less docile in accepting the inconvenience of living in 'digs' than their predecessors. Many prefer to live in flats or bed-sitting rooms, and we have not the staff or resources to provide any adequate supervision or to operate a licensing system for lodgings. The attractions of a Bohemian life are real enough, no doubt, but so are its disadvantages, whether expressed in terms of the economics of catering on a precarious student grant budget, or of the possibility of ill-health without adequate care and attention.*

Nor was it simply a problem of residential space. Social spaces continued to be limited and in his final report as Principal, Chapman warned that the College might have problems in competing with 'other better provided institutions' for full-time students unless some solution was found.

Finding accommodation for students continued to be a real headache for the Polytechnic. In September 1975 over a hundred students were obliged to sleep on mattresses and camp beds in the two senior common rooms, many of them not being housed for three weeks. This was just at a time when the Polytechnic was experiencing cutbacks in capital building programmes and further Halls of Residence places seemed unlikely. In 1980, as local people faced large increases in both interest and inflation rates, the Polytechnic mounted a major campaign to encourage households to take in students.

**MORTGAGE RATE 15%**
**RENT & RATES UP 20%**
Can YOU afford
to leave your spare room empty?

**FILL THE GAP WITH A**
**STUDENT LODGER**
CONTACT:—
Marian Gaskins, Accommodation Officer,
Accommodation Services,
The Hatfield Polytechnic.
Telephone: Hatfield 68100, ext. 305.

In 1982, the Polytechnic took delivery of a two-storey mobile unit, formerly used to house oil workers, to help as a 'stop gap solution' in relieving pressure on Halls of Residence and local accommodation. Accommodation Officer Anna Brown told the local press that this was 'an idea born out of desperation'. By September 1982 Pembroke Hall was open and able to take an additional 220 students. But the search for solutions to the housing problem continued and in 1986 the Polytechnic was able to announce the inauguration of their Head Leasing Scheme. Starting with 80 properties, by June 1986, 900 students were being housed in 180 properties, with a target of 1,000 places for September 1986. Negotiations were also entered into to take on Trident House (renamed Asquith House, after former Chief Executive of the Welwyn Hatfield Council, Leslie Asquith) in Hatfield town centre from the District Council with the intention of housing 150 students in 66 self-contained furnished flats. A dramatic increase in enrolment in 1990 made it necessary to resort to yet another prefab solution with the creation of Roehyde Hall, providing 221 new rooms. By this time the first phase of the Roberts Way student village was well under way, leading eventually to the building of 72 shared accommodation houses.

## Gender balance

The social life of the students was also influenced to a considerable degree by the gender balance. Of 2,143 students in 1963 only 196 were women. Still, social events were organised with the predominantly

*'The room was painted yellow, which sounds quite nice, but it was literally painted on brick. It was tiny, and it had a sink in the corner, and this big wardrobe and a little table and single bed, and it was stark, and I just looked at it ... My mum just stood there, and she just looked at it, and she said, "Well, no one said it was going to be the Ritz – Bye!".'*

*Jane Blacklock, one of the few female Engineering students in the late 1980s, on her first impressions of her room in a College Lane Hall of Residence.*

*An impressively tidy student communal kitchen in the 1970s.*

female students of the Colleges of Education. The ratio of male to female students was a constant theme in the Polytechnic's Annual Reports, and the considerable effort to promote courses to both women and mature students saw a change in the ratio of male to female, from just under 8:1 in 1971 to 2:1 by 1986. The Polytechnic also continued the drive to attract more women into the engineering industries with day courses targeting talented sixth-formers. Progress, however, was slow in this area. Christine Rayner was the first woman to graduate with a Civil Engineering degree in 1969, but women Engineering students remained the exception. In 1981 the School of Engineering was able to report only a slight increase in the numbers of women applying.

> *'We had the College dance in the main hall, and we would all be there with our girlfriends, dancing around, and Dr Chapman would be there with his wife. And Dr Chapman would be going around the dance floor, this is the honest truth, and for couples he'd be parting them so that they didn't touch. And he would go up to them and push them apart!'*
>
> **Sir Stuart Matthews,** *Mechanical Engineering student who graduated from Hatfield Technical College in 1958.*

In the age of feminism and women's liberation any whiff of sexism was fought in what had long been a male-dominated environment. In 1974 there were complaints from some female students, dubbed 'Women's Libbers' by the local press, when the Polytechnic Rag magazine *Oops* carried a large number of pictures of female nudes. Six of the ten pairs of breasts on display appeared in a 'pick your favourite' competition, the prize for which was a day for two in 'Sunny Hatfield' with expenses of fifty pence thrown in. The local press reported that the Rag magazine was a particular favourite with 'publand customers', and in the first week alone sales had topped the one thousand mark. Rag organiser Paul Thompson, confronted by complaints from the female students, defended the magazine and said it contained much more than just nudity: 'There are original jokes written by college students'. He argued that they took care not to sell the magazine to children and, ultimately, 'the important thing is that it sells better with nudes and as the cash goes to charities that cannot be bad'. Four years later the Rag magazine *Reject 78* again raised eyebrows when the front cover carried a photograph of the editor, Steve Earle, wearing only a jock strap. Students' Union (SU) President Alistair Cormie called for it to be changed, but the Rag Committee defended the photograph:

> *We do not feel that this publication is in any way offensive to the majority of students in this college. The majority of complaints seem to come from a small group of political activists within the college who seem to believe that the general public are a bunch of mindless idiots.*

The sexual politics of the era also impacted on accommodation policy. Responding to 'student demand and the recent lowering of the age of adult-hood to eighteen', in 1972 the Polytechnic decided to relax the regulations regarding overnight guests, permitting twenty-four-hour mixed visiting for an experimental period, 'subject to safeguards to prevent permanent multiple occupation'. A year later mixed floors were introduced into Chapman Hall as an experiment. Whilst all Halls other than Fairshot Court had

*Hatfield Technical College Students' Union Council, 1955. Image courtesy of Sir Stuart Matthews.*

housed men and women, this had been on the basis of separate floors or wings for each gender. It was planned to extend the experiment to other Halls, although there were some problems associated with the high male to female ratio. As the report noted, mixed floors were not the answer for everybody: a survey of Hatfield Polytechnic students in 1972–73 had shown that 'although 50 per cent of the men would prefer mixed floors, only about 20 per cent of the women would do so'.

# The Students' Union

In 1958–59 the Students' Union affiliated to the National Union of Students and also developed a closer working relationship with staff. Union representatives met regularly with those from the College's Staff Association. The Union also donated £100 to a fund for a dedicated Union building – it took a long time to arrive. The latter part of the 1960s saw a change in the expectations of young people. Whilst recent research has dispelled some of the myths regarding students' enthusiasm for protest, nevertheless this was a time of student sit-ins, marches and calls for greater student representation on policy-making bodies. At Hatfield, this period also coincided with the move towards Polytechnic status, and the Students' Union seems to have seen this as an opportune moment to make its claim for greater representation. Students' Union President Malcolm Felgate saw negotiation, rather than confrontation, as the way forward. Indeed, he expressed his annoyance at the unofficial boycott by some students who were complaining at the extension of the full-time day into the evening: 'Last year we found that negotiations between the principal and ourselves achieved a great deal and we do not want to see this work dashed by any irresponsible actions.'

The timing of the boycott was unfortunate as negotiations for student representation on internal committees, up to and including Board level, were in the process of being finalised. The following week the local paper announced the appointment of two students to sit on the Board of Governors of the new polytechnic. In his report for the 1967–68 session, Norman Lindop made particular mention of the approach taken by Hatfield students:

> During a session in which the activities of students elsewhere received much publicity, it is perhaps of interest that the student body of this College, while by no means uninterested in the issues agitating some academic institutions, found the channels of communication with the staff and the administration adequate for the expression of their views.

By 1975 there were four student representatives serving on the Board of Governors and representation on all internal committees, although this fell short of the rather optimistic call from SU President Denny Adam in 1979 for 50 per cent of all such bodies to be made up of students since, 'after all this place exists for the students, not the other way round'. Relations between Polytechnic students and staff nevertheless wobbled at times, with SU presidents reminding the administration on a couple of occasions that the Polytechnic's primary function was to support students in their studies and future development. In 1981 SU President Simon Gulliford called on

> all governors to take a more active interest in student life at the Polytechnic; unfortunately the majority are concerned only with finances and current political dogma. Very few of you seem to care about the students. Please can we reach a situation where students' problems become paramount and get away from the present situation which now exists whereby the problems of the country are regarded as being greater than the problems of individual students.

The Elephant House.

Cartoon of the Ele House from the Students' Union handbook 1978–79.

Yet, in general, students and staff fashioned a good working relationship, in many cases drawn together by the impact of cuts to funding. In his report for 1981–82, John Illston made special mention of the support given by the Union and the rest of the student body who had 'tolerated conditions that were, at times, far from tolerable'.

The Students' Union finally got its own building in 1977. With its pyramidal roofs and apex skylights, it was considered a noteworthy new structure in the region by the Royal Institute of British Architects, and certainly attracted a strong reaction from the student body. The Polytechnic authorities apparently wanted to call it 'The Focus', but students quickly invented derogatory names for it – the 'Have a Dump House', 'Effluent House' and 'THAT building'. It was the students who finally settled on the 'Elephant House' due to its resemblance to the Elephant House at London Zoo. It later became known more affectionately as the 'Ele House'. Shortly after it opened for business, with its shop, SU offices, bar, games room and television, the Students' Union noted how well maintained everything was, thanks to porters Bert Bray and George Crouch, and cleaners Edie Kemp and Nellie Dolling.

Further need for space led to new wrangles with the University administration. The Battle of the Toilet Space broke out in 1994 when the Union requested to take over the Hutton Block foyer and old toilet area, refurbish it, and make it the centre of the Union's commercial activities. The administration,

*The Font Bar, 1974.*

*(Below) Students' Union bar staff, 1974–75. In 1976 the Union renamed one of their bars the Vale Bar in memory of bar steward Vic Vale (second from right).*

*(Bottom) Crush Radio studio, 1990.*

however, wanted the toilet area to continue serving its original function. The frustrated Union grumbled that its short-term development had been thwarted 'because of a toilet block, which is probably the worst kept toilet block in the whole University. The University cannot be expected to care for its students when something as vital as disused toilets are involved – long live the Jobsworths of the University!'

The SU made contact with the student body through its newspaper *Universe* and Crush FM – the first campus radio in the country. It was started in 1960 as Campus Radio Hatfield on a 'pirate radio' basis, and was then renamed Crush 1278 and broadcast on 1278 AM frequency. By the late 1970s it had three studios and a radio director, with its output being available in Halls of Residence, student bars and the refectories. Other student media enterprises came and went over the years, such as the Hatfield-Welwyn independent student newspaper *Embryo* in 1961, which cost three pence. In the early 1990s the Literature Society at Wall Hall produced a magazine called *Writing on the Wall*, and Wall Hall students also produced their own enjoyably rude but short-lived student magazine, the *Plagiarist*, mocking the foibles of staff.

## Clubs, societies and crazy stunts

Dr Chapman concluded his third Annual Report with thanks for the support given to the students by their parents and landladies: 'The life of a serious student is strenuous and if he is to succeed amidst the distraction of the present world he requires all the sympathy he can obtain.' How did the 'serious student' enjoy him- or even herself? The College did face particular problems, as the student body was diverse in terms of its mix of classes and ages, and with only a small minority being full-time students. Furthermore, there was no residential accommodation for students, nor at first did it have a Students' Union bar offering a natural social space for students until the Font Bar was created in 1974, using accommodation vacated by Hatfield School.

In spite of the challenges, students did organise themselves, forming a range of societies. Within only two years of the founding of the College, they were able to choose from football, hockey, badminton, cricket, judo, drama, music, debating, photography, modern languages and motor clubs, although the report from the Students' Union of 1953–54 did note that the response from students in general was 'disappointingly small'.

Much of the College students' 'latent talent' was devoted to spending their time on projects that reflected their interest in building on existing engineering skills. In 1954 a group of students formed themselves into the T.K. Flying Group with the intention of building a Druine 'Turbi' two-seater light aircraft. This ambitious project took three years' work and its progress was featured in the June edition of *Flight* magazine as 'the first amateur-construction project to be undertaken under the simplified system of supervision by the Popular Flying Association'. Finally, in August 1958, the plane took to the skies, and a maiden voyage to Bordeaux was successfully completed – a tribute to the dedication of a group of students who blurred the line between work and pleasure.

Other engineering projects also caught the headlines, including the journey of five students from the Motor Club – Tom Hudson, Mike Savage, Mike Smith, Hugh Tansley and John Wilson – who travelled non-stop from Edinburgh to London on a Ransome Matador motor-mower during the Easter holidays in 1959.

# Dave Rayment, de Havilland trainee:

'I was on day release to College and we done a sponsored lawnmower drive from Edinburgh to Hyde Park and in the grass box of the lawnmower was a haggis and we were going to give this to the Lord Mayor of London, and, they'd asked at the College for people to accompany the lawnmower, as a "guard of honour" as it were, along its route. Well I was meant to be at College on this particular day and it was the day that it came through Hatfield, so I thought "nobody will miss me; I'm going to go an' accompany this lawnmower".

So I got on me bike, duly dressed in my scarf from the college and accompanied it all the way from Hatfield to Hyde Park. Thought no more of it; went back to work the next day. Nobody said anything. I thought, "I've got away with that one again". It was alright, until the *Hertfordshire Mercury* came out the following week. Who was on the front page of the *Hertfordshire Mercury* riding his bike along the side of this lawnmower? Me! Clear as a bell. Next day; another note on my clock card: "please come and see me". So I had to go into the Manager's office and got a right dressing down for not attending College and I lost a day's pay over it.'

*The epic 1959 mower journey.*

In the same year, two teams represented the College in the *Daily Mail* Bleriot Centenary Cross-Channel Race, the only college or university team to enter. The race started from Marble Arch and the two teams joined thirty-eight other competitors trying to reach the Arc de Triomphe and return in the shortest possible time. Not all the teams were bent on the quickest time: there was also a prize for the most original method of reaching the finishing line. One Hatfield student, D. Mott, received an honourable mention in *The Times* and a £100 prize for his 'notably enterprising entry', which saw him complete the course in two cars and an aeroplane, all built by fellow students at the Technical College for a total cost of £460. An unnamed veteran of the Edinburgh motor-mower trip also took part, driving his mower to an airfield where he then piloted a Tiger Moth across the Channel and thence by mower again to the Arc de Triomphe, before repeating the journey in reverse.

In October 1961 six students put their heads together to come up with a trip that would 'maintain the tradition and reputation at this college in the field of unconventional travel'. Mike Bright, Peter Comben, Pat Culshaw, Robin Dandy, David Field and Donald McNicholl successfully completed the 1,000 mile journey from Land's End to John O'Groats in a specially adapted 197cc, two-stroke engine go-kart, complete with side-lights, handbrake, number plates, speedometer and mudguards. Chapman commented on the 'combination of fortitude and good organisation' shown by all concerned. Hatfield students did not have a monopoly on crazy ideas, of course. In 1960 Hatfield was one of fifteen college and university teams taking part in a ninety-eight mile London to Leicester Pram Race, organised by Leicester University. The Hatfield team came in sixth, in a time of seven hours and twenty-two minutes, with the best performance coming from student Anthony Slater who averaged twenty miles per hour on the final leg. Two years later, the team performed even better, taking first place in icy conditions – the result, in Chapman's opinion, of 'careful selection, training and a modicum of sharp practice on the day'. Their reward was a 4½ gallon barrel of beer, which was consumed by the twenty-man team in less than thirty minutes. A spokesman for the happy team told reporters, 'We were in tremendous spirits at the end of the race and quickly consumed the beer. Then we joined in a big rock and roll session and had a happy journey home.' Alcohol seems to have been the prize of choice for students in these years. In 1966 a Hatfield team of sixteen men and one woman beat nine local colleges of further education to take the prize of a crate of beer in a chariot race from Marble Arch to St Albans. The sole female was Barbara Lawrence, who took the role of charioteer behind her team of four 'horses', with changeovers at every mile staging post.

*The 1961 Land's End to John O'Groats go-kart team. Image courtesy of Peter Comben.*

'The most ill-conceived, but superbly produced show in Hertfordshire. It is a constant source of wonder to all concerned that so much effort is put into producing such a load of drivel.' This mock quote from the Students' Union Handbook for 1964 began a pitch for student volunteers to get involved in the annual Christmas revue, which at the time drew in some hundred or so students. 'Whether your intentions are honourable or not, the Revue is by far the best way to get to know your fellow students.'

*Rag Day procession leaving the College in 1960.*

In the very first academic year, the Drama Society mounted an ambitious performance of Jean Anouilh's *Ring Round the Moon* and the local press commented on their first-rate production of this 'charade with music'. Much of the report was concerned with the innovative stage production, which used coloured lighting to make the back of the stage 'look like the sky, complete with moving clouds, during daylight, and at night with the stars out'. It was perhaps appropriate for this new college that it was the clever use of technology that most impressed the critics. The Students' Union report of 1953–54 seemed somewhat taken aback at their early successes, commenting that they had 'surprised everyone with a magnificent production of Thornton Wilder's *The Skin of our Teeth*', although sadly it was only an artistic rather than a financial success. However, it is in the nature of student societies to wax and wane in their popularity, and in the years that followed only one further production appeared under the auspices of the Drama Society – *Playboy of the Western World*, in 1958–59 – before the Society folded in 1959–60. The theatrical flag was, however, kept flying by the Rag Society, whose Revue Committee mounted productions of Christmas pantomimes such as *Aladdin* as well as an annual Rag Revue which, in the words of the Students' Union, 'showed the considerable latent talent in the College'.

Rag Week, of course, brought out the inventive side of Hatfield students. The first College Rag Day was held in October 1955, and in its second year of operations Chapman was able to report that the Rag celebrations, which were 'conducted with

commendable decorum', had raised £440 for the
Red Cross. In 1961 John Clubley circled the statue
of Eros in Piccadilly Circus 225 times in his vintage
car, stopping only in the end 'because his neck was
aching from looking to the right'. He was joined by
cyclist Roger Duncan, who began his circuit of Eros
at 1.30am to avoid the traffic, completing 80 circuits
before having to stop and mend a rear light. He then
transferred to Trafalgar Square, where there was less
traffic, and amassed a total of 372 circuits.

Inventive as these ideas were, the students who took
part in Rag Week 1966 raised themselves to another
level. A group of students set a world record for racing model cars by completing over
10,000 laps in a 48-hour period on a specially built circuit set up in the Co-operative
Store in White Lion Square. A three-legged pub crawl, street procession, fashion show,
wrestling match and Rag Ball were just some of the events, which raised over £767 for
charity. There was also an auction of 'Lost Property', which included as Lot No. 103:

*Setting the world record for racing model cars, 1966. Welwyn and Hatfield Advertiser, 25 March 1966, image courtesy of HALS.*

> *She's blonde. She's 35, 24, 36. Physical condition superb. Mental condition cheerful. She
> has promised to go out on this Friday evening with the highest bidder. This is only a date.*

The 'item' in question was student Christine Gaire,
and the winning bid of £12 came from a syndicate
of students who then drew lots for the honour
of her company on the date. The photograph
accompanying the article should have reassured her
mother, as the couple were pictured enjoying a cup of
tea together.

The highlight of Rag Week 1966, however, was the
sailing of a bedstead across the English Channel.
The intrepid team consisted of six young men, 'Gus'
Blanchard, Leslie 'Blod' Mountain, Johnny Hatch,
John Rice, Malcolm Birch and Alec Curmi, and one young woman, Sue Spearing.
They had responded to the call for volunteers to sail a 10ft by 12ft metal bedstead the
twenty-two miles from Dover to Calais. The bedstead was acquired from a local Scout
troop and fitted with flotation tanks supplied by British Aerospace in Stevenage and an

*Christine Gaire with the lucky winner, 1966. Welwyn and Hatfield Advertiser, 1 April 1966, image courtesy of HALS.*

outboard motor from a company in Acton, North London. The idea originated with Leslie 'Blod' Mountain and, coincidentally, the event marked the 900th anniversary of the Battle of Hastings. As the Captain of the Bed, 'Gus' Blanchard, remarked, 'this will be our way of showing British initiative'. A remarkably relaxed Chapman commented, 'This is a very good thing for students to do and if it is carried out properly the exercise is a good thing for the college. It gives them a chance to do some organising and to carry out schemes which test their resourcefulness.'

*'An 18-year-old girl student at Hatfield College of Technology, Sue Spearing, of Telford Avenue, Campshill, Stevenage, who describes herself as "a basically mad bird", will be rafting across the Channel with the six young men on the floating bedstead. This will not be the first time Sue has been afloat but it will be her maiden voyage on this sort of "vessel". "It's going to be just great," said Sue, sorting out a weather-resisting ensemble for the trip.'*
**Welwyn and Hatfield Advertiser, *11 March 1966.***

A few days before setting sail, the bed boat was taken on the back of a lorry to test its sea-worthiness on the waters of the Abbey Cross Pit, near Cheshunt. The testing consisted of a large number of students jumping up and down on the raft in a deliberate attempt to sink it: 'They climbed onto the bed and started rocking it up and down, but eventually it gathered so much momentum that it toppled over on top of them.' Only moments before, the deputy warden of the Abbey Cross Pit had told all those who could not swim to get off the raft, which was probably fortunate as when the bedstead capsized it temporarily trapped some of the sixteen remaining volunteers underneath the 'weighty oil drums and bulky superstructure'. The raft was declared safe – although it is not clear by whom – and ready for the crossing.

Poor weather meant the start was postponed for two days, but on the afternoon of Monday 14 March the bedstead was launched, its crew dressed in 'nightshirts and bed caps with polythene under-sealing for warmth'. Progress was slow, as once beyond the harbour wall the boat's speed of three knots was unfortunately met by an incoming tide of three knots. Two of the smaller oil drums were discarded and three of the crew taken onto the support boat in an effort to reduce weight and improve speed; the three re-joined their crew mates once the bed was further into the journey. Finally, after eight hours, they reached Calais harbour, and the Hatfield contingent was greeted by representatives from the French press and a meal of steak and chips. Revitalised by their *repas* and sense of a job well done, they now faced the problem of what to do with the bed. The escort boat that was due to take the students back to England was not able to tow the bed, nor could it return under its own steam, so it was towed just beyond the harbour walls where escort boat owner Mr Dennis Cox fired 115 bullets into the floats. The bed, however, was not to be got rid of so easily and refused to sink. The coastguard was called in and agreed to tow the bed back to England, where it was hoped it would provide a centrepiece for the Rag Week. However, the story did not end there, as, once out to sea, the bed broke free of its tow and 'was last seen drifting past Ramsgate at a steady two knots', its final resting place a mystery.

Not all Rag stunts involved engineering skills. In 1963, in a precursor of the 1985 Nick Kamen advert for Levi jeans, customers in a Hatfield laundrette were treated to a group of students taking off their trousers and putting them in a washing machine. That same year, the *Welwyn and Hatfield Advertiser* carried photographs of a group of athletic students performing somersaults over a wooden horse as part of the Rag Week procession. In a re-enactment of the English POW escape using a wooden horse to mask the building of a tunnel, the Hatfield students used the cover of the gym equipment to cement a lavatory pan to the pavement. This all took place in Hatfield, as permission to hold Rag events in Welwyn Garden City had only been given on the understanding that students would behave themselves and cause no damage, as the previous year had seen an expensive clean-up operation after walls were daubed with graffiti. The year 1963 passed without further comment, but the following year saw the staging of 'an unfortunate, but none the less memorable, incident', which brought national attention to the Rag Week events, jointly staged that year by Hatfield College of Technology and Mid-Herts Further Education College.

*Rag Day, 1962.*

In response to 999 calls, police cars from across the county raced to cover the main exit roads from Welwyn Garden City in an attempt to capture three masked robbers who had carried out a raid on Lloyds Bank. Three hundred police were involved in tracking down the culprits, who were eventually revealed as a group of students on a Rag Week stunt. Three young men, wearing silk stockings, goggles and balaclava helmets to conceal their appearance, ran from the bank to a waiting car, shooting toy cap guns as they went and carrying a briefcase supposedly packed with cash.

A fourth student pretended to be a passer-by knocked to the ground by the fleeing robbers, whilst a fifth staggered from the bank with his face covered in an unspecified red substance, screaming, 'Stop, thieves!' Once apprehended, the students were kept in the local police cells for an hour before being sent on their way with no further action taken.

The only repercussion seems to have been that the students involved were not allowed to attend the Rag Ball. Dr Chapman was silent on this particular escapade, but Dr W.V. Lloyd, Principal of Mid-Herts Further Education College, did tell the press that 'any

*Rag Day stunt. How many people can fit in a telephone box?*

more of these stunts' would be met with serious consequences. It is not clear from the newspaper accounts whether the stunt involved students from both colleges. The stunt was to collect funds for the Hertfordshire Fund for the Blind and the King George Fund for Sailors.

The Polytechnic did not get the affectionate name the 'Jolly Poly' for nothing. It continued the College tradition of student mischief and adventure, although students fell foul of local people on occasions. In 1971 Hertford Borough Council refused the students permission to collect in the town, threatening prosecution

for any students caught asking for money. This meant that the good people of Hertford were denied the experience of an invasion of students dressed as Martians, but Hertford's loss was Welwyn Garden City's gain. A year later, there were problems when the white painted slogan 'Poly Rag 1972' appeared on streets and buildings around Hatfield, St Albans and Welwyn Garden City. One of the events staged that year was the opportunity to throw wet sponges at students pinned into stocks in the town centre, thus allowing local people to vent any anger and raise money for good causes in one move. In 1976 a three-legged pub crawl was organised that visited every public house in the Hatfield area. Unfortunately, not all the local pubs were flattered by the attention. Entrants were warned not to visit the Horse and Groom in Park Street, as the landlord had made some unwelcome comments about their behaviour. He was quoted in the local paper as saying, 'The students are not particularly welcome here. Like most people in large crowds they make it unpleasant for others. They are noisy and they pile all their coats and bags on the seats.' Other Hatfield pubs were more welcoming. 'I think they are a tremendous group of people. They always make a happy atmosphere here. The pub crawl competitors came here on Monday night and we all joined in the spirit of the thing,' said 'Greg' Gregory of the Cavendish Arms in Bishops Rise. Barman James Wallace at the Red Lion, Great North Road, Hatfield, gave a similar endorsement: '[T]he pub crawl came here and all the students were very well-behaved.' The winners of the competition completed the course of thirteen pubs in one hour and thirty minutes. The pub crawl became a feature of Rag Week events, although there were some concerns in 1979 when three students ended up in hospital having their stomachs pumped after downing double shots in each of fourteen pubs.

In 1971 a team of six students took part in a trolley race, pushing a tea trolley 237 miles from Hatfield to Blackpool. On the way they were hijacked by a group of students from Preston who kept the trolley for a few hours before letting them on their way. The trolley needed eight new sets of wheels during the journey, but on their arrival they were rewarded with a cheque for £60, presented to them by the manufacturers of the trolley. The 'ace trolley navigators' were Sheila Milne, Ian Day, Colin Day, Peter Stanley, Roger Riseley and David Carr.

That same year the Polytechnic staged its first Drag Queen contest. The photograph which accompanied the item in the local paper showed the contestants wearing what appeared to be their girlfriends' clothes rather than a full-on Danny-La-Rue-style get-up, and beards were well represented amongst the winners. The idea came about when two male students tried to join in the Rag Queen contest and were refused. The winner was twenty-year-old Business Studies student Bob Moore, whose alter-ego, 'Ruby', was deemed 'quite attractive' by Rag chairman Alan Rawbone. His prize for coming first was twenty-four pints of beer, and indeed all contestants were rewarded with beer for their bravery. Three fourth-year Computer Science students, Chris Holder, Ray Lewis and Tony Dennett, entered as a singing group, 'The Kronettes', and were given fourteen pints between them. By 1978 gender equality had hit the Polytechnic and both a Drag Queen and Drag King competition were held. Second-year Humanities student Mark Davidson retained his title under the guise of Ann Lucer Brasi Capon-Rivet, winning a bottle of whisky and a £5 record token. His Drag King was Mary Thompson, a third-year Biology student, who also won a bottle of vodka and a record token.

Kidnapping was an oft-used ploy to raise money. In 1971 students kidnapped the red model plane outside the Comet Hotel and demanded a ransom for its return. A donation of £50 was made by the manager, who was quite happy with the exchange as the plane had been given a fresh coat of paint, along with a new cockpit and propeller. Then, years later, students in black leather and khaki kidnapped three lecturers from the departments of Electrical Engineering and Mathematics. They demanded a ransom of £10 for each of them, but negotiations stalled somewhat when the departments concerned offered double that if students would keep the hostages. Eventually the ransom was paid after it was warned that failure to do so would result in 'a fate worse than death' for the hostages – a night in the Halls of Residence.

*Hatfield Polytechnic Motorcycle Club sponsored push, 1989.*

# More memorable student achievements

**1969** John Arthur of St Albans won first prize in a fruit gum sucking event, making his sweet last for 1 hour 31 minutes.

**1971** People were invited to build a mile of pennies – old or new. The idea was inspired by the switch to decimalisation, which took place on 15 February that year.

**1972** In a homage to Benny Hill's Ernie, which had topped the charts the previous Christmas, students invited the public to join them in Hatfield town centre in throwing yoghurts and stale meat pies in a series of duels to find The Fastest Milkman in the West.

**1972** Students claimed two world records playing games of Monopoly and Snakes and Ladders non-stop for 100 hours and 50 hours respectively. The Snakes and Ladders' team consisted of Sally Duncan, Ashley Drury, Kevin Reid, Bob Jewett, Martin Budd and Dianne Harvey. The Monopoly team was Peter Rushing, Tony Whitehorne, Bob Green, Alan O'Dell and John Carlie.

**1973** A sponsored hitchhike was held to see how far students could travel in 24 hours. A team consisting of Nilam Sharma and Andy Meesem approached an air taxi service operating out of Elstree Aerodrome and persuaded it to find spaces for them on a five-seater executive plane bound for Manchester, from where they then thumbed a lift to Edinburgh. Extra points were awarded to the team of Debbie Clarke and Mary Stoddart, who managed to find a boat willing to give them passage from the east coast of Scotland to Holy Island.

**1976** The inaugural game of Pubopoly – a drinking game which became a feature of Rags in the years that followed. Invented by an unnamed student, it involved teams of two who had to get round the board as many times as possible before closing time. Rather than buying houses, contestants bought pubs – all named after local hostelries in Hatfield. Whenever a team landed on a pub, one of the pair had to drive the other to its real-life counterpart to drink a half, whilst the remaining teams continued the game.

**1971** Students played a marathon game of table soccer over a week, a task made particularly hard as the game was set up on the back of a lorry driven around the town by a team of drivers. A non-stop game of hopscotch was played out over two days, and student Bob Wilkinson stayed at his drums for 24 hours.

*(Left to right)*
*Building a mile of pennies.* Welwyn and Hatfield Advertiser, *26 February 1971.*
*Week-long table football match.* Welwyn and Hatfield Advertiser, *26 February 1971.*
*Setting a world record for playing Monopoly.* Welwyn and Hatfield Advertiser, *25 February 1972.*
*All images courtesy of HALS.*

**1976** A special rugby match that saw a fifteen-man team face an opposition made up of thirty girls. Rag magazine editor Steve Earle said of the rugby match: 'The mixed Rugby match would be very good, with the fifteen fellas playing to international rules, except they cannot run with the ball, and the girls playing to very few rules at all.' Sadly, history does not relate the score of this game.

**1979** Student Craig Simmonds took the 24-hour sponsored hitchhike to a new level when he travelled as far as Luxembourg in the allotted time.

**1979** Business Studies student Martin Rock performed a 24-hour sponsored drum solo, raising £70, and carrying on regardless when he was joined in the Sports Hall by a netball match.

**1980** The residents of Hatfield were invited to attend a 'slave market' in the town centre, to buy a student for just fifty pence and then ask them to do anything they wished – 'within reason, of course'.

**1989** Computer Studies student Pat Bateman ate 186 squares of ravioli in just over five minutes, beating the previous Guinness Book of Records holder by 15 squares.

Sports societies were an important part of student life for many. In 1953–53 the Annual Report noted that the Football Society was now firmly established within the College, 'even though it did not win a single game during the session and came bottom of its league'. The 1958–59 academic year saw the inauguration of the Fern Cup, a competition held between the three Hertfordshire technical colleges of Hatfield, Watford and North Herts, named in honour of the Chair of Governors and played out through eight different sports. The report for that year was rather coy about the result other than noting that 'North Herts won this time, but we hope it will be our turn this coming year'. The following year's report mentioned an 'honourable second place'. It is somewhat likely that performances across the sporting field reflected that of the football field or, indeed, the athletics track, as Hatfield in that year organised an Athletics Meeting for seven colleges and 'came very low on the results list'.

*'That was quite an exciting thing in my first week as well, because not only are you signing up for your classes, and where you are going to be, you are also signing up for clubs and societies, and looking to see if there is anything of interest to you. I just happened to get sucked into water polo. Never played before.'*

UH water polo team member Gobi Ranganathan, who graduated in 1999.

The institution's students would, nevertheless, go on to have considerable national and international success in the sporting world. In 1979, for instance, Computer Science PhD student Martin Dew made his debut for England in the Men's Badminton team and went on to win medals at the World and European championships. A former Polytechnic student, Adrian Pierson, joined Warwickshire Cricket Club in 1985 and became 'the first Polytechnic cricketer to take a wicket in county cricket – his victim being no less than Viv Richards'. Numerous notable individual sporting successes followed in the university years.

# Clubs and Societies on offer at Fresher's Fair October 1996

- 41 Productions
- Aerobics
- Afro-Caribbean
- Aikido Yoshinkan
- Alpha
- Amateur Radio
- American Football
- Archery
- Arts
- Arts and Theatre
- Asian
- Astro Physical
- Athletics
- Badminton
- Basketball (Men)
- Basketball (Women)
- Canoe
- Car
- Chess
- Chinese
- Christian Fellowship
- Christian Union
- Climbing & Walking
- Cricket (Men)
- Cricket (Watford)
- Cycling/Mountain Biking
- Drama
- Environment Group
- Exploration

- Fencing
- Flying
- Football (Hertford, Hatfield and Watford)
- Football (Women)
- Free Weight Users
- Gaelic Athletic Association
- Golf
- Gymnastics & Trampolining
- Hellenic Cypriot
- History (Watford)
- Hockey (Men)
- Hockey (Mixed)
- Hockey (Women)
- International (Hertford & Hatfield)
- Irish
- Islamic
- Jewish
- Jiu Jitsu
- Kick Boxing
- Kyshatiya Dharma
- Lesbian, Gay, Bisexual
- Live Band
- Living Marxism
- MASH
- Morpheus Project
- Motorcycle
- Myth and Magik (Watford)
- Netball
- Parachute

- Philosophy (Watford)
- Photography
- Politics
- PSIFA
- Red Cross
- Riding
- Rowing
- Rugby (Hatfield & Watford)
- Rugby (Women)
- Rugby League
- Sailing & Windsurfing
- Shotokai Karate
- Shotokan Karate
- Skiing
- Squash
- St John's Links
- Student Law
- Sub Aqua
- Surf and Skate
- Swimming
- Tae Kwon-Do
- Tennis (Hertford & Hatfield)
- Turkish
- Ving Tsun Kung Fu
- Volleyball (Hertford & Hatfield)
- Waterpolo
- Waterski
- Zeu Wei

## Student protest

One morning in the 1958–59 academic year the words 'Communist Chapman' were spelt out in large black letters on the College front entrance. Not the most subtle of political statements, and contrary to the usual perception of the political inclinations of students. But it shows that the politicisation of the student body did not begin with the election of the Thatcher government. From its first days as a polytechnic, there were signs of a willingness amongst students to take direct action in order to influence decisions being taken at both the local and national level.

*Gobi Ranganathan and the University water polo team. Image courtesy of Gobi Ranganathan. Gobi is currently the No.1 British Men's singles wheelchair badminton player, ranked 8th in the world.*

As we have already seen, the move of courses to both Wall Hall and Balls Park led students to mount protests by occupying academic buildings. In 1970, as a protest against the cramped conditions in the College Lane refectory caused by the large increase in student numbers, there was an invasion of the staff dining room, with students having to pay a 9d waitress service charge each – later refunded by the Union. The occupation of the telephone exchange was a tactic first used in March 1974 as part of an ongoing campaign calling for an increase in grants and the end of means testing. Bob Sterling, SU President, told the local press that they were calling on the government to raise grants from the existing £485 to £655 a year, a rise which would still only return grants to their 1962 level. The same edition of the paper carried a photograph of a female student holding up a pamphlet calling for change, with four male students manning the phones in the background. The grant was eventually set at £605.

In February 1973 the Polytechnic was the centre for a demonstration by 1,000 students from Hatfield and associate colleges calling for a universal grant. SU President David Carr addressed the rally and was quoted as saying, 'equal opportunity for rich and poor in education cannot exist with the means test'. Labour MP for Bedwelty and former Cardiff University SU President Neil Kinnock also attended and spoke to students. The local press carried a photograph of a young female student bearing the placard:

**HEATH = £20,000     STUDENTS = £275**

Students went on strike in March 1982 as a protest against the increase of grants by only 4 per cent. In his report for the year 1981–82, SU President Simon Gulliford warned of students facing serious hardship:

*A disturbing number of students are now finding it almost impossible to keep body and soul together on the grant provided by the state. Some students are fortunate enough to have parents who are able to top up their children's grant in order that they may eat properly and buy the necessary text books. Other students come from families whose parents have recently been made redundant, whose grant has yet to be re-assessed and as a result are unable to help financially. The result is the student must enter into debt which bank managers are now eager to accommodate.*

This was at a time when interest rates were at record highs. In 1979, prior to the general election, the Bank of England rate stood at 12 per cent; by November 1979 it was 17 per cent; and in November 1981 it was still high at 15 per cent.

*Students demonstrating during a visit to the Polytechnic by Keith Joseph in 1986.*

The campaign against cuts to grants took a new twist when the Conservative Education Minister, Sir Keith Joseph, called for students to be financed by loans rather than grants. In that same year, 1981–82, Gulliford spelt out his vision for any future education system built on a framework of loans rather than grants as envisioned by Sir Keith Joseph:

*He fails to realise that those parents who can afford to pay for their children's education will continue to do so whilst those who cannot, will, if they are to educate themselves, have to enter into a long-term debt in order to acquire further qualifications. It does not need a great deal of imagination to realise that such a system would be an enormous disincentive to those from a depressed area with a poor family background.*

A visit by Sir Keith Joseph to the Polytechnic in 1986 was greeted by a large student demonstration which was reported in the national news. The Annual Report for that year carried a photograph of Sir Keith on the steps of the main entrance, flanked by policemen with banner-waving students in the background. He was not the last government minister to receive such a welcome. In December 1987 around 200 students dressed in black staged a mock execution of a tailor's dummy labelled 'Grant', for the benefit of visiting Junior Education Minister Robert Jackson. In February 1989 an anti-loan song, composed by an unnamed Students' Union official, received its premiere at a day of action. Campaigners argued that the loan system would leave students with a typical debt of £1,400 at the end of their three-year course.

Other demonstrations were aimed at a more international audience, with students involved in protests in support of miners, the Campaign for Nuclear Disarmament and anti-apartheid movements. In December 1971, in a move against apartheid, the Students' Union was successful in preventing the South African Cape Coloured 'Proteas' rugby team from staying in their Halls of Residence during their tour of the country. In May 1974, in the words of the local paper, there was 'a near riot' when students at the Polytechnic protested at a lecture given by a Chilean economics lecturer, who wanted to speak in defence of his country's military junta.

The year the Polytechnic became a university, students from Hatfield joined in national demonstrations against cuts to student grants and housing benefit. Hatfield SU President Leonie Howard Phillips argued that the situation had been steadily deteriorating over the past twelve years, with students finding themselves with average overdrafts of £8,900 at graduation: 'Students should be free to concentrate on their studies, rather than [face] constant anxiety about financial problems.'

*Kelly Goldsworthy and fellow UH students marching against tuition fees in 2000. Image courtesy of Kelly Goldsworthy.*

# A global community

Whilst numbers of students as a whole were rising, the figures for those from overseas were hit by decisions made at central government level both at home and abroad. At the start of the 1978 academic year, there were 326 students (11.9 per cent of the total student body) studying at Hatfield whose home was overseas; the largest groups came from Malaysia (82), Iran (71), Sri Lanka (29), Rhodesia (now Zimbabwe, 17), Hong Kong (14) and Nigeria (12). The following year two events occurred which were to have an impact on the numbers of overseas students: the election of Mrs Thatcher's Conservative government and the overthrow of the Shah and subsequent revolution in Iran. Under pressure from central government, Hertfordshire County Council introduced a major increase in fees for new overseas students, a policy regretted by Sir Norman Lindop in his report of that year, when he referred to 'his dislike of the methods used' to increase revenues. Within a year, numbers had fallen to 302 students (9.2 per cent of the total student body). The School of Engineering's report for 1980–81 noted that the number of applications from overseas students had 'dropped dramatically', the result of a rise in fees. In his report for the year 1979–80, SU President Denny Adam referred to the ongoing fight against 'a reactionary Tory government' and the need to confront their 'racist attacks on overseas students'. By 1985 the number of overseas students had fallen to only 172, representing 41 different countries; the largest groups were from Malaysia (32) and Hong Kong (28).

The overthrow of the Shah in Iran caused severe difficulties for many students from that country. The disruption of the transfer of funds from families caught up in the turmoil of the revolution meant that calls on a special hardship fund increased, with many Iranian students forced to sell personal belongings to make ends meet. The situation continued to deteriorate and some students found themselves in real peril and obliged to seek political asylum, as their government refused to allow sponsors to pay fees and maintenance on the grounds of 'alleged counter-revolutionary activities'.

One Iranian student, 23-year-old Babak Kia, found himself at the centre of an immigration battle after the refusal of the British authorities to allow him back into the country following a placement in Germany as part of his course. Sent back to Germany, in spite of proof of his status at the Polytechnic, he contacted the Students' Union before flying back to Heathrow for a second attempt. With deportation imminent, he was given a temporary stay of execution only after Denny Adam went to Heathrow to speak to officials on Babak's behalf. After a further month of paperwork, he was given the right to stay in the country to complete his course.

*Students graduating in Shanghai, 2005–06.*

When, in 1992, the fortieth anniversary of the opening of the Hatfield Technical College was celebrated, former students travelled from as far afield as Bahrain and the United States to attend. Distance was no barrier to involvement in university life. Civil Engineering student Alan Hudson's home was the South Atlantic island of St Helena; his journey to Hatfield took fourteen days and the journey home had to be timed to coincide with the ship which called at his home only once every six weeks. Married with two young children, Alan had been given a British Council grant to study in Britain and 'his sponsors chose Hatfield for his education because of its reputation for training engineers'.

## Alumni

With the help of volunteer alumni over the years, the University of Hertfordshire has endeavoured to keep in touch with its past. The University's broad alumni community is comprised of the graduating classes of today's institution, as well as alumni of Hatfield Polytechnic, and back to the former 'de Havilland Apprentices', who studied here as part of the first cohorts at Hatfield Technical College. The current Alumni Association was formally established with a representative body in 2007. Through a consistent, innovative communications programme, the last few years have seen the number of alumni the University is in contact with more than double, with applications for alumni membership cards rising from around two to over a hundred per month on average. Through the website, publications, online social networks and reunions, the alumni relations programme facilitates the lifelong relationship the University has with its former students, and to date the Alumni team is in regular contact with around 170,000 of them. Through the *Futures* magazine (shortlisted at the annual Heist Awards for 'Alumni Publication of the Year' in 2008) and *e-Futures* (the monthly e-newsletter) alumni regularly find out about all the news and events going on at the University and amongst their fellow alumni – with professional, sporting and leisure benefits also available to them for life.

- In 1977 over 10% of the 4,000 students at the Polytechnic were from overseas.

- In 2002 6.9% of 21,695 students were from overseas.

The President of the Alumni Association, MSc graduate Kate Bellingham (Broadcaster, Engineer, Keynote Speaker and Ambassador for Women in Engineering, has been in the role since being personally invited in 2007 by former Vice-Chancellor Sir Tim Wilson. Some of the best-known alumni include: Helen Lederer (actress, comedian, writer and television and radio presenter), Alistair Spalding (Chief Executive and Artistic Director of Sadler's Wells theatre, London), Nitin Sawhney (world-renowned music producer, songwriter, DJ, multi-instrumentalist, orchestral composer and cultural pioneer), Sir Stuart Matthews (who has had a highly decorated career in the aviation industry) and Diane MacLean (world-renowned sculptor and environmental artist). To celebrate the importance of alumni to the University, in 2010 an annual Alumnus of the Year Award was created as a way of formally recognising an alumnus who represents outstanding achievement in their field or has made a major contribution to the lives of others or has overcome very significant personal adversity. The Association continually supports reunions, campus tours, fundraising projects and get-togethers of former classmates, housemates and team-mates – helping to facilitate events and connections all around the world.

## Deljit Singh, Applied Biology graduate in the 1980s, telling how he first came to Hatfield ... and how he returned twenty-five years later

'At the conclusion of the application process [after A Levels] I was left with two firm offers, one from Queen Elizabeth College in London for a BSc [in] Life Sciences and the other from Hatfield Polytechnic for a BSc [in] Applied Biology. My main reason for selecting Hatfield Polytechnic was that, unlike the three-year degree course at Queen Elizabeth College, the course at Hatfield was a four-year sandwich course with the third year spent working in industry and gaining real work experience. Also, around this time, in 1982, a report in the *Sunday Times* listed Hatfield Polytechnic as the fourth best UK College for genetics after the universities of Oxford, Cambridge and St Andrews, and ahead of many other so-called 'top' universities. Lastly and importantly for me, Hatfield Polytechnic had a great reputation for putting on live bands and I looked forward to an excellent social life.

When I first arrived at Hatfield Polytechnic, the college campus appeared huge. The fact we had an entire building, the C.P. Snow Building, dedicated to our Biology degree seemed amazing. Unlike school, we no longer had to share one piece of equipment between us and the equipment was modern and not out of the ark. I was fortunate to get a room in Chapman Halls of Residence, a proper brick building, unlike Pembroke Hall which was basically a pre-fabricated building. In terms of socialising facilities at Hatfield the main places were the Elephant House and the Font Bar. In hindsight neither of these facilities was plush but as students they were our refuge from the real world and great places to unwind with friends.

In January 2011 I was contacted by an old student friend, Fiona. As it was the twenty-fifth anniversary of our graduating from Hatfield she suggested a reunion. I was quite sceptical but I agreed we should give it a go. The world of Facebook and Friends Reunited now meant we could start searching for our old college cohorts online and, with the help of the alumni office at Hatfield Polytechnic, now the University of Hertfordshire, we set about contacting former students and faculty staff from the Applied Biology Class of 1986. Twenty-five students (just over fifty per cent of the course) and three faculty staff signed up to attend.

As the reunion date neared I became more and more excited; receiving emails from colleagues I had not spoken to for almost a quarter of a century brought back some fond memories.

As I put together a slideshow of photographs from our Hatfield days for the reunion I was reminded of just how wonderful my time at Hatfield had been. Finally the day arrived and I began to welcome my old college buddies. On meeting them I immediately recognised each and every one. Clearly we had all changed – gravity had taken its toll as had good living, a lack of exercise and of course kids – most of us were greyer now. After meeting in the Ele House, which looked nothing like the venue of the same name we frequented twenty-five years earlier, we were invited on a tour of the campus and were amazed to see how the college had grown in becoming a university. Friendships were rekindled and everyone agreed that we should all try harder to stay in touch in future.'

# 6. Building our future

2012 is an opportune time to reflect on higher education. The political environment for higher education is certainly a challenging one. The sector has seen considerable expansion recently but is now entering a period of great financial uncertainty due to changes in the funding regime for undergraduate students. As the balance of funding shifts from the state to individuals through tuition fees, there will be pressure on universities to be even more responsive both to the task of preparing students for the world of work and to the priorities of the businesses and organisations that employ them. How universities respond to these pressures will shape their future trajectories. Let us begin by looking at some numbers.

The Further and Higher Education Act (1992) permitted all polytechnics to become universities, thereby almost doubling the number of universities to 84. Since then, new entrants have appeared on a regular basis. As of September 2011 there are 115 universities in the UK. In addition to this there are a further 50 institutions including university colleges, specialist higher education institutions and other higher education colleges. So, all together, there are now 165 Higher Education Institutions (HEIs), including new private providers that the government is keen to see enter the higher education market.

In 1999 the Labour government set a target of getting 50 per cent of young adults into higher education by 2010. Whilst this target was not achieved, there was a major increase in numbers. The Department for Business, Innovation and Skills (BIS) recorded that 47 per cent of English domiciled seventeen- to thirty-year-olds were attending Higher Education Institutions in the year 2009–10, up from 39 per cent in 1999–2000. To put it in more human terms, there were 2,493,425 students in HEIs in 2009–10, roughly two-thirds of whom were full-time and one third part-time. This expansion represents a 55 per cent increase in undergraduate enrolments and a 73 per cent increase in postgraduate enrolments at HEIs since 1994–95. The impact of this growth in student numbers is striking in financial terms. HEIs in the UK had a total income of £26.8 billion in 2009–10. To give some context to this, it is roughly the equivalent to the combined income of Sainsbury's and Marks & Spencer. These numbers show the scale of the HEI sector up and down the country. A key element of this financial expansion has been the growth in non-UK domiciled students. In 2009–10, 405,805 such students were registered (16 per cent of the total), with fee income from these students totalling around £2.5 billion. Additionally, other spending by these students in our economy was worth almost double the amount they spent on tuition fees. In this respect, then, the international reputation of UK higher education translates into substantial revenue for UK plc and many local communities.

So the higher education sector has seen rapid expansion as successive governments have looked to invest in the expansion of the knowledge and skills base of the population to enable the UK to compete in global markets, particularly the new technology and creative markets. A 2011 BIS report argued that this had been done in a way that was working for students and the economy. It looked at the careers and earnings of graduates compared to non-graduates with two or more A Levels or equivalent and calculated a mean net graduate premium (i.e. earnings net of the student's education costs) associated with an undergraduate degree of approximately £108,000 over a working lifetime. Such figures have been bandied around for decades on both sides of the Atlantic, based on decidedly crude analyses of generational earning power. Whilst some graduates will benefit from such a 'degree premium' through their working lives, many will not. Pertinent questions are raised about whether degrees should be 'sold' to prospective students in such narrow financial terms. A degree is a life-changing investment intellectually, culturally and socially as well as financially. It provides skills and knowledge that open up opportunities throughout graduates' lives. The previous chapter of this book provides ample demonstration of the richness of student life and learning beyond an individual's speculative life earnings. Still, a degree should not be seen as the be-all and end-all of education. One of the fascinating insights provided by the history of this institution from college to university has been how the diverse array of non-degree courses and qualifications it has provided over the decades have had equally life-changing consequences for those studying them. Taking a degree should be a choice and not a political, educational or social obligation.

This leads us to the withdrawal of the government teaching grant for most undergraduate courses and its replacement by the student paying the tuition fee via a loan from the government that becomes repayable from post-graduation earnings. This is a very significant change and it is difficult to predict how this will impact on the sector. Increased restrictions are also being placed on international students coming to study in the UK at a time when many other countries are aggressively expanding their marketing for these students – China, for instance, has for the first time become a net importer of students. The model that funded the expansion of the higher education sector has changed and the full effects of this remain to be seen.

One of the key aims of the current coalition government is to increase competition between universities and an expanding group of other higher education providers as a way of improving choice and quality. Yet the future of an institution is probably most clearly understood as being about its brand – what it is and what it aspires to be. As the sector seeks to become more differentiated, challenging the outmoded medieval/redbrick/post-1992 divides, more questions are going to be asked about the distinctiveness of a university's brand. How clearly and persuasively that distinctiveness can be communicated to prospective students and their parents, to businesses, to government, to the media and to donors and other advocates will be at the heart of university strategy.

In July 1997 a bronze statue of Sir Geoffrey de Havilland, created by sculptor Keith Maddison, was unveiled at the College Lane campus by the Duke of Edinburgh. The actress Olivia de Havilland (a cousin of Sir Geoffrey) was present to see forty de Havilland aircraft fly past in tribute. The statue was funded by the Sir Geoffrey de Havilland Memorial Fund, which was set up in the 1990s. The fund also provides financial support for postgraduate studies in aerospace engineering at the University.

As new types of Higher Education Institution have emerged, from the redbricks of the late nineteenth century to the colleges of advanced technology and the polytechnics of the twentieth, and, indeed, the further education colleges now moving into greater higher-level provision in the twenty-first century, they have all tended to emphasise their newness. Looking to create clear space in the higher education landscape, their founders and leaders have stressed the distinctiveness of their missions. Often such missions have been infused with a form of civic pride, a commitment to meet the educational and training needs of local industry and of local people to allow the area to thrive and prosper. Over time, such expressions of newness and distinctiveness have sometimes given way, perhaps understandably, to a greater identification with the established sector. There has been greater convergence in universities' stated aims and aspirations. Now, perhaps, the time has come to rediscover our differences, to imagine new alignments of shared interests and values. As part of this process we can explore our histories and see how they can inform our future development.

Universities' strategies are about preparation for the future, and the importance of developing sound and successful strategies is increasing as they come to take less than half of their funding from government. But strategy by its nature takes a long view, a view that can stretch as far into the past as it does into the future. The idea of a 'business-facing' university was defined in the 2000s to encapsulate the ethos and spirit of Hertfordshire and differentiate the institution in a more competitive emerging environment. Yet in many ways 'business-facing' is simply the latest expression of the mission that the Technical College embraced on its foundation in 1952 and which was taken on by the Polytechnic in 1969. Over time, the language changes, as does the institution. What and how students learn, lecturers teach or researchers investigate, why managers take the decisions they do, cannot and should not remain static. Yet innovation and change are often most likely to gain traction when there is awareness of the past.

*September 2009 saw the opening of the £38 million state-of-the-art Student Forum complex, providing some of the best student facilities in the sector and a new cultural venue for the wider community. It is named after the now demolished Hatfield Forum Theatre, which opened in 1977.*

The University is currently halfway through its Strategic Plan for 2010–2015, which identifies five 'strategic drivers': student experience; learning and teaching; employability and entrepreneurship; research, innovation and enterprise; and international engagement. These are to be achieved through developing the University's academic profile, people and culture, financial strengths, infrastructure and sustainability, and community engagement. All modern universities strive for similar goals, of course, although with varying emphases. What makes the University of Hertfordshire well placed to build on its success is that it has a history and record of triangulating the needs of students, communities (local, national and international), and the wider worlds of business, the public sector and cultural and charitable organisations. The Board of Governors, whose members represent this spectrum of external interests, plays an important part in assessing the degree to which the University follows the higher education agenda and government policy, challenges it, or leads it.

In the 2011 White Paper on higher education and student finance it was announced that former Vice-Chancellor of the University of Hertfordshire, Professor Sir Tim Wilson, had been asked to lead a review into how to make the UK the best place in the world for university–industry collaboration. The choice owed much to his promotion of 'business-facing' as a new university descriptor, where working with companies, public sector organisations and charities was a core part of its activities, integrated with teaching and research. The review's remit was wide: from student employability to graduate recruitment, knowledge exchange to entrepreneurship, local economic development to inward investment. The report recognised that no one university could cover all these domains; hence the need for a policy of 'collaborative advantage' – that is, seeking collaborations with other institutions to achieve objectives that could not be fulfilled alone – if the UK was to realise its world-class ambitions.

This acknowledgement of the differentiation and complementary strengths of universities is a theme that has shaped the University of Hertfordshire's business-facing strategy from the outset. A pragmatic yet ambitious understanding of the sector provided the context, rejecting the idea that universities can – or should – try to be the same. In a sense this understanding was informed by an awareness of the different purposes for which institutions were established and the paths they have taken over time, in response as much to local circumstances as to national patterns and policies. It was also reflected in the way the recommendations for the Wilson review were framed: not as prescriptions but as invitations to consider evidence of good practice.

Hertfordshire had already embraced many of the practices advocated in the review as part of its developing strategy, from waiving fees for placement years to having advisory panels of relevant industry and enterprise experts contributing to curriculum design, to taking a lead locally in economic and cultural development. The University has also, in the course of the last decade, made a powerful case for how the Arts and Humanities can contribute to the business-facing agenda by demonstrating their important role in cultural and social entrepreneurialism. There are also areas where there is real scope for innovation at the University of Hertfordshire in response to the review's recommendations, such as structuring in work experience for postgraduate students and developing Master's programmes to complement a strong portfolio of doctoral study options for research on professional practice. By embracing such innovation the University is continuing a journey begun in the 1950s with an institution where the boundaries between study and work, between knowledge and its application, were highly permeable.

The University's Jubilee year heralds a further revision of the institution's academic structure with the removal of faculties – a tier of management introduced in 1997. As we have seen in previous chapters, such restructuring has taken place periodically within the institution as it has grown, in response to the changing higher education environment, and has been shaped by the vision of incoming directors and vice-chancellors. The current restructuring has its origins in the creation of Strategic Business Units (SBUs) in 2004. Each academic school became an SBU responsible for balancing its own budget and striving to create a surplus by external income generation through research and knowledge transfer partnerships with industry and charities, offering continuing professional development services to the private and public sector, and short courses to the local community. Professional SBUs were also created to support the running of the institution (Academic Registry; Dean of Students; Enterprise and Business Development; Estates, Hospitalities and Contracts; Finance; Information Hertfordshire; Marketing and Communications; Office of the Vice-Chancellor).

With the SBU model deeply embedded in the management structure and working practices of the University, faculties have served their purpose and are being phased out in order to streamline bureaucracy, provide more direct and responsive flows of information and ideas between SBUs and the Office of the Vice-Chancellor, and to foster closer ties between different schools with shared academic interests.

The University also begins its Jubilee year with the commencement of the first phase of the ambitious 2020 Estates Masterplan. Its aim is to reshape the built environment, particularly on the College Lane campus, which has grown considerably and incrementally since the 1950s. The Masterplan is not about expanding the University but about improving and enhancing the campuses for students, staff and the wider community. It is about preparing for the future, providing spaces and facilities that will meet the needs of all those who will use them. The Estates vision reminds us of how crucial the strategic development of the institution's physical presence has been in shaping its success, aiding the transformation from college to polytechnic and university. The built and landscaped environments in which students study, staff work, and visitors engage with the institution are crucial to future success in achieving its mission.

*The de Havilland campus today. It is built on the site of the aerodrome and associated aeroplane and rocket industry complex founded by the de Havilland Aircraft Company in the 1930s.*

The institution's past achievements and strengths can be demonstrated in its fabric, so that everyone – staff, students, visitors – can feel and understand the character of the place. The message being that whilst we are a new university – although that term becomes more and more redundant – and are focussed on the ability to adapt quickly when appropriate to the needs of students, we can draw upon our past and hold on to the strengths and values that will sustain our development in the rapidly changing higher education sector. Such visible initiatives help connect people with our university's history, not as something consisting solely of memories of the past but also as something with relevance, interest and significance for the present and future.

Whilst student experience, through teaching and research, lies at the heart of the University's vision for the next decade, the University's mission is also inspired by broader concerns. The task of meeting local and global environmental challenges is embedded in the current and future plans of the University, and in the activities of

*The University's current College Lane site, developed around the original Hatfield Technical College buildings.*

the people who work and study there. The University has invested in a Centre for Sustainable Communities, which works closely with the University's Social Enterprise Unit and Heritage Hub to encourage staff and students from across the Sciences, Arts and Humanities to get involved in community projects that seek to understand, adapt to and rethink the way we need to live in the future. The Environment Team has received national recognition for its work in promoting energy efficiency, recycling, and wildlife conservation. The University's active role in providing a bus network for the region also makes it an important player in shaping sustainable transport initiatives

What is the recipe for the University's continued success? For one, an understanding of where we have come from and the lessons that have been learnt during the journey from college to university – lessons about widening participation, the importance of research, the need for a broad curriculum, the value of international engagement and the importance of working with business and the public and voluntary sectors. As this history of the University has highlighted, that means putting students' needs first but at the same time trusting staff to identify and assess the nature of those needs. The University of Hertfordshire has a sixty-year record of doing all this well, and it has a heritage that represents the essence of what a university should be about: the collaboration between the Arts, Humanities and Sciences for the benefit of society.

# Appendix 1
## University Chancellors

### Sir Brian Corby

Visitor to Hatfield Polytechnic 1991–92
Chancellor of the University of Hertfordshire 1992–96

Brian Corby was born in 1929 near Northampton, where his father was employed in the town's shoe industry. After leaving school, Brian completed his National Service with the RAF, and then went on to read Mathematics at St John's College, Cambridge. He graduated in 1952 with a Master's degree and joined the Prudential Assurance Company, the organisation with which he would serve his entire working career. He qualified as an actuary in 1955 and held a series of posts within the company before being appointed as Chief Executive in 1982; in 1990 he took on the position of non-Executive Chairman of the company, combining this with a period as President of the Confederation of British Industry (CBI). A supporter of a stronger European market, he was invited to chair a number of groups examining implications and opportunities for European businesses. He was also a member of the Court of the Bank of England between 1985 and 1993. He was knighted in 1989.

When Corby joined the Prudential Assurance Company, its image was very much that of 'the man from the Pru', with a business model derived from its nineteenth-century origins of door-to-door collectors in the industrial heartlands. As the Chief Executive during the economically challenging years of the 1980s, Corby was instrumental in overseeing expansion and modernisation of the company, making it competitive during a period in which high interest rates and recession were defeating many. Away from the world of business, Corby was Chairman of the South Bank Arts Complex (1990–98) at a time when there were calls for this cash-strapped institution to be privatised, calls which he successfully defeated.

In 1973 Corby and his family moved to the Hertfordshire village of Albury, where he took a keen interest in local affairs. In 1991 he was invited to take on the honorary position of Visitor to Hatfield Polytechnic as it made the transition to University status; a year later he became the first Chancellor of the new University of Hertfordshire, delivering the inaugural Chancellor's lecture, 'On Risk and Uncertainty in Modern Society'.

Sir Brian Corby died on St George's Day, 2009. He was once described as 'an actuary with a distinctly austere, mathematical appearance', but in reflecting upon his life a friend of Corby's, writing in the *Albury Newsletter*, concluded with a reference to his 'dry sense of humour and willingness to help', and the quote chosen for his funeral service summed up his outlook on life for those who knew him best: 'Don't cry because it's over. Smile because it's happened.'

## Lord MacLaurin of Knebworth DL
Chancellor 1996–2005

Ian Charter MacLaurin was born in 1937 and educated at Malvern College in Worcestershire. Upon leaving school he spent two years fulfilling his National Service requirement with the RAF, and it was during the latter part of this period that a chance encounter with Jack Cohen, the founder of Tesco, set the course of his future career. MacLaurin, a keen sportsman, was playing cricket at Eastbourne, and Cohen, who was a spectator, invited him and the rest of the team to consider applying for a job with his retail organisation which was then in the process of expansion. MacLaurin began his career at Tesco in 1959 as a management trainee, learning his trade from the bottom up; after a period in the warehouse loading vans, he moved on to manage his first shop, in Neasden, North London; by 1973 he was Managing Director of the company, and oversaw the shift from smaller stores to out-of-town developments. As Chairman of the company between 1985 and 1997, he introduced many of the initiatives which saw Tesco secure the largest share of the supermarket sector.

Upon leaving Tesco in 1997 he took on a number of non-executive roles with companies such as Vodafone, Guinness, Whitbread and NatWest. His continuing love of cricket saw him invited to become the first Chairman of the English and Wales Cricket Board – latterly the Test and County Cricket Board – a role he held from 1997 to 2002.

MacLaurin was knighted in 1989 and given a life peerage in 1996. At that time he chose to take as his title Lord MacLaurin of Knebworth, in recognition of his Hertfordshire connections. He was appointed as a Deputy Lieutenant of the County of Hertfordshire in 1992.

# The Most Honourable, the Marquess of Salisbury PC DL
Chancellor 2005–

Robert Michael James Gascoyne-Cecil, the seventh Marquess of Salisbury, was born in 1946. His Hertfordshire credentials are impeccable; his family have lived at Hatfield House since the early seventeenth century when Robert Cecil, the first Earl of Salisbury, built the current Jacobean mansion to house his family after King James I, taking a fancy to the then Cecil estate at Theobalds, near Cheshunt, 'persuaded' Robert to do a house swap.

The Cecil family has a long history of public service, a tradition which the current Marquess has continued. Educated at Eton and Oxford, the then Viscount Cranborne entered the House of Commons as the Conservative MP for Dorchester South in 1979, a seat he held for the next eight years. In 1992 the Prime Minister, John Major, introduced a Writ of Acceleration enabling Viscount Cranborne to take a seat in the House of Lords whilst his father was still living; he took Baron Cecil of Essendon as his title. He then served the Conservative government as Parliamentary Under-Secretary of State for Defence (1992–94), before being appointed Lord Privy Seal and Leader of the House of Lords in 1994. He served as a member of the Shadow cabinet, following the election of Tony Blair in 1997, and led the Opposition party in the House of Lords.

Lord Salisbury has served as Deputy Lieutenant in both Dorset (1987–2006) and Hertfordshire (2007 to the present), reflecting his family's long-held ties with both counties. His other interests have included an appointment as Chairman of the Council of the Royal Veterinary College (1999–2007), Chairman of the Friends of Lambeth Palace Library since 2008, and President of the Friends of the British Library since 2005. He recently took up the post of Chairman of the Thames Diamond Jubilee Foundation, which organised a Jubilee Pageant to celebrate the sixtieth anniversary of the accession of Queen Elizabeth II: a royal barge, carrying the Queen and escorted by a flotilla of over a thousand boats, progressed along the river Thames from Hammersmith towards the Tower of London.

Lord Salisbury is patron of several organisations including the Friends of the Welwyn Hatfield Museums, the Central Hertfordshire Branch of the YMCA, and Groundwork Hertfordshire. For the 2012 London Olympic and Paralympic Games, he took on the role of patron to the Hertfordshire is Ready for Winners partnership, which sought to maximise the opportunities the Games offered for improving the sporting, social and economic profile of the county.

# Appendix 2
## Honorary appointments and degrees awarded

## Doctor of Education

| | | |
|---|---|---|
| 1989 | Donald Fisher CBE | County Education Officer, Hertfordshire County Council |
| 2006 | Dr Priscilla Chadwick | Principal, Berkhamsted Collegiate School |
| 2011 | Dr Wang Kim Ha | Founder and Group Executive Director of Smart Reader Worldwide |

## Doctor of Laws

| | | |
|---|---|---|
| 1992 | Joyce Rose CBE | Hertfordshire Magistrate and former Deputy Lieutenant of the County |
| 1994 | Morris Le Fleming DL | Chief Executive of Hertfordshire County Council, 1979–90 |
| | Dato' Lim Kok Wing | Communications and Design Expert, founder of the Society for the Mentally Handicapped in Malaysia |
| 1995 | Viscount Cranborne | Leader of the House of Lords, Marquess of Salisbury of Hatfield House |
| | Sir Ian MacLaurin DL | Chairman of Tesco Ltd – resident of Hertfordshire |
| | Michael Mansfield QC | Lawyer and civil liberties campaigner |
| | His Honour Judge Eric Stockdale | Circuit judge for Hertfordshire, 1972–94, Visiting Professor of Law at the University |
| | The Right Reverend John Taylor | Bishop of St Albans, 1980–95 |
| 1996 | T.G. Mercer OBE | Former Chairman of the Governing Body of Hatfield Polytechnic |
| | The Right Honourable Lord Justice Staughton | Lord Justice of the Court of Appeal |
| 1997 | David Pannick QC | Recorder and Fellow of All Souls College, Oxford |
| 1999 | The Right Honourable Eddie George | Governor of the Bank of England |
| | Joshua Rozenberg | BBC Legal Correspondent |
| | Iris Tarry CBE | Leader of Hertfordshire County Council, 1993–97 |
| 2000 | Rodney Bickerstaffe | General Secretary of UNISON |
| | His Royal Highness Prince Hassan of Jordan | Crown Prince of Jordan |
| | Eryl McNally MEP | MEP for the East of England |
| 2002 | Professor Sir Robin Auld | Lord Justice of the Court of Appeal and member of the Privy Council |
| | Dr Drakoulis Fountoukakos | Co-founder and Director of Independent Science and Technology Studies, Athens |
| | Professor Rhea Martin OBE | Former Pro-Director of Hatfield Polytechnic and Visiting Professor in the Faculty of Law |
| 2003 | Tan Yew Sing | President of the INTI International Education Group, Malaysia |
| | The Right Honourable Lord Slynn of Hadley | Senior Judge and former Advocate-General at the European Court of Justice in Luxembourg |
| 2004 | Sir Brian Briscoe | Chief Executive of the Local Government Association and former Chief Executive of Hertfordshire County Council |
| | Jim McGown | Former Managing Director of Three Valleys Water Company and Chairman of the Board of Governors |
| 2005 | Lt. Col. Jack Fielder MBE | Chairman of the HCC Further Education Committee and Governor of the Polytechnic and University |
| | Roger Gochin | Former Principal of North Hertfordshire College |
| | Sir Stephen Lander KCB | Former Director General of MI5 |
| | Lady Parkinson DL | Deputy Lieutenant of Hertfordshire, Trustee of the Hertfordshire Community Foundation and Governor of the University |

| 2006 | The Right Honourable Peter Lilley MP | MP for Hitchin and Harpenden |
| | Baroness Shirley Williams | Former MP for Hitchin and for Hertford and Stevenage |
| 2007 | Professor Chen Dasen | Former President of Shanghai University of Electric Power, partner in a Foundation Programme collaboration with the University of Hertfordshire |
| | Brian Hall | Leader of Stevenage Borough Council |
| | Sir Simon Bowes Lyon KCVO | Lord Lieutenant of Hertfordshire, 1986–2007 |
| | Sir Phillip Mawer | Former Principal Private Secretary to the Home Secretary, 1987–89, and Parliamentary Commissioner for Standards, 2002–07 |
| 2008 | The Right Honourable the Baroness Catherine Ashton of Upholland | European Commissioner for Trade and former Chair of the Hertfordshire Health Authority |
| 2009 | Professor Neil Buxton | Former Vice-Chancellor of the University, 1987–2003 |
| | Lord Dholakia of Waltham Brooks OBE DL | Activist and Ambassador for Improving Community Relations |
| | Sir Terry Leahy | Chief Executive of Tesco PLC |
| 2010 | Barbara Follett | Former MP for Stevenage |
| | Stuart Kenny | Director General of the Letchworth Garden City Foundation |
| | Lord Thomas McNally | Politician and Leader of the Liberal Democrats in the House of Lords |

## Doctor of Letters

| 1990 | David Kossoff | Actor, writer and storyteller – resident of Hatfield |
| 1992 | Sir Nigel Hawthorne CBE | Actor – resident of Baldock |
| | The Right Reverend Lord Runcie | Bishop of St Albans, 1970–80, Archbishop of Canterbury, 1980–91 |
| 1993 | Professor John Lill OBE | Classical pianist and Professor at the Royal College of Music |
| | Derek Prag MEP | Member of the European Parliament for Hertfordshire |
| 1994 | PD James, Baroness James of Holland Park | Author |
| 1995 | Alan Davie CBE | Scottish artist – resident of Hertford Heath, Hertfordshire |
| | Humphrey Lyttelton | Jazz musician and broadcaster – resident of Barnet, Hertfordshire |
| 1996 | Barry Norman CBE | Author, journalist, film critic and television presenter – resident of Datchworth, Hertfordshire |
| 1997 | Peter Kellner | Journalist and political commentator |
| | Stan Tracey OBE | Jazz pianist and composer |
| 1998 | Pat Barker CBE | Author |
| | Olivia de Havilland | Oscar-winning actress and cousin of Sir Geoffrey de Havilland |
| | Tom Karen | Industrial designer and creator of the Chopper bike |
| | Professor Norman Thomas CBE | Specialist adviser on education and HMI of Schools |
| 1999 | The Very Reverend Dr Christopher Lewis | Dean of the Abbey Church and Cathedral of St Alban |
| 2000 | Reverend Martin Eggleton | Former Secretary of Higher Education Chaplaincies of the Methodist Conference and author |
| | Professor Max Stafford-Clark | Theatre director |
| | Professor Jeff Thompson CBE | Educationalist and alumnus of Hatfield Polytechnic |

| 2001 | The Right Reverend Bishop James O'Brien | Auxiliary Bishop of Westminster with responsibility for the Roman Catholic community of Hertfordshire |
| | Mary Russell MBE | Executive Director of Universities' Council for the Education of Teachers |
| | Hugh Richard Walduck OBE | Former High Sheriff and Deputy Lieutenant of Hertfordshire and founder member of the University of Hertfordshire's Development Committee |
| 2002 | Tim Gilligan DL | Deputy Lieutenant of Hertfordshire and former Chairman of the University of Hertfordshire's Development Committee |
| | Neville Reyner CBE | Deputy Chairman of the East of England Development Agency |
| 2003 | Sanjeev Bhaskar OBE | Writer, comedian and alumnus of Hatfield Polytechnic |
| | The Right Reverend Christopher Herbert | Bishop of St Albans |
| | Donovan Leitch | Singer and songwriter – native of Hatfield |
| 2004 | Lord Digby Jones | Director General of the CBI |
| | John Mole | Poet and jazz musician and Visiting Poet to the University – Hertfordshire resident |
| 2005 | Michael Morpurgo MBE | Author and Children's Laureate – born in St Albans |
| 2006 | John Motson OBE | Sports journalist and BBC commentator |
| | Professor F.M.L. Thompson CBE MA DPhil FBA | Historian – resident of Hertfordshire |
| 2007 | Dr Bruce Mallen | Academic, film producer and Visiting Professor in Motion Picture Industry Studies at the University |
| 2009 | Caroline Tapster | Former Chief Executive of Hertfordshire County Council |
| | Jonathan Steele | Journalist and foreign correspondent for the *Guardian* |
| 2010 | Richard Lambert | Former editor of the *Financial Times* |
| | Dr Roger Lewis | Biographer, journalist and alumnus of the University |
| 2011 | Larry Elliott | Economics editor of the *Guardian* and Visiting Fellow of the University |
| | The Right Reverend C.R.J. Foster | Former Bishop of Hertford and member of the Board of Governors |
| | Tony Marchant | Television dramatist and creator of *Garrow's Law*, which drew inspiration from the archives of the Old Bailey Online Project |

## Doctor of Science

| 1987 | David Jack CBE | Pharmacologist, Research and Development Director of Glaxo Holdings |
| 1988 | Hugh Metcalfe OBE | Managing Director of British Aerospace, Hatfield Division |
| 1989 | Sir Patrick Moore CBE OBE | Astronomer and presenter of the BBC's *The Sky at Night* |
| 1990 | David Shepherd OBE | Artist and wildlife conservationist |
| 1992 | Sir Nick Faldo MBE | Golfer and winner of the 1992 British Open Golf Championship – born and educated in Welwyn Garden City, Hertfordshire |
| 1993 | Professor Sir James Black FRS | Medical Researcher and holder of the Nobel Prize for Medicine |
| | Denis Filer CBE | Director General of the Engineering Council |
| | Misu Negritoiu | Romania's Chief Economic Adviser |

| 1994 | Professor Heather Couper | Broadcaster and writer on astronomy |
|------|--------------------------|-------------------------------------|
| | Dr David G. Hessayon | Author of the bestselling *Gardening Expert* series of books |
| | Dr Adrian V. Stokes OBE | Expert on computer technology and former Senior Research Fellow of the Polytechnic |
| | Sir Richard Sykes | Chief Executive of Glaxo Holdings |
| 1995 | Dr Mary Archer | Lecturer in Chemistry and the first Official Visitor to the University |
| 1996 | Sir Brian Corby | Chancellor of the University of Hertfordshire, 1992–96, President of the CBI, 1990–92 |
| | Mary E. McClymont | Education Officer for the Queen's Institute of District Nurses and leader of the Health Visitor course at Stevenage College |
| | Barbara A. Webber | President of the Association of Chartered Physiotherapists in Respiratory Care |
| 1997 | Joan Greenwood OBE | Midwifery Officer, Department of Health |
| | Sir Herbert Laming CBE | Former Director of Hertfordshire Social Services |
| | Sir Norman Lindop DL | Principal of Hatfield College of Technology, 1966–69, Director of Hatfield Polytechnic, 1969–1982 |
| | Alec H.M. Moir | Chairman of Oscar Faber, Consulting Engineers |
| | Baroness Young of Old Scone | Chief Executive of the Royal Society for the Protection of Birds |
| 1998 | Sir Colin Chandler | Chairman of Vickers and alumnus of Hatfield College of Technology |
| | Professor Michael Elves | Director of Scientific and Educational Affairs, Glaxo Wellcome PLC |
| | Professor R.J. (Jan) Pentreath | Director of Environmental Strategy at the Environment Agency |
| 1999 | Professor John Barrow | Research Professor of Mathematical Sciences at the University of Cambridge |
| | Baroness Helene Hayman | Former MP for Welwyn and Hatfield |
| | Arsène Wenger OBE | Manager of Arsenal Football Club |
| 2000 | Dr John Cordingley | Former member of the Board of Governors at Hatfield Polytechnic |
| | Barbara Doherty | Chair of Isabel Hospice, Hertfordshire |
| | Dato' Dr. Ir. Abu Hashim bin Abdul Ghani | Engineer and alumnus of Hatfield Polytechnic |
| | Professor David Lawson CBE | Chairman of the Medicines Commission |
| | Martin Leach | Vice-President of Product Development Ford Europe and alumnus of Hatfield Polytechnic |
| | François Pienaar | Captain of the 1995 World Cup-winning South African Rugby Team |
| 2001 | Hilary Cropper CBE | Executive Chair of Xansa, a business consulting and information technology company, and former Governor of the University |
| | Dr Joseph Farman | Member of the British Antarctic Survey team and discoverer of the ozone hole over the Atlantic Ocean |
| | Francis Ogilvie | Deputy Head of Overall Aircraft Design for the Airbus A380 and alumnus of Hatfield College of Technology |
| | Peter Sachs | Former Director General of the Electronics Engineering Association |

| 2002 | Professor Sir Tim Hunt FRS | Holder of the Nobel Prize for Medicine and Principal Scientist at Cancer Research UK, Clare Hall Laboratories, Hertfordshire |
|------|---------------------------|---------------|
| | Professor Jon King | Director of Corus Automotive, Visiting Professor of the Royal Academy of Engineering and alumnus of Hatfield Polytechnic |
| | Brian May CBE | Astronomer and rock guitarist with Queen |
| | Professor Roger Needham CBE | Managing Director of Microsoft Research Ltd |
| | Graham Taylor OBE | Former Watford and England Football Manager |
| 2003 | Professor Douglas Chamberlain CBE | Founder member of the European Resuscitation Council |
| | Professor Peter Lines | Former Pro-Vice-Chancellor (Academic Quality) of the University of Hertfordshire |
| | The Dowager Marchioness of Salisbury | Vice-President of the Royal Horticultural Society |
| 2004 | Joanne Goode MBE | Olympic, World, Commonwealth and European medallist in badminton and alumnus of the University |
| | Richard Hill MBE | Saracens and England rugby player |
| | Professor Hamid Mughal | Director of Manufacturing Engineering at Rolls Royce and Visiting Professor at the University |
| | Dr Roger Neighbour | President of the Royal College of General Practitioners – native of Hertfordshire |
| 2005 | Ir Andy Seo Kian Haw SMS | Vice-President of the Federation of Malaysian Manufacturers and alumnus of the University |
| | Dr Diana Hodgins MBE | Managing Director of European Technology for Business |
| | Reverend Dame Sarah Mullally DBE | Chief Nursing Officer for the Department of Health |
| | Professor Michael Richards | National Cancer Director for the Department of Health |
| 2006 | Professor Dame Carol Black OBE CBE | President of the Royal College of Physicians |
| | Hertfordshire Fire and Rescue Service | For their bravery in tackling the Buncefield Oil Depot fire |
| | Mike Newton | Former Vice-President of Apple and Dell and alumnus of the University |
| 2007 | Tore Laerdal | Chairman and CEO of Laerdal Medical AS, developer of SimBaby |
| | Dr Julia Schofield MBE | Computer consultant, first totally blind graduate in Computer Science in the UK and alumnus of the Polytechnic |
| | Professor Sir Nicholas Wright | Warden and Vice-Principal at St Bartholomew's Hospital and the London School of Medicine and Dentistry |
| 2008 | Nigel Wray | Chairman and owner of Saracens Rugby Club |
| 2009 | Andrés Duany | Architect and urban planner |
| | Phillip Friend OBE | Chairman of RADAR and founder of Phil & Friends |
| | Professor Peter Noyce CBE | Professor of Pharmacy Practice at the University of Manchester |
| | Dr Lee Fah Onn | President of INTI International University |
| 2010 | Dr Peter Carter OBE | General Secretary and Chief Executive of the Royal College of Nursing |
| | Stephen Joseph OBE | Executive Director of Campaign for Better Transport – resident of Hertfordshire |
| | Mike Norris | Chief Executive Officer of Computacenter PLC |
| | Dr Malcolm Skingle CBE | Director of Academic Liaison, GlaxoSmithKline |

| 2011 | Professor John Burland CBE | Emeritus Professor and Senior Research Investigator at Imperial College |
| | Professor Thom Hanahoe | Chairman of the West Herts Hospital Trust and former Pro-Vice-Chancellor of the University |
| | Dr Paul Robinson | Medical Director at Merck, Sharp and Dohme |

## Master of Arts

| 1985 | Charles Wallace | Film and television producer and director |
| 1998 | The Reverend Bill Taylor | Former Chaplain to the University |
| 1999 | Tony Rook | Teacher, broadcaster, local historian and archaeologist – resident of Welwyn, Hertfordshire |
| | George Wenham | Teacher and representative for Welwyn and Hatfield on Town, District and County Councils |
| 2001 | Tony Grounds | Stage, television and film writer – Hertfordshire resident |
| | Megs Wilson | Co-founder of the Willow Foundation Charity with husband Bob, and resident of Brookmans Park, Hertfordshire |
| 2007 | David Mitchinson | Head of Collections and Exhibitions, the Henry Moore Foundation |
| 2009 | Gemma Metheringham | Creative Director for fashion designer Karen Millen |
| 2010 | Kitty Hart-Moxon OBE | Holocaust Survivor and member of the Holocaust Educational Trust |

## Master of Education

| 2005 | Nigel Gates | Principal Lecturer in Education |
| 2008 | Russell Ball | Director of the Stevenage Partnership |
| | Gareth Humphreys MBE | Education and Young Person's Adviser at MBDA, Stevenage |
| | Thow Ngee Lim | Teacher Trainer in the University's School of Education, Malaysia |

## Master of Laws

| 2000 | Dr Michael Clark OBE | Chairman of the Mid-Herts Magistrates Bench and former Vice-Chairman of Hatfield Polytechnic Board of Governors |
| 2004 | Pat Ingram | Former Registrar of the Faculty of Engineering and Information Sciences |
| | Dr Dennis Lewis | Former Chairman and Leader of Welwyn Hatfield Council |

## Master of Letters

| 2002 | Margaret Jones | Former Assistant Secretary at the University |
| 2004 | Terry Mitchinson | Editor of the *Welwyn and Hatfield Times* |
| 2011 | Naomi Simmons | International bestselling author of children's books and English language teaching materials for primary schoolchildren – resident of Hertfordshire |

## Master of Science

| | | |
|---|---|---|
| **1993** | J.C.D. Marsh | Former Lecturer in Engineering, Hatfield College of Technology, and Director of the Hatfield Polytechnic Observatory |
| **1995** | Gillian Ballance | Lecturer in Social Work at Hatfield Polytechnic, 1971–94 |
| | Dawn Lee | Nursing Officer at Hatfield Polytechnic, Head of Health Centre Services for the University |
| | Joan Wiggall MBE | Services to the British Red Cross Society, Hertfordshire |
| **1997** | Dr Frank Baker | Former Principal of West Herts College |
| | Adrienne Finch | Education Chair for Europe for the International Society of Radiographers and Radiological Technologists |
| | Keith I. Gardner | Former Principal of Oaklands College |
| | John R. Guppy | Engineer and Visiting Fellow at the University |
| **1998** | Gary Mabbutt MBE | Former Tottenham Hotspur and England footballer – resident of Brookmans Park, Hertfordshire |
| | Heather Coates | Director of Studies (Physiotherapy) |
| **2002** | John Evans | Former Principal and Chief Executive of Hertford Regional College |
| | Christine Ryan | Former Head of Midwifery at the University of Hertfordshire |
| **2003** | Colin Johnson | Technical Manager of the Faculty of Engineering and Information Sciences |
| **2004** | Valerie Booth | Former Headmistress of St Albans Girls' School |
| **2005** | Andrew Bern | Manager of Human Resources Six Sigma – Ford Motor Company Ltd |
| | Lorraine Nuttall | Radiographer, Luton and Dunstable NHS Trust |
| **2006** | Jim Messenger | Coach of the University's American football team, the Hertfordshire Hurricanes |
| **2008** | Gary Lewin | Head of Physiotherapy to the England Senior Men's Football Team |
| **2009** | Margaret Jackson | Director of Coaching for the Superleague Netball club, the Mavericks |
| | Jean Pickering | Founder and Secretary of the Ron Pickering Memorial Fund to support young athletes |
| **2010** | Stuart McKay MBE | Writer and historian of the aircraft industry |
| **2011** | David James | Premier League and England goalkeeper – native of Welwyn Garden City |
| | Philip Mayo | Managing Director of Premier EDA Solutions and a mentor to students of the University |

# Appendix 3
## Academic structures 1952–2012

| Hatfield Technical College 1952–60 | | | | | | | |
|---|---|---|---|---|---|---|---|
| **Departments** | | | | | | | |
| **1952** | | | | | | | |
| Building | Commerce & Retail Trades | Social & Professional Studies | Science | Works & Production Engineering | Technical & Design Engineering | | |
| **1954** | | | | | | | |
| | Commerce, Social & Professional Studies | | | | | | |
| **1955** | | | | | | | |
| | | | | Mechanical & Production Engineering | Aeronautical & Mechanical Design | Electrical Engineering | |
| **1958** | | | | | | | |
| Transferred to Hertfordshire College of Building | | | | | | | |
| **1959** | | | | | | | |
| | | | | | | | Mathematics |

## Hatfield College of Technology 1960–69

### Departments

| Social Studies | Management Studies | Humanities | Science | Industrial Engineering | Mechanical & Aeronautical Engineering | Electrical Engineering | Mathematics & Statistics | Computer Science |
|---|---|---|---|---|---|---|---|---|
| **1960** | | | | | | | | |
| Business & Social Studies | | | Science | Industrial Engineering | Mechanical & Aeronautical Engineering | Electrical Engineering | Mathematics | |
| **1963** | | | | | | | | |
| | | | | | Mechanical, Aeronautical & Civil Engineering | | | |
| **1964** | | | | | | | | |
| | | | Chemistry & Biology | | | Electrical Engineering & Physics | | |
| **1967** | | | | | | | | |
| Social Studies | Management Studies | Humanities | | | | | | |
| **1968** | | | | | | | | |
| | | | | | | | Mathematics & Statistics | Computer Science |

## Hatfield Polytechnic 1969–92

### Departments

| Psychological & Social Studies | Administration & Business Studies | Management Studies | Humanities | Biological Sciences | Chemical Sciences | Civil Engineering & Construction | Mechanical & Aeronautical Engineering | Industrial Engineering | Electrical Engineering & Physics | Control & Optimisation | Mathematics & Statistics | Computer Science |
|---|---|---|---|---|---|---|---|---|---|---|---|---|
| **1969** | | | | | | | | | | | | |
| Social Sciences | | Management Studies | Humanities | Biological Sciences | Chemical Sciences | Civil Engineering & Construction | Mechanical & Aeronautical Engineering | Industrial Engineering | Electrical Engineering & Physics | | Mathematics & Statistics | Computer Science |
| **1970** | | | | | | | | | | | | |
| Psychological & Social Studies | Administration & Business Studies | | | | | | | | | | | |
| **1974** | | | | | | | | | Electrical Engineering & Physics | Control & Optimisation | | |

### Schools of Study

| Social Sciences | Humanities | Natural Sciences | Engineering | Information Sciences |
|---|---|---|---|---|
| **1975** | | | | |
| Social Sciences | Humanities | Natural Sciences | Engineering | Information Sciences |
| **1981** | | | | |
| Business & Social Sciences | | | | |
| **1988** | | | | |
| Business | Humanities & Education | Health & Human Sciences | | |

## University of Hertfordshire 1992–2012

### Schools of Study

**1992**

| Business | Humanities & Education | | Natural Sciences | Health & Human Sciences | Art & Design | Engineering | Information Sciences |
|---|---|---|---|---|---|---|---|
| | | | | | | | |

**1994**

| | | Combined & Continuing Studies | | | | | |
|---|---|---|---|---|---|---|---|

### Faculties

**1997**

| Business School | Law | Humanities, Languages & Education | Interdisciplinary Studies | Natural Sciences | Health & Human Sciences | Art & Design | Engineering & Information Sciences |
|---|---|---|---|---|---|---|---|

**2003**

| | | Humanities & Education | | | | | |
|---|---|---|---|---|---|---|---|

**2004**

| | Humanities, Law & Education | | | | Creative & Cultural Industries | | |
|---|---|---|---|---|---|---|---|

**2009**

| Business School | Humanities, Law & Education | | Health & Human Sciences | | Science, Technology & the Creative Arts | | |
|---|---|---|---|---|---|---|---|

**In 2012 the University structure is formed around four faculties comprising fourteen different Schools of Study.**

| BUSINESS | HUMANITIES, LAW & EDUCATION | HEALTH & HUMAN SCIENCES | SCIENCE, TECHNOLOGY & THE CREATIVE ARTS |
|---|---|---|---|
| **SCHOOLS OF STUDY** | | | |
| Business | Education | Health & Emergency Professions | Computer Science |
| | Humanities | Life Sciences | Creative Arts |
| | Law | Nursing, Midwifery & Social Work | Engineering & Technology |
| | | Pharmacy | Physics, Astronomy & Mathematics |
| | | Post-Graduate Medicine | |
| | | Psychology | |

**In addition there are three interdisciplinary Research Institutes.**

| Social Sciences, Arts and Humanities (SSAHRI) | Health and Human Sciences (HHSRI) | Science and Technology (STRI) |
|---|---|---|

# Appendix 4
## Hatfield Technical College: Examinations taken 1952–62

| Year | Awarding Body | Subject | No. of Students |
|------|---------------|---------|:---------------:|
| **1952–53** | Royal Aeronautical Society | Part I | 19 |
| | | Part II | 18 |
| | Institution of Production Engineers | Part I | 2 |
| | | Part II | 4 |
| | | Part III | 7 |
| | Ordinary National Certificate | Mechanical Engineering | 27 |
| | | Mechanical Engineering with Aeronautical Engineering | 16 |
| | | Electrical Engineering | 5 |
| | | Endorsement in Mechanical Engineering (Production) | 3 |
| | City and Guilds of London Institute | Brickwork | 2 |
| | | Builders' Quantities | 1 |
| | | Carpentry and Joinery | 5 |
| | | Plumbing | 4 |
| | | Machine Shop Engineering | 24 |
| | | Motor Vehicle Mechanic's Course | 4 |
| | | Sheet Metalwork – Intermediate | 2 |
| | | Electrical Installation | 3 |
| | | Mathematics for Telecommunications II | 3 |
| | | Telecommunication Principles | 4 |
| | | Telephone Exchange Systems II | 1 |
| | | Radio | 4 |
| | Local Government Examination Board | Intermediate | 2 |
| | Institute of Export | First Examination | 2 |
| | Institute of Certified Grocers | Intermediate | 4 |
| | Institute of Meat | Craftsman's Certificate | 4 |
| | Royal Society of Arts & Pitman's | Intermediate and Advanced | 26 |
| | General Certificate of Education | Unspecified | 18 |
| | | | |
| **1953–54** | Royal Aeronautical Society | Part I | 7 |
| | | Part II | 14 |
| | Institution of Production Engineers | Part III | 4 |
| | Ordinary National Certificate | Mechanical Engineering | 37 |
| | | Mechanical Engineering with Aeronautical Engineering | 25 |

| | | | |
|---|---|---|---|
| | | Electrical Engineering | 18 |
| | Higher National Certificate | Production Engineering | 6 |
| | | Mechanical Engineering | 15 |
| | | Mechanical Engineering with Aeronautical Engineering | 12 |
| | Ordinary National Certificate | Endorsement in Mechanical Engineering | 20 |
| | | Endorsement in Electrical Engineering | 14 |
| | Higher National Certificate | Endorsement in Mechanical Engineering | 14 |
| | City and Guilds of London Institute | Aircraft Servicing and Maintenance | 7 |
| | | Brickwork | 5 |
| | | Carpentry and Joinery – Intermediate | 10 |
| | | Plumbing | 3 |
| | | Machine Shop Engineering – Final | 1 |
| | | Machine Shop Engineering – Intermediate | 41 |
| | | Motor Vehicle Mechanic's Course | 6 |
| | | Sheet Metal – Final | 1 |
| | | Sheet Metal – Intermediate | 3 |
| | | Oxy-Acetylene Welding Technology | 3 |
| | | Electrical Installation Work | 7 |
| | | Telecommunication Principles | 9 |
| | | Mathematics for Telecommunication Part II | 8 |
| | | Telephone Exchange Systems Part I | 2 |
| | | Radio Part I | 7 |
| | | Radio Amateur's Examination | 2 |
| | Institute of Certified Grocers | Advanced | 3 |
| | | Intermediate | 3 |
| | Institute of Meat | Meat Trades Diploma | 3 |
| | | Craftsman's Certificate | 5 |
| | Institute of Export | First Examination | 1 |
| | | Intermediate Examination | 1 |
| | National Certificate | Commerce | 2 |
| | Royal Society of Arts and Pitman's | Intermediate and Advanced | 40 |
| | General Certificate of Education | A Level | 11 (20 passes) |
| | | O Level | 54 (93 passes) |
| | College Certificate | Boiler House Practice | 2 |
| | | Unspecified | 15 |
| | | | |
| 1954–55 | Institution of Mechanical Engineers | Section A | 1 |
| | Institution of Production Engineers | Part I | 1 |
| | Royal Aeronautical Society | Part I | 4 |
| | | Part II | 9 |

| | | | |
|---|---|---|---|
| | Society of Licensed Aircraft Engineers | Unspecified | 2 |
| | Ordinary National Diploma | Mechanical Engineering | 3 |
| | Ordinary National Certificate | Mechanical Engineering | 16 |
| | | Mechanical Engineering with Production | 77 |
| | | Mechanical Engineering with Aeronautical Engineering | 34 |
| | | Electrical Engineering | 5 |
| | | Building | 3 |
| | | Chemistry | 12 |
| | Higher National Certificate | Mechanical Engineering | 25 |
| | | Mechanical Engineering with Aeronautical Engineering | 14 |
| | | Production Engineering | 8 |
| | | Electrical Engineering | 7 |
| | Ordinary National Certificate | Endorsement in Mechanical Engineering | 31 |
| | | Endorsement in Electrical Engineering | 4 |
| | Higher National Certificate | Endorsement in Mechanical Engineering | 40 |
| | | Endorsement in Electrical Engineering | 2 |
| | City and Guilds of London Institute | Aircraft Service and Maintenance – Intermediate | 7 |
| | | Aircraft Service and Maintenance – Final | 5 |
| | | Brickwork – Intermediate | 6 |
| | | Brickwork – Final | 4 |
| | | Carpentry and Joinery – Intermediate | 11 |
| | | Carpentry and Joinery – Final | 2 |
| | | Concrete Practice – Grade I | 5 |
| | | Machine Shop Engineering – Intermediate | 42 |
| | | Machine Shop Engineering – Final | 11 |
| | | Mechanical Engineering Design | 1 |
| | | Mechanical Engineering Inspection | 4 |
| | | Motor Vehicle Mechanic's Work | 7 |
| | | Motor Vehicle Technician's Work | 3 |
| | | Plumbing – Intermediate | 8 |
| | | Plumbing – Final | 2 |
| | | Radio Servicing – Intermediate | 6 |
| | | Sheet Metalwork – Intermediate | 1 |
| | | Sheet Metalwork – Final | 1 |
| | | Elementary Telecommunications Practice | 3 |
| | | Telecommunications Principles Part I | 4 |
| | | Telecommunications Principles Part II | 6 |
| | | Telecommunications Principles Part III | 2 |
| | | Mathematics for Telecommunications Part I | 3 |
| | | Mathematics for Telecommunications Part II | 7 |

| | | Mathematics for Telecommunications Part III | 9 |
|---|---|---|---|
| | | Radio Part I | 6 |
| | | Radio Part II | 7 |
| | | Line Plant Practice | 1 |
| | | Electrical Installation | 7 |
| | | Oxy-Acetylene Welding – Final | 2 |
| | | Electric-Arc Welding – Final | 4 |
| | Institute of Certified Grocers | Advanced | 3 |
| | | Intermediate | 3 |
| | | First | 2 |
| | Institute of Management | | 1 |
| | Institute of Meat | Meat Trades Diploma | 2 |
| | | Craftsman's Certificate | 5 |
| | Royal Society of Arts and Pitman's | Intermediate and Advanced | 81 |
| | General Certificate of Education | A Level | 30 (58 passes) |
| | | O Level | 58 (83 passes) |
| | College Certificate | Boiler House Practice | 4 |
| | | | |

**Lower Level Subjects**

| | Added | Lost |
|---|---|---|
| **1955–56** | ONC Chemistry | |
| | ONC Building | |
| | HNC Chemistry | |
| **1956–57** | Intermediate Certificate – Management Studies | |
| | ONC Commerce | |
| | Institute of Linguists | |
| **1957–58** | C&G – Painters and Decorators | |
| | Television Servicing | |
| | Institute of Cost and Works Accountants Intermediate Pts I & II | |
| **1960–61** | Institute of Bankers Exams | Building Department – plumbing, brickwork, carpentry and joinery, etc. |

# Appendix 5
## Advanced level courses 1952–77[1]

| First offered | CNAA Degrees | Attendance[2] | HNC/HND & Advanced Courses | Attendance |
|---|---|---|---|---|
| *Hatfield Technical College* | | | | |
| 1952 | | | HNC Mechanical & Aeronautical Engineering | PTD |
| | | | HNC Production Engineering | PTD |
| 1953 | | | HNC Electrical Engineering | PTD |
| | | | HNC Chemistry | PTD |
| *Hatfield College of Technology* | | | | |
| 1960 | BSc & BSc (Hons) Aeronautical Engineering | SW | | |
| | BSc & BSc (Hons) Electrical & Electronic Engineering | SW | | |
| 1961 | BSc & BSc (Hons) Mechanical Engineering | SW | | |
| 1962 | | | HNC Business Studies | PTD |
| 1963 | BSc & BSc (Hons) Applied Chemistry | SW | HND Production Engineering | SW |
| | BSc & BSc (Hons) Mathematics | SW | | |
| 1965 | BSc & BSC (Hons) Civil Engineering | SW & FT | HND Mechanical Engineering | SW |
| | BSc (Hons) Computer Science | SW | | |
| 1966 | BSc Computer Science | SW | | |
| | BSc Applied Chemistry | SW | | |
| | BA (Hons) Business Studies | SW | | |
| 1967 | BSc & BSC (Hons) Industrial Engineering | SW | | |
| | BSc & BSC (Hons) Applied Biology | SW | | |
| | BSc Mathematics | PT | | |
| | BA Business Studies | SW | | |
| 1968 | BSc Applied Chemistry | PT | HNC Applied Biology | PTD |
| | | | HND Business Studies | FT |
| | | | Diploma in Management Studies | PT |
| 1969 | MSc Control Engineering | PT | HNC Engineering | PTD |
| | BA Applied Social Studies | SW | | |
| 1970 | MSc Computer Science | PT | | |

1  'Table 1. Growth of the Academic Work of the Hatfield College of Technology and Polytechnic 1960–77', Hatfield Polytechnic, *Annual Report 1976–77*, pp. 24–5.
2  BR = Block Release, FT = Full-Time, PTD = Part-Time Day Release, PT = Other forms of part-time study, including evening, SW = Sandwich Course.

| | | | | |
|---|---|---|---|---|
| | BSc & BSc (Hons) Applied Biology | PT | | |
| | BSc Physics | PT | | |
| | BA English | PT | | |
| **1971** | BSc (Hons) Psychology | FT | HND Civil Engineering | SW |
| | | | HND Measurement & Control | SW |
| | | | HND Computer Studies | SW |
| **1972** | Postgraduate Diploma in Engineering Studies | PT | HND Agriculture | |
| | BSc & BSc (Hons) Sociology | PT | | |
| **1973** | MSc Operational Research | BR | Diploma in Accounting & Finance | PT |
| | MSc Industrial Chemistry | PT | | |
| | Diploma in Higher Education Mathematics | FT & PT | | |
| | BA (Hons) Humanities – Linguistics & English Literature major | FT | | |
| **1974** | Postgraduate Diploma Structural Engineering | PT | HNC Metallurgy (Materials Studies) | PTD |
| | Postgraduate Diploma Computer Education | PT | | |
| | MSc Pharmacological Biochemistry | PT | | |
| | BEd & BEd (Hons) | PT | | |
| | BA (Hons) English | PT | | |
| | BA & BA (Hons) Contemporary Studies | PTD | | |
| | Diploma in Higher Education Contemporary Studies | PTD | | |
| **1975** | BSc & BSc (Hons) Computer Science | PT | HND Electrical & Electronic Engineering | SW |
| | Diploma in Higher Education Computer Science | PT | HND Mathematics, Statistics & Computing | FT |
| | BA (Hons) Humanities – Philosophy major | FT | | |
| | Postgraduate Diploma Careers Education & Counselling | FT | | |
| **1976** | BSc & BSc (Hons) Environmental Studies | SW | | |
| | BSc & BSc (Hons) Physics & Engineering Science | PT | | |
| | MSc Optimisation | PT | | |
| | MSc Information Systems | PT | | |
| | MSc Engineering | PT | | |
| | Postgraduate Diploma Applied Educational Studies | PT | | |
| | BA (Hons) Humanities – History major | FT | | |
| **1977** | MSc Astronomy & Astronautics | PT | | |
| | BA & BA (Hons) Social Sciences | FT | | |

# Appendix 6

## Hatfield Technical College: Students enrolled 1952–86

| Academic Year | Number of Enrolled Students | | | | | |
| --- | --- | --- | --- | --- | --- | --- |
| | Full-Time Day | Part-Time Day | Evening Classes | Total | Total Male | Total Female |
| 1952–53 | 55 | 813 | 870 | 1,738 | 1,469 | 269 |
| 1953–54 | 112 | 1,073 | 1,359 | 2,544 | 2,151 | 393 |
| 1954–55 | 140 | 1,371 | 1,386 | 2,897 | 2,617 | 280 |
| 1955–56 | 149 | 1,656 | 1,712 | 3,517 | 3,206 | 311 |
| 1956–57 | 150 | 1,956 | 1,773 | 3,879 | nd | nd |
| 1957–58 | 187 | 2,154 | 1,506 | 3,847 | 3,620 | 227 |
| 1958–59 | 229 | 1,788 | 1,583 | 3,600 | 3,394 | 206 |
| 1959–60 | 262 | 1,500 | 1,483 | 3,245 | 2,975 | 270 |
| 1960–61 | 257 | 1,387 | 1,443 | 3,087 | 2,870 | 217 |
| 1961–62 | 261 | 1,266 | 1,227 | 2,754 | 2,562 | 192 |
| 1962–63 | 254 | 995 | 894 | 2,143 | 1,947 | 196 |
| 1963–64 | 342 | 1,038 | 1,329 | 2,709 | nd | nd |
| 1964–65 | 449 | 969 | 656 | 2,074 | nd | nd |
| 1965–66 | 591 | 825 | 571 | 1,987 | nd | nd |
| 1966–67 | 887 | 619 | 281 | 1,787 | nd | nd |
| 1967–68 | 1,090 | 675 | 263 | 2,028 | nd | nd |
| 1968–69 | 1,335 | 673 | 135 | 2,143 | nd | nd |
| 1969–70 | 1,622 | 900 | 102 | 2,624 | nd | nd |
| 1970–71 | 1,558 | 917 | nd | 2,475 | 2,198 | 277 |
| 1971–72 | 1,662 | 934 | nd | 2,596 | 2,231 | 365 |
| 1972–73 | 1,760 | 986 | nd | 2,746 | 2,266 | 480 |
| 1973–74 | 1,864 | 1,056 | nd | 2,920 | 2,322 | 598 |
| 1974–75 | 2,070 | 1,282 | nd | 3,352 | 2,598 | 754 |
| 1975–76 | 2,383 | 1,226 | 133 | 3,742 | 2,861 | 881 |
| 1976–77 | 2,491 | 1,276 | 141 | 3,908 | 2,951 | 957 |
| 1977–78 | 2,624 | 1,285 | 100 | 4,009 | 3,014 | 993 |
| 1978–79 | 2,752 | 1,470 | 119 | 4,341 | 3,229 | 1,112 |
| 1979–80 | 2,916 | 1,465 | 108 | 4,489 | 3,245 | 1,244 |
| 1980–81 | 3,012 | 1,419 | 121 | 4,552 | 3,271 | 1,281 |
| 1981–82 | 3,461 | 1,399 | 186 | 5,046 | 3,512 | 1,534 |
| 1982–83 | 3,554 | 1,426 | 272 | 5,252 | 3,523 | 1,729 |
| 1983–84 | 3,821 | 1,446 | 346 | 5,613 | 3,749 | 1,864 |
| 1984–85 | 3,895 | 1,449 | 320 | 5,664 | 3,724 | 1,940 |
| 1985–86 | 3,913 | 1,380 | 236 | 5,529 | 3,562 | 1,967 |

Source: Hatfield Technical College *Annual Reports (1952–86)*. 'nd' = no data available.

# Detailed timeline of achievements and events 1941 – 2012

## Hatfield Technical College

**1941**  Hertfordshire County Council enters into partnership with the de Havilland Aircraft Company to train fifteen- and sixteen-year-old aircraft apprentices.

**1944**  Hertfordshire County Council responds to the 1944 Education Act requirement to restructure secondary education with a comprehensive plan for technical and further education within the county.

Alan S. Butler offers to donate ninety acres of land at Roe Green, on condition it be used for further educational purposes. The offer is accepted by Hertfordshire County Council in May.

**1945**  The first post-war emergency women's teacher training college is established at Wall Hall, Aldenham, and opened by R.A. Butler, Education Minister.

**1946**  The New Towns Act, designed to meet the housing needs of a bomb-damaged London, poor-quality national housing stock and a growing population, sees an extensive building programme within Hertfordshire including the New Towns of Hatfield, Hemel Hempstead, Stevenage and Welwyn Garden City.

The Deed of Gift and Conveyance resulting from Alan S. Butler's offer is signed: 'the County Council shall and will establish and maintain on the land hereby conveyed a college for the provision of further education (with special regard to education of a technical type) and with such provision (if any) for secondary education (of such a type as aforesaid) as the County Council may deem necessary or desirable'.

**1949**  Dr W.A.J. Chapman is appointed first Principal of Hatfield Technical College.

**1952**  The first students enrol in Hatfield Technical College – 55 full-time and sandwich, 813 part-time, 870 evening (total 1,738). Ann Copus is the very first student to enrol, opting for secretarial and language courses.

Eleanor Lyen of Hong Kong is the first overseas student to enrol. She is awarded a College Certificate for her success in the Intermediate and Advanced Pitman's RSA exam.

The official opening ceremony is performed by HRH Prince Philip, Duke of Edinburgh.

**1953**  Hatfield Technical College's Dramatic Society gives its first performance: a production of *Ring Round the Moon* by Jean Anouilh.

The College mounts its first exhibition, celebrating the England of Queen Elizabeth I and the newly crowned Queen Elizabeth II.

Hatfield School opens on the campus. The architects' plan (December 1946) names the school as Hatfield Day Technical School, but it is always called Hatfield School.

**1955**  The First College Rag Day is held.

The National Council for Technological Awards (NCTA) is established.

| 1956 | Gordon H. Wright is employed as County Technical Librarian and begins the expansion of the Hertfordshire College Library Network. |
|---|---|
| | The first course on computing is provided, 'The Application of Computers to Automation' – a Specialist Short Course held under the auspices of the Department of Mechanical and Production Engineering. |
| 1958 | A Druine 'Turbi' two-seater light aircraft built by students of the T.K. Flying Group makes its maiden flight. |
| 1959 | John Hall is appointed as Head of the newly formed Mathematics Department. |
| | The first students to be awarded the degree of BSc (Engineering) as external students of the University of London are N. Cadoux-Hudson, J.E. Hackett, A.E. James, I.J. Langley, A. Stephenson and D.H. Wilkinson. |
| | D.H. Wilkinson is the only external candidate in that year to be awarded a University of London BSc (Eng) degree with First Class Honours. |
| | Four students from the Motor Club drive a Ransome Matador motor-mower non-stop from Edinburgh to London. |
| | Two teams enter the *Daily Mail* Bleriot Centenary Cross-Channel Race, from Marble Arch to the Arc de Triomphe and home again – the only college or university teams to participate. |

# Hatfield College of Technology

| 1960 | Hatfield Technical College is renamed Hatfield College of Technology. |
|---|---|
| | The College achieves recognition from the NCTA of its four-year sandwich courses leading to a Diploma in Technology in both Aeronautical and Electrical Engineering. |
| | The Mathematics Department hosts a conference on 'Computers in Education'. It proves to be a key moment in the development of Computer Science as an academic discipline. |
| | A College team makes its first appearance in the ninety-eight-mile London to Leicester Pram Race. |
| 1961 | The College is recognised as a Regional College, one of twenty-five Regional Colleges in England and Wales. |
| | Six students race from Land's End to John O'Groats on a 197cc, two-stroke engine go-kart. |
| 1963 | The Robbins Report, which calls for doubling the numbers of students in higher education by 1980, is released. |
| | The first digital computer at the College is purchased – a National Elliott 803B digital computer, at a cost of £24,010. |
| | The Computer Unit within the Mathematics Department, headed by Dr R.W. Sharp as Director, is formed. Its two main functions are (1) teaching and research in Computer Science and (2) provision of a computing service to students and staff. |
| | The first students to be awarded a Diploma in Technology (Engineering) in Aeronautical Engineering are P.R. Edwards, R.G. Gawthorpe, J.R. Jones, M.D. Mant, A. Middleditch, B.G. Pearce, N.K. Richardson and D.A. Sutcliffe. |

**1964** The first students to be awarded a higher degree, an MSc in Chemistry, as external students of the University of London are L.B. Austin, R. Munden and Miss M. Gawluk. Miss Gawluk is the first female student to be awarded a higher degree.

Miss J. Hornby and Miss G.S. Sumner are the first female students to be awarded the BSc (General) as external students of the University of London.

**1965** The NCTA is replaced by the Council for National Academic Awards (CNAA).

The first research student to be awarded a PhD by the University of London (External), for research undertaken whilst a student of the Department of Chemistry and Biology, Hatfield College of Technology, is Dr Brian Coffin.

Fairshot Hall, Sandridge, becomes the College's first Hall of Residence.

**1966** Norman Lindop joins the College as Principal.

The government White Paper 'A Plan for Polytechnics and other Colleges' lists Hatfield amongst proposed polytechnics to be established in England and Wales.

The first female students to be awarded a BSc degree in Engineering (CNAA) by the College are Miss B.E. Murphy and Miss P.D. Baker.

Seven students cross the English Channel from Dover to Calais on a specially adapted bed in order to publicise Rag Week.

**1967** Hertfordshire County Council approves the use of Bayfordbury Mansion as additional teaching space for the College.

The CNAA approves the introduction of a part-time Ordinary degree course in Mathematics, the first part-time course to be approved by the CNAA. This course is aimed at members of the teaching profession who wish to improve their skills.

The first female research student to be awarded a PhD by the University of London, for research undertaken whilst a student in the Department of Chemistry and Biology, Hatfield College of Technology, is Dr Mary Chisholm.

**1968** Two student representatives are to sit on the Board of Governors of the new Polytechnic.

The Secretary of State for Education and Science, Edward Short, approves the provision of a multi-access computer system at a cost not exceeding £300,000.

The first lectures in Descriptive Astronomy introduced.

# Hatfield Polytechnic

**1969**  Hatfield College of Technology is designated as Hatfield Polytechnic.

Birklands Mansion is acquired as an additional teaching site and is occupied by the Design Centre of the Department of Mechanical and Aeronautical Engineering.

A part-time MSc in Control Engineering is introduced, the first postgraduate course at Hatfield to gain CNAA approval.

A part-time degree in English is introduced, the first such course to gain CNAA approval in the country.

The first CNAA PhD degree is awarded to a member of the Polytechnic: Dr W.G. Burrows, a member of the Department of Electrical Engineering and Physics.

**1970**  The Astronomical Observatory, housing a sixteen-inch multi-purpose telescope, is formally opened in the grounds of Bayfordbury Mansion.

Two new Halls of Residence are opened: Butler Hall, named in honour of Alan S. Butler; and Fern Hall, named in honour of Alderman Harold Fern, first Chair of the Board of Governors of the Technical College.

The first students to be awarded a BA (Hons) degree by the Polytechnic, an Honours degree in Business Studies, are D.A. Beauchamp, T.M. Berridge, D. Brameld, J.A. Britton, D.J. Bromley, M.S. Butler, G.A. Clark, P.J. Collins, R.C. Collins, J.J. Copley, M. Daglish, L.R. Geary, B.A. Hamilton, G.L.J. Hayes, R.J. Holdaway, N.G. Jones, J. Ostle, S. Powell, J.D. Robins, A.R. Russell, M.J. Sims and A.J. Thornhill.

The best equipped and staffed Computer Centre in the public sector in education is formed, and, following the purchase of a DEC PDP-10 costing £256,500, the first multi-access computer system in education – linking schools, colleges and the Polytechnic – goes live.

The first Fellowship of the Hatfield Polytechnic is conferred upon Dr W.A.J. Chapman, founder Principal of the College.

**1971**  The Polytechnic occupies the former Hatfield School building. The south building is named the Hutton Building, in honour of the first headmaster of Hatfield School, Dr Kenneth Hutton; it is one of the first technical schools to be built under the provisions of the 1944 Education Act.

A new Hall of Residence is opened: Chapman Hall, named in honour of Dr W.A.J. Chapman.

An Honorary Fellowship is conferred upon Alan S. Butler.

**1972**  C.P. Snow is appointed the Polytechnic's first Visitor.

**1973**  The Polytechnic introduces the Common Modular Structure, which allows for a wider choice of courses taken across different departments.

Norman Lindop receives a knighthood in recognition of his role as Chairman of the Committee of Directors of Polytechnics.

**1974**  Two new Halls of Residence are opened: Sidney Broad Hall, named in honour of Sidney T. Broad, County Education Officer (1957–73); and John Coales Hall, named in honour of Professor John F. Coales, founder Governor of Hatfield Technical College.

The Students' Union moves into the Hutton Building. A new bar, named The Font, is opened.

**1975**    The Polytechnic is reorganised into five schools of study and a Centre for Management Studies.

Julia Schofield becomes the first totally blind graduate in Computer Science in the UK.

**1976**    Wall Hall and Balls Park teacher training colleges merge to form the Hertfordshire College of Higher Education.

The Students' Union Oracle Bar is renamed the Vale Bar in honour of Bar Steward Vic Vale, who died during the year.

**1977**    The Students' Union Social Centre is opened, which soon becomes known as the 'Elephant House' due to its unusual design.

**1978**    Lord Todd, Nobel Laureate in Chemistry, is appointed the second Visitor to the Polytechnic.

The Polytechnic takes possession of Balls Park, which offers additional space for the teaching of Business Studies and Social Sciences.

**1979**    Alan McCall is awarded the first British CNAA-approved PhD in Astronomy.

**1980**    A free inter-site bus is introduced to connect Balls Park and Hatfield. Fares are introduced in September of this year.

**1981**    Hatfield Polytechnic is the first to introduce short courses in Genetic Engineering.

**1982**    Dr John Illston PhD DSc (Eng) CEng FICE is appointed Director of the Polytechnic. He first joined the Polytechnic in 1977 as Director of Studies, Civil Engineering.

**1984**    The Sports Hall on the Hatfield site is opened.

Birklands Mansion is closed and the Management Centre relocates to Balls Park.

Bayfordbury Mansion is handed back to the County Council. The College continues to maintain the Observatory and a Science Block on the site.

**1987**    Professor Neil Buxton, an economics historian and former Scottish hockey international, is appointed Director of the Polytechnic.

The first Professors at the Polytechnic are appointed: Dr Bob Barrett, Dean of the School of Engineering; Dr Mike Evans, Head of Division (Chemical Sciences) School of Natural Sciences; Dr Bill Jenkins, Associate Dean (Civil Engineering) School of Engineering; Dr Derek Nowell, Associate Dean (Chemical Sciences and Schemes) School of Natural Sciences.

The Polytechnic merges with the Hertfordshire College of Higher Education. The Wall Hall Mansion becomes the new home of the Faculty of Humanities and Education.

**1988**    In March, Hatfield Polytechnic receives accreditation from the CNAA, allowing it to initiate and periodically review its courses within the CNAA regulations. In July, the Polytechnic becomes one of only eight polytechnics accredited for research degrees.

The Polytechnic, in partnership with Writtle College, introduces the first BSc (Horticulture) course outside the university system.

Nursing as a discipline is introduced to the Polytechnic as academics from Stevenage College merge their programmes into the Health and Social Work Group.

**1989**   The Polytechnic is given corporate status, removing it from County Council control.

Private developers begin work on three buildings between the newly opened A1(M) and College Lane. They are leased by the Polytechnic and are named the Todd, Lindop and Mercer Buildings in honour of the Polytechnic's former Visitor, Director and Chair of Governors.

Gordon H. Wright, former County Technical Librarian, returns from his retirement in Canada as guest of honour to attend the naming of the building in his honour, which will house the School of Health and Human Sciences.

**1990**   Professor Maureen Lahiff is appointed the Professor of Nursing and Midwifery Studies, the first female Professor at the Polytechnic.

The Polytechnic wins a contract with the North-West Thames Regional Health Authority to provide degrees in Diagnostic Radiography and Radiotherapy.

**1991**   The Polytechnic forms an Associate College Network with Hertford Regional College, North Herts College, Oaklands College and West Herts College. The first courses are introduced in September 1992.

# University of Hertfordshire

**1992**   The Polytechnic becomes a university.

Sir Brian Corby is appointed the first Chancellor of the University.

Dr Mary Archer is appointed the first Visitor to the University.

The University merges with the St Albans-based Hertfordshire College of Art and Design.

The University is the first to run its own bus service, named Universitybus and set up to address the problems of poor public transport for students and staff travelling east to west across the county.

The University wins a contract with the North-West Thames Regional Health Authority to provide a BSc (Hons) degree in Physiotherapy.

The first Smith Kline Beecham Fund Chair in Pharmacology is awarded to Professor Mike Parsons.

The University's Organisational Development Centre collaborates with Bucharest Polytechnic to set up a Centre for the Improvement of Management Performance.

The Business School establishes a franchise with the Independent Science and Technology Institute in Athens to teach the BA degree course in Business Administration.

The University of Hertfordshire Press is launched. The first publication is *Our Heritage: The Story of the Campuses and Buildings of the University of Hertfordshire* (1992) by Tony Gardner.

**1993**   The Great Hall is renamed as The Prince Edward Hall in honour of the visit of HRH Prince Edward to commemorate the new status of the University of Hertfordshire.

Redland Aggregates donates three granite rocks to mark the entrance to the University.

Lt. Col. Jack Fielder, former Chair of the County Council Education Committee and a Governor of the University, formally opens the new training and conference centre named in his honour.

The Right Honourable Viscount Tonypandy, Patron of the College of Radiographers, opens the new Radiography Suite named in his honour.

The University merges with the Hertfordshire College of Health Care and Nursing Studies, and the Barnet College of Nursing and Midwifery. The first thirty students join the newly validated BSc (Hons) in Pre-Registration Nursing.

The University's School of Health and Human Sciences introduces courses in radiography and physiotherapy.

The University signs an Inter-University Co-operation Pact with the Hogeschool Gelderland in Arnhem, Holland, for closer links in Biosciences, Business, Social Work and Education.

The University is a founder partner with Hertfordshire Training and Enterprise Council, Hertfordshire Chambers of Commerce and Industry, and Hertfordshire County Council in the county's new single business help and advice centre in St Albans, called Business Link.

Glaxo and the School of Natural Sciences collaborate in developing the UK's first university-based centre into research alternatives to animal testing for new drugs.

Mitsubishi and the School of Engineering collaborate on offering training courses in a newly established Electronics and Electrical Engineering Centre.

The School of Humanities and Education launch the Historical Resources Project under Professor Nigel Goose with the aim of collecting and analysing data from the 1851 census in Hertfordshire.

**1994**
The University is named 'Top New University' in *The Times Good University Guide*.

The School of Art and Design moves from St Albans to the former British Aerospace Design Block, Hatfield.

Graduation ceremonies are moved to the Cathedral and Abbey Church of St Alban.

The University begins to develop links with China.

UH*Arts* is launched to raise the cultural profile of the University. The first event is a performance of works by Dvorak and Smetana by the Symphony Orchestra of Bohemia.

Pembroke Hall, prefabricated buildings brought in to provide temporary accommodation for students in 1982, is removed. Telford Court and Asquith House are opened.

Dr Richard Wiseman takes part in the country's largest ever live experiment to test which of three media – radio, television or print – is best at deceiving an audience.

**1995**
The Law Department takes over the former premises of the School of Art and Design.

The University is the first in the UK to offer a degree-level course for registered paramedics.

The University signs a formal agreement with the INTI College in Malaysia, allowing the College to provide accredited university courses.

The University signs a Memoranda of Co-operations with the Health Care Institute of Mikkeli in Finland, providing specialist courses in same-day care surgery nursing.

**1996**
Sir Ian MacLaurin is appointed Chancellor of the University.

The University's Centre for Research in Primary and Community Care (CRIPACC) is established with initial funding support from the Department of Health.

The first degree ceremony is held in Kuala Lumpur, the capital city of Malaysia, in response to the large number of students from Singapore and Malaysia.

**1997**   HRH Prince Philip, Duke of Edinburgh, returns to the University to unveil a statue of Sir Geoffrey de Havilland. The guests include Olivia de Havilland, the actress and cousin of Sir Geoffrey, and former employees of the de Havilland aircraft factory.

In September the four-storey Learning Resources Centre, designed by Architects Co. Partnership, is opened. *Building* magazine headlines the opening with 'One day, all libraries will be like this'.

Novelist and Hatfield resident Dame Barbara Cartland opens the Learning Resources Centre at Balls Park, Hertford.

The Science and Technology Research Centre is opened.

The Hatfield Philharmonic, conducted by Professor Howard Burrell, gives a gala performance of all five of Beethoven's piano concertos, with John Lill at the piano, to celebrate its new partnership with UH*Arts*.

Dr W.A.J. Chapman, founder Principal of Hatfield Technical College, dies in December.

**1998**   A two-storey regional art gallery opens, as part of the purpose-built Faculty of Art and Design.

The Rhea Martin Courtroom is formally opened. The interior of Hatfield Magistrates Court No. 1, donated by the Mid-Hertfordshire Magistrates and Hertfordshire Magistrates Court, is named in honour of the former lecturer in Law at the Polytechnic and Chair of the Hatfield Magistrates Bench.

The University introduces the first BSc (Hons) Paramedic Science degree in the country. This course is commissioned by the London Ambulance Service.

Students from the University's Midwifery degree course are featured in a fly-on-the-wall documentary for Channel 5 entitled *Baby School*.

The University competes in the first ever Formula Student competition held in the UK. The team wins the prize for the Best Presented Team.

The University's American football team, the Hertfordshire Hurricanes, wins the UK national championship.

**1999**   The Voyager Information Service is introduced.

The University's Psychology Department receives funding from the Higher Education Funding Council for England to establish a National Centre for Tactile Diagrams, which will help develop educational material to assist blind students, and diagrams and maps that can be read by the visually impaired.

Exemplas Ltd is established as part of the Business Link initiative to offer skills and business support to local companies.

Students Kane Ashton and Anthony Pritchard enter a robot called Behemoth in the BBC2 television programme *Robot Wars*.

**2000**   Work begins on the building of the new de Havilland campus at Hatfield on a site formerly occupied by British Aerospace.

The University receives the Investors in People Award.

The University introduces a BA/BA (Hons) degree course in Early Childhood Studies for those working as nursery nurses, classroom and childcare assistants. This is the first degree course of its kind.

The University establishes the Hertfordshire Intensive Care and Emergency Simulation Centre, a joint venture between the departments of Electronic Engineering and Nursing and Paramedic Science.

A racing car built by students under the guidance of Automotive Programme Tutor Dr Phil Green is featured on BBC2's *Top Gear*.

Visiting Research Fellow Andy Goldsworthy and thirty Art and Design students install giant snowballs at fourteen sites across London as part of the 'Snowballs in Summer' event.

The Minister for Sport, Kate Hoey, opens the new facilities for Sports Science teaching, consulting and research.

Astronomer Patrick Moore opens the newly upgraded Bayfordbury Observatory, which includes eight optical telescopes housed in domes. The rotunda building is named the Patrick Moore Building in his honour.

The University joins with the Associate College Network in forming the Hertfordshire Higher Education Consortium.

The *Times Higher Education Supplement* names Dr Richard Wiseman as the fourth most quoted scientist in the country, after Richard Dawkins, Raj Persaud and Lord Winstanley.

**2001**
The Key Centre, a multi-faith, multicultural centre, is opened by Lady Rosalind Runcie, widow of the late Robert Runcie, former Bishop of St Albans and Archbishop of Canterbury.

Studynet is introduced, giving greater access to information and support to both students and staff.

The Business Partnership Office is opened as a 'one-stop' shop for the business and commercial community.

Student Tim Edwards, studying software systems for arts and media, wins a national television competition. His animated film, *The Vortex*, is shown on Channel 4.

The University introduces the first UK Internet-based Master of Science degree: MSc Manufacturing Management.

**2002**
The University wins the contract to deliver radiography and radiotherapy courses for the Thames Valley Strategic Health Authority, making it the largest radiography provider in the UK.

The College Lane campus Learning Resources Centre is awarded both the SCONUL Design Award for 2002 and the RIBAS East Spirit of Ingenuity Award 2002 for its pioneering design.

The de Havilland Sports and Social Club is formally opened.

Dr Richard Wiseman publishes the results of the search for the world's funniest joke.

**2003**
Professor Neil Buxton retires and Professor Tim Wilson is appointed Vice-Chancellor of the University in his place.

HRH Prince Philip, Duke of Edinburgh, returns again to open the new £120 million de Havilland campus. The sites at Wall Hall, Aldenham and Balls Park, Hertford, are closed and students studying Education, Humanities and Business Studies transfer to the new campus.

The £15 million Hertfordshire Sports Village complex opens on the de Havilland site.

The £500,000 Automotive Engineering Centre, on the College Lane campus, is opened.

A joint project led by Professor Tim Hitchcock (of the University's History Department) and Dr Robert Shoemaker (University of Sheffield) sees the publication online of the Proceedings of the Central Criminal Court (Old Bailey) 1674–1834. The website wins two Cybrarian awards for ease of navigability and appeal to a wider audience.

**2004**
The University receives the Queen's Award for Enterprise in International Trade.

Collaboration with the China University Training Center for Science-Technology (CUTC) in Beijing and Fuzhou University in Fujian Province sees the establishment of the new Fuzhou University Hertfordshire College (FUHC).

On the College Lane campus, a £4.5 million Innovation Centre offering hi-tech office space for spin-out and start-up companies is opened by Alan Johnson MP, Minister for Lifelong Learning. The intention is to facilitate the development of excellence in academia, industry and business.

Seven Paralympic athletes train at the Hertfordshire Sports Village in the build-up to the Athens Olympics; they bring back seven medals between them, including a bronze medal in swimming for Hatfield Swimming Club member Jody Cundy.

**2005**    Lord Salisbury becomes Chancellor of the University upon the retirement of Lord MacLaurin.

The Bedfordshire and Hertfordshire Postgraduate Medical School and the School of Pharmacy are established.

The University introduces the first Postgraduate Diploma in Medical Care Practice to enable healthcare professionals to support General Practitioners.

The School of Law introduces a 'pro-bono' clinic for members of the public seeking legal advice.

Universitybus changes its name to Uno to reflect its service to the general public as well as staff and students.

A team from the University of Hertfordshire appears on the BBC television programme *University Challenge*. Team members Bob Chapman, Adrian Lewis, Avril Day Jones and Sarah Williamson reach the quarter finals.

**2006**    The School of Film, Music and Media is established.

The University BioPark is opened, offering laboratory, conference and office space for the region's bioscience and healthcare industries, and start-up companies.

The University introduces a three-year pre-registration BSc (Hons) Dietetics course with integrated work placement – the first of its kind in the East of England.

Saracens Rugby Club relocates its training and administrative facilities to the University.

Over 1,000 people attend the Grand Ballroom of the International Convention Centre in Shanghai for the University's first graduation ceremony in China. This is the largest graduation ceremony ever held overseas by a UK university.

**2007**    The MacLaurin Building is officially opened, named in honour of the University's former Chancellor, Lord MacLaurin of Knebworth.

The University enters the first ever hydrogen-powered Formula Student racing car in the UK Formula Student event.

**2008**    The University receives its first nomination for the *Times Higher Education Supplement* 'University of the Year' Award.

The University becomes the first of the post-1992 universities to be listed on the Shanghai Jiao Tong world research league table.

The School of Nursing and Midwifery introduces a shortened work-based Midwifery Programme, a first within Midwifery education.

The School of Creative Arts signs a partnership agreement with the British Higher School of Art and Design in Moscow.

Hertfordshire Sports Village Netball Team wins the Netball Super League Grand Final.

**2009**    The University is shortlisted for the *Times Higher Education Supplement* 'Entrepreneurial University of the Year' Award.

The College Lane Learning Resources Centre is named the Buxton Centre, in honour of former Vice-Chancellor, Professor Neil Buxton.

The new entertainments venue, The Forum, is opened.

The School of Creative Arts signs a partnership agreement with The One Academy in Kuala Lumpur.

Hertfordshire Sports Village is selected as one of seventeen training camp venues for athletes competing in the London Olympics in 2012.

The University enters the first wholly electric Formula Student car in the UK Formula Student event and wins the prize for lowest carbon production.

The UNESCO Chair in Information and Computer Ethics is established and held by Philosophy Professor Luciano Floridi. It is one of fourteen UNESCO Chairs in the UK.

**2010**   The University is named as the *Times Higher Education Supplement* 'Entrepreneurial University of the Year'.

Professor Tim Hitchcock (of the University's History Department) and Professor Robert Shoemaker (University of Sheffield) are awarded the Longman *History Today* Trustees Award for their work on the development of the digital projects, Old Bailey Proceedings Online, and London Lives.

The first Alumnus of the Year award is made to Sir Stuart Matthews, a former Aeronautical and Mechanical Engineering student who graduated in 1958.

**2011**   Professor Tim Wilson retires and Professor Quintin McKellar is appointed Vice-Chancellor of the University.

Professor Wilson receives a knighthood in the Queen's New Year Honours List.

Professor McKellar receives a CBE for services to science as Principal of the Royal Veterinary College.

The St Albans campus is closed and the Law Faculty moves into a purpose-built building on the de Havilland campus.

The Law Court building is awarded Hertfordshire's Building Futures Award for Most Sustainable Construction.

The University takes third place overall in the UK Formula Student event, including first place in the Business Presentation class, and second place in the Endurance Performance class.

The restored de Havilland Beacon, which guided pilots back to the pre-Second World War airfield, is installed at the entrance to the de Havilland campus.

The University opens its own Campus Pharmacy, run by staff from the School of Pharmacy.

**2012**   The University's Midwifery Team wins the Royal College of Midwives Annual Award for Excellence in Midwifery Education.

Dr Avice Hall receives an MBE for her services to higher education and to the community of St Albans.

Mrs Jo Connell DL, Pro-Chancellor and Chair of the Board of Governors at the University, receives an OBE for her services to older people through her work as a trustee of Help the Aged.

# References

Two invaluable sources for the college and early polytechnic years are the unpublished histories written by Peter Jeffreys and Peter Kingsford. Both made considerable use of County Council and College minutes, which made the task of completing this book much easier. Published sources casting light on the history of the institution include:

Argles, Michael [Librarian, A.S. Butler Library], 'The Technical College Library', *Vocational Aspects of Education*, 7 (1955), pp. 8–14.

Baxter, E.G., 'Technical College at Hatfield', *Architectural Review* (February 1953), pp. 8–87.

Chapman, W.A.J., 'Hatfield College of Technology', *Chemistry and Industry* (1962), pp. 472–83.

Gardner, Tony, *Our Heritage: The Story of the Campuses and Buildings of the University of Hertfordshire* (Hatfield, 1992).

Hall, J.A.P., Gordon Brand and Alan Davies (eds), *Computers in Education II* (Hatfield, 2009).

Lindop, Norman, 'Hatfield Polytechnic Today', in W. Roy Niblett, R. Freeman Butts and Brian Holmes (eds), *Universities Facing the Future* (London, 1972), pp. 281–97.

Parker, David, *John Newsom: A Hertfordshire Educationalist* (Hatfield, 2005).

Robinson, Brian, and Simon Tanner, 'Higher Education Digitisation Service: Access in the Future, Preserving the Past – the UK Perspective', *Bibliothek*, 23 (1999), pp. 66–9.

Tilley, Daphne, and Joan Beagle (eds), *Wall Hall: From Farmhouse to University* (Aldenham, 2003).

## Chapter 1: Our place in history

### Post-war Hertfordshire:

'County Rate up by 1s. 4d.', *Hertfordshire Mercury*, 7 March 1952; *200 Years of the Census* www.statistics.gov.uk/census2001/bicentenary/pdfs/hertfordshire.pdf. The population in 1931 = 401,206, 1951 = 609,775, 1971 = 924,632, 1991 = 975,829; '1,000th New House in Hatfield', *Hertfordshire Mercury*, 8 May 1953.

### Post-war Hertfordshire education plans:

'Details of Herts County Council's Budget', *Hertfordshire Mercury*, 7 March 1952; 'Local Schools' Accommodation Problems', *Hertfordshire Mercury*, 15 April 1952; 'Secondary Technical School Head Appointed', *Hertfordshire Mercury*, 23 January 1953; A. Jackson, 'The Politics of Architecture: English Architecture 1929–1951', *Journal of Architectural Historians*, 24, 1 (1965), pp. 97–107.

### History of the College Lane site:

HCRO D/EX824/E1 (1920) Sale Particulars of the Gape Settled Estate; F.M.L. Thompson, 'English Landed Society in the Twentieth Century. I Property: Collapse and Survival', *Transactions of the Royal Historical Society*, 5th series, 40 (1990), pp. 1–24; A.F. Cooper, *British Agricultural Policy 1912–36* (Manchester, 1989), p. 45; Gardner, *Our Heritage*.

**Alan S. Butler:**

'Obituary of Mr. Alan Butler', *The Times*, 27 May 1987; 'Flying at Public Schools', *The Times*, 26 November 1925.

**The building of the Technical College:**

'New Technical College', *The Times*, 16 December 1952; 'How it began: reminiscences of the foundation of Hatfield Technical College by the founder Principal, Dr. W.A.J. Chapman', Hatfield Polytechnic, *Annual Report 1976–77 and review of the twenty-five years 1952–1977*, pp.16–21; HCRO HCC21/29 'Signed Copies of Abstracts of Minutes of the Education Committee. Report of Finance and General Purposes Sub-Committee', 7 April 1952, p. 42, Item 109.

**Art at the Technical College:**

'New Technical College', *The Times*, 16 December 1952; 'Nicholson, Benjamin Lauder (1894–1982)', *Oxford Dictionary of National Biography*; J. Read, 'Butler, Reginald Cotterell (1913–1981)', *Oxford Dictionary of National Biography*; 'Sculpture Daubed With Paint' and 'Man Threw Model on Ground', *Hertfordshire Mercury*, 27 March 1953; 'Points from the Budget Debate', *Hertfordshire Mercury*, 7 March 1952; S. Maclure, 'Newsom, Sir John Hubert (1910–1971)', *Oxford Dictionary of National Biography*; Parker, *John Newsom*.

**The opening ceremony:**

'Speech made by His Royal Highness, the Duke of Edinburgh at the Opening Ceremony on 16 December 1952', Hatfield Technical College, *Annual Report 1952–53*, p. 2; 'Duke of Edinburgh Opens Technical College at Hatfield', *Hertfordshire Mercury*, 19 December 1952; 'How it began: reminiscences of the foundation of Hatfield Technical College by the founder Principal, Dr. W.A.J. Chapman', Hatfield Polytechnic, *Annual Report 1976–77 and review of the twenty-five years 1952–1977*, pp. 16–21.

**The Elizabethan Exhibition:**

'Elizabethan Exhibition', Hatfield Technical College, *Annual Report 1952–53*, p. 7; 'Glimpse of Life Four Centuries Ago', *Hertfordshire Mercury*, 19 June 1953.

**On Dr W.A.J. Chapman:**

'University's Founding Father Dies', *Welwyn and Hatfield Times*, 3 December 1997; 'Technical Book Sets Record', *Welwyn and Hatfield Advertiser*, 9 February 1973; 'Opening of the Conference', *Journal of the Institution of Production Engineers*, 26, 7 (1947), pp.148–9; 'Whitehall Delay Riles Town', *Welwyn and Hatfield Advertiser*, 17 January 1969; 'They Met At A Wedding', *Hertfordshire Mercury*, 21 September 1962; 'Desert Probe', *Welwyn and Hatfield Advertiser*, 6 June 1969.

**On Dr Peter Kingsford:**

www.brookmans.com/news/november08/Dr_Peter_Kingsford_hits_100.shtml; P. Kingsford, 'Paddington at War', *TSSA Journal*, 105, 1191 (May, 2008), p. 21; 'University Challenge', *The Times*, 17 April 2003; 'Account of a Life as a Lecturer in Social Studies December 1946–November 1952', Essex Record Office T/Z445 http://seax.essexcc.gov.uk/result_details.asp?DocID=315246; 'Why David Evans Felt Sick When the Monsignor Proposed a Toast', *Welwyn and Hatfield Times*, 31 December 1987; 'Staff Resignations and Retirements', Hatfield Polytechnic, *Annual Report 1973–74*, p. 43; www.brookmans.com for details of his books on local history, available for reading online; 'Headteacher's Newsletter', Chancellor's School, Brookmans Park, 11 June 2010 .

**The first departments:**

'Departmental Reports', Hatfield Technical College, *Annual Reports 1952–53 to 1959–60.*

**A.S. Butler Library:**

Michael Argles, 'The Technical College Library', *Vocational Aspects of Education*, 7 (1955), pp. 8–14; 'The A.S. Butler Library', Hatfield Technical College, *Annual Report 1952–53*, p. 14; 'The A.S. Butler Library', Hatfield Technical College, *Annual Report 1955–56*, p. 11; 'Technical Library and Information Service and the A.S. Butler Library', Hatfield Technical College, *Annual Report 1959–60*, p. 19.

**Links with industry:**

'The de Havilland Aircraft Company', *The Times,* 30 May 1953; 'Relationship with Industry' and 'Social and Professional Studies Department', Hatfield Technical College, *Annual Report 1952–53*, pp. 6, 11; 'Table III. Day Release Students Industrial Distribution', Hatfield Technical College, *Annual Report 1952–53*, p. 15.

**Hatfield in the 1960s:**

T. Rook, *A History of Hertfordshire*, 2nd ed. (Chichester, 1997), p. 132; 'Bold £1m. plan for Hatfield town centre', *Welwyn and Hatfield Advertiser*, 9 March 1962; 'Queensway House – the signpost to Hatfield', *Welwyn and Hatfield Advertiser*, 21 September 1961; 'St. John's Church, Hatfield', *Welwyn and Hatfield Advertiser*, 9 March 1962; 'To-Day's Arrangements', *The Times*, 14 June 1958; 'Swim pool "foolishness"', *Welwyn and Hatfield Advertiser*, 11 January 1961; 'Rates and obligations', Letter from Heather Conway of St. Albans, *Welwyn and Hatfield Advertiser*, 11 January 1963; 'Hatfield housing "ugly, drab, sordid"', Letter from Mrs. Hugh McCorquodale, *Welwyn and Hatfield Advertiser*, 3 March 1961; 'Hatfield's Ugly Housing', Letters from Rev. D. Farnborough and F.H. Bradbeer of Elm Drive, Oxlease, Hatfield, *Welwyn and Hatfield Advertiser*, 10 March and 24 March 1961; Companies advertising for staff in the 'Situations Vacant', *Welwyn and Hatfield Advertiser*, 24 January 1969; 'Hatfield could become a ghost town – union man', *Welwyn and Hatfield Advertiser*, 29 September 1961; 'New name for de Havilland – now a division', *Welwyn and Hatfield Advertiser*, 21 June 1963.

# Chapter 2: Coming together

**Hatfield College of Technology:**

Departmental Reports, Hatfield College of Technology, *Annual Reports 1959–60 to 1968–69*; Norman Lindop, 'Hatfield Polytechnic Today', in W. Roy Niblett, R. Freeman Butts and Brian Holmes (eds), *Universities Facing the Future* (London, 1972), pp. 281–97.

**Proposed University:**

'Principal's Report', Hatfield College of Technology, *Annual Report 1960–61*, p. 6; 'Noisy Scenes at Stevenage Public Inquiry', *The Times*, 20 October 1960; 'University may be built at St. Albans', *Herts Advertiser*, 10 April 1964; 'University proposal causing concern', *Herts Advertiser*, 17 April 1964; 'Criticism of St. Albans as site of university', *Herts Advertiser*, 7 May 1965; 'University – no decision yet says Minister', *Herts Advertiser*, 14 May 1965. [Shirley Williams was Labour MP for Hitchin 1964–74, and Hertford and Stevenage 1974–79. She was awarded an honorary doctorate by the University of Hertfordshire in 2006.]; 'University plan turned down by Minister', *Herts Advertiser*, 9 July 1965; 'Principal's Report', Hatfield College of Technology, *Annual Report 1964–65*, p. 2; 'Department of Industrial Engineering', Hatfield College of Technology, *Annual Report 1964–65*, p. 9.

**Towards Polytechnic status:**

'Latest Appointments', *The Times*, 3 February 1966; 'Principal's Report', Hatfield College of Technology, *Annual Report 1962–63*, p. 6; *Annual Report 1964–65*; *Annual Report 1965–66*, p. 2; *Annual Report 1966–67*, pp. 5, 9, 13; *Annual Report 1967–68*, pp. 4, 15; 'Department of Electrical Engineering', Hatfield College of Technology, *Annual Report 196–62*, p. 15; 'Department of Humanities', Hatfield College of Technology, *Annual Report 1967–68*, p. 21; 'Poly will turn to face town', *Welwyn and Hatfield Advertiser*, 20 March 1970.

**On Bayfordbury:**

Gardner, *Our Heritage*; G. Robinson, *Barracuda Guide to County History: Hertfordshire* (Chesham, 1978); H. Prince, *Parks in Hertfordshire since 1500* (Hatfield, 2008), pp. 190–92.

**Hatfield Polytechnic:**

J. Pratt, *The Polytechnic Experiment: 1965–1992* (Buckingham, 1997); 'Polytechnic Extensions', *Welwyn and Hatfield Advertiser*, 22 January 1971; 'Halls of Residence', Hatfield Polytechnic, *Annual Report 1971–72*, p. 17, and *Annual Report 1974–75*, p. 76; 'New Poly library could become a prototype', *Welwyn and Hatfield Advertiser*, 30 April 1971; 'Building Development Programme', Hatfield Polytechnic, *Annual Report 1971–72*, p. 14, and *Annual Report 1972–73*, p. 18; 'New Year Honours – Poly chief is knighted', *Hatfield and Welwyn Advertiser*, 5 January 1973; Hatfield Polytechnic, *Annual Report 1973–74*, p. 6; Norman Jackson and Patricia Gregg, 'Is the modularisation of courses a stepping stone or a stumbling block?', *Times Higher Education*, 29 September 1995; 'Director's Report', Hatfield Polytechnic, *Annual Report 1969–70* and *1985–86*; 'More Academic Freedom for Polytechnics Urged', *The Times*, 25 April 1985; 'New era opens as the poly goes private', *Welwyn and Hatfield Times*, 5 April 1989.

**Birklands, St Albans:**

Gardner, *Our Heritage*; 'Invitations – Parkins and Gotto', *The Times*, 4 January 1883; 'St. Albans – New Barnes Estate', *Herts Advertiser and St Albans Times*, 26 June 1886.

**Wall Hall, Aldenham:**

Gardner, *Our Heritage*; K. Harwood, 'Some Hertfordshire Nabobs' in A. Rowe (ed.), *Hertfordshire Garden History: A Miscellany* (Hatfield, 2007), pp. 4–77; 'New plans "could destroy the Poly"', *Welwyn Times and Hatfield Advertiser*, 10 December 1987.

**Ball's Park, Hertford:**

Gardner, *Our Heritage*; 'Students occupy College', *Welwyn Times and Hatfield Advertiser*, 25 February 1977; 'Students' demo disrupts Poly', *Welwyn Times and Hatfield Advertiser*, 11 March 1977; H. Prince, *Parks in Hertfordshire since 1500* (Hatfield, 2008), p. 41; F.M.L. Thompson, 'Townshend, John Villiers Stuart, fifth Marquess Townshend (1831–1899)', *Oxford Dictionary of National Biography*; 'An Ex-Lord Mayor London. Death of Sir George Faudel-Phillips', *The Times*, 29 December 1922; 'A City Alderman in "Darkest Hertford"', article by 'Ishmaelite', City Press, reprinted in *Hertford Mercury*, 24 January 1891; 'Hertford – All Saints Infant School', *Hertford Mercury*, 3 January 1891; 'New Year's Treat to the Workhouse Inmates', *Hertford Mercury*, 10 January 1891; 'Hertford Penny Dinners', *Hertford Mercury*, 24 January 1891.

**On Hatfield in 1992:**

'End of an Era-plane!', *Welwyn and Hatfield Times*, 29 January 1992; 'BAe workers' desperate bid to delay factory closure', *Welwyn and Hatfield Times*, 30 September 1992; 'BAe's office shocker', *Welwyn and Hatfield Times*, 18 March 1992; 'More jobs gloom as firm sheds 30', *Welwyn and Hatfield Times*, 5 February 1992; 'Now we are one', *Welwyn and Hatfield Times*, 9 September 1992; 'UCI The Galleria', *Welwyn and Hatfield Times*, 8 July 1992; 'Classified Advertisements', *Welwyn Hatfield Times*, 6 January 1992; 'Students are facing increasing poverty', *Welwyn and Hatfield Times*, 19 February 1992.

**Naming the new University:**

'Name upset delays Poly bid for university status', *Welwyn and Hatfield Times*, 18 March 1992; 'Charles Meynard's Times Diary – A New Chapter', *Welwyn and Hatfield Times*, 24 June 1992; 'Painful decision over the University's name', Letter from Professor Neil Buxton, *Welwyn and Hatfield Times*, 22 July 1992.

**Marking the new University of Hertfordshire:**

'Ode to a New University', *Horizon. News of the University of Hertfordshire*, 57 (1992), p. 2; 'Cash boost puts town on map as major nurse training centre', *Welwyn and Hatfield Times*, 13 October 1993; 'Artistic vision for the future', *Welwyn and Hatfield Times*, 2 September 1992; 'The Art of Moving', *The Insider* (November 1994), p. 1; University of Hertfordshire, *Annual Review 1994–95*, p. 34.

**The de Havilland campus:**

'Moving on?', *Horizon. News of the University of Hertfordshire*, 1 (1998), p. 1; Owen Davies (ed.), *The de Havilland Legacy: Hatfield Aerodrome Remembered* (Hatfield, 2010), p. viii; 'A campus for the 21st century', *Horizon. News of the University of Hertfordshire*, Special Edition Issue 42 (2003), p. 1; 'de Havilland', *Horizon. News of the University of Hertfordshire*, 26 (2001), p. 2; 'de Havilland Sports and Social Club Opens', *Horizon. News of the University of Hertfordshire*, 32 (2002), p. 1; 'The millennium campus is envisaged', *Horizon. News of the University of Hertfordshire*, 15 (2000), p. 1; 'New campus, on time and on budget', *Horizon. News of the University of Hertfordshire*, 41 (2003), p. 1; University of Hertfordshire, *Annual Review* 2002–03, p. 8.

# Chapter 3: Building success

**Information on all departments and schools over the years:**

Hatfield Technical College, *Annual Reports 1952–53* to *1959–60*.

Hatfield College of Technology, *Annual Reports 1960–61* to *1967–68*.

Hatfield Polytechnic, *Annual* Reports *1968–69* to *1990–91*.

University of Hertfordshire, *Annual Review 1991–92* to date.

**Further information:**

'Losing money is a "drag", says Marcus', *Welwyn and Hatfield Times*, 20 May 1992; 'Star Turn: Hut and Super Hut' and 'Formula team races on', *Horizon. News of the University of Hertfordshire,* 1 (1998), pp. 1, 4; 'The sky's the limit for vintage jet', *Horizon. News of the University of Hertfordshire*, 5 (1999), p. 1; 'Giant "brain" will think for schools', *Welwyn and Hatfield Advertiser*, 2 January 1970; 'Rocket girl's a star guest', *Welwyn and Hatfield Times*, 16 September 1992; 'Now, sky's the limit at university', *Welwyn and Hatfield Times*, 21 October 1992; obituary for John Hall published in *The Times*, 8 October 2008, compiled and later revised by Gordon Brand, Gabriel Newfield, with the assistance of Peter Lines; 'Inventors with a handy handle angle', *Welwyn Times and Hatfield Advertiser*, 19 April 1989; Ranjit K. Arora, *Race and Ethnicity in Education* (Aldershot, 2005), p. 113; 'New Poly library could become a prototype', *Welwyn and Hatfield Advertiser*, 30 April 1971; 'Novelist is first official Visitor', *Welwyn and Hatfield Advertiser*, 7 April 1972; 'New mace will grace graduation ceremony', *Welwyn and Hatfield Times*, 19 November 1997; 'All rise for new court', *Horizon. News of the University of Hertfordshire,* 1 (1998), p. 4; 'Radiography Suite is Launched', *Horizon. News of the University of Hertfordshire*, 63 (1993), p. 1; 'Medics move up', *Horizon. News of the University of Hertfordshire,* 4 (1999), p. 1; 'Research points finger at hospital hygiene', *Welwyn and Hatfield Times,* 28 December 2000; 'Industry–university collaboration leads to new course', *The Insider* (March 1996), p. 5; 'Degree course scheme for budding opera stars', *Welwyn and Hatfield Times*, 30 December 1992.

**International connections:**

Annual Departmental Reports; 'Overseas News' and 'PM opens centre in Romania', *Horizon. News of the University of Hertfordshire*, 57 (1992), pp. 2, 3; 'Poly hosts Russians', *Welwyn and Hatfield Times*, 8 April 1992; 'Poly expert called in to identify war dead', *Welwyn and Hatfield Times*, 27 May 1992; 'Varsity Success', *Welwyn and Hatfield Times*, 8 July 1992; 'University forges new friends', *Horizon. News of the University of Hertfordshire*, 60 (1993), p. 3; 'Nursing franchise in Finland', *The Insider* (December 1995), p. 2; 'INSET in Turkey', *The Insider* (March 1996), p. 2; 'Malaysian franchise agreed', *The Insider* (June 1995), p. 2; 'Anglo-Sino University College Announced', *Horizon. News of the University of Hertfordshire*, 47 (2004); 'University to open new China Campus', *Welwyn and Hatfield Times*, 14 July 2004.

**Research:**

Annual Departmental Reports; P. Kingsford, *History of the University* (n.d., typed manuscript held by the University of Hertfordshire), Chapter 3, pp. 17–18; 'Boffins in action to test those Pakistan swingers', *Welwyn and Hatfield Times*, 19 August 1992; 'Former Polytechnic weighs mixed blessing', *The Independent*, 18 December 1992.

# Chapter 4: Working with communities

**On the growth of the New Town of Hatfield:**

'Redevelopment stalemate causes concern', *Welwyn and Hatfield Advertiser*, 3 January 1969; 'Superstore – and another forecast', *Welwyn and Hatfield Advertiser*, 27 February 1970; 'Planners give go-ahead to tunnel road', *Welwyn and Hatfield Times*, 23 March 1979; 'Why a motorway could bring the quiet life', *Welwyn and Hatfield Times*, 18 January 1980; 'Upstairs, downstairs!', *Welwyn and Hatfield Times*, 6 March 1981; 'A1 Eyesore flats are coming down', *Welwyn and Hatfield Times*, 12 February 1982; 'Student flats hit by flood', *Welwyn and Hatfield Times*, 12 January 1979; www.hatfield-herts.co.uk/history. html; 'Council decides on £¼ million centre', *Welwyn and Hatfield Advertiser*, 3 March 1972; 'South Hatfield campaign for buses', *Welwyn and Hatfield Advertiser*, 7 March 1969; 'Cinema Petition', *Welwyn and Hatfield Advertiser*, 7 January 1972; 'Churches' investigation at Hatfield', *Welwyn and Hatfield Advertiser*, 27 June 1969; 'College clamp-down to beat vandalism', *Welwyn and Hatfield Advertiser*, 7 April 1972; 'Plea for closer college links', *Welwyn and Hatfield Advertiser*, 28 April 1972; '"Don't fence us in" say angry residents', *Welwyn Times and Hatfield Advertiser*, 25 March 1977.

**Community shows**:

'Record Rag After Ban on Pranks', *Hatfield and Welwyn Advertiser*, 23 February 1973; 'Rag-time band out to make a new record', *Hatfield and Welwyn Advertiser*, 30 January 1976; 'Rag to riches plan for charity', *Welwyn Times and Hatfield Advertiser*, 8 February 1980; 'Personal Services Unit', Hatfield Polytechnic, *Annual Report 1980–81*, p. 44 for account of the £500 raised for the third annual Christmas party for local pensioners; 'Those Happy Days are here again', *Welwyn and Hatfield Times,* 24 December 1987, for account of OAP's Christmas Party; 'Students Union', Hatfield Polytechnic, *Annual Report 1971–72*, p. 20; 'Fighting stops the dancing at Poly Rag Ball', *Welwyn Times and Hatfield Advertiser*, 4 March 1977.

**Community involvement:**

http://extragalactic.info/Bayfordbury/main.php; 'School of Natural Sciences', Hatfield Polytechnic, *Annual Report 1975–76*, p. 33; 'The Observatory', Hatfield Polytechnic, *Annual Report 1982–83, 1983–84, 1985–86*; 'Cultural Activities', Hatfield Polytechnic, *Annual Report 1970–71* to *1985–86*; 'Drama', Hatfield Polytechnic, *Annual Report 1977–78*, p. 42; 'Making a drama out of a crisis', *Welwyn and Hatfield Times*, 10 December 1987; 'Would-be soccer stars helped by UH students', *Welwyn and Hatfield Times*, 4 October 2000; 'A campus for the 21st century', *Horizon. News of the University of Hertfordshire*, 42 (2003), pp. 1–2; University of Hertfordshire, *Annual Review 1998–99*; 'Poly hosts arts festival', *Welwyn and Hatfield Times*, 17 June 1992; University of Hertfordshire, *Annual Review 1994–95*, p. 38; 'Exhibition is Master Stroke', *Horizon. News of the University of Hertfordshire*, 2 (1998), p. 1; 'Artistic Journey', *Welwyn and Hatfield Times,* 10 January 2001; www.herts.ac.uk/about-us/arts-and-galleries/home.cfm.

**Working with business:**

'Traders Can Cope', *Hatfield and Potters Bar Gazette*, 8 July 1955; 'Hatfield Trades Fair', *Hatfield and Potters Bar Gazette*, 8 July 1955; 'Director's Report', Hatfield Polytechnic, *Annual Report 1971–72, 1979–80, 1984–85*, pp. 5, 3, 7; 'Department of Computer Science', Hatfield Polytechnic, *Annual Report 1968–69*, p. 10; 'Centre for Management Studies', Hatfield Polytechnic, *Annual Report 1975–76, 1977–78*, pp. 74, 37; 'School of Information Sciences', Hatfield Polytechnic, *Annual Report 1979–80, 1983–84* pp. 26, 24; 'Department of Mechanical and Aeronautical Engineering', Hatfield Polytechnic,

*Annual Report 1969–70*, p. 17; 'School of Humanities', Hatfield Polytechnic, *Annual Report 1983–84*, p. 22; 'Your Own Business – Get into a Poly Team', *The Times*, 25 October 1985; 'A Founding Partner in Business Link', University of Hertfordshire, *Annual Report 1994–95*, p. 18; 'UH supports 3,600 jobs', *The Insider* (March 1996), p. 1.

### Working with the region's schools:

'Principal's Report', Hatfield College of Technology, *Annual Report 1961–62*, p. 9; 'Department of Mathematics', Hatfield College of Technology, *Annual Report 1963–64, 1957–68*, pp. 20, 30; 'School of Information Sciences', Hatfield Polytechnic, *Annual Report 1975–76*, p. 32; 'School of Natural Sciences', Hatfield Polytechnic, *Annual Report 1975–76, 1983–84*, pp. 30, 28; 'Varsity gets a top award', *Welwyn and Hatfield Times*, 10 February 1993; 'Science is Fun – That's a Fact!', *The Insider* (May 1995), pp. 4–5; 'Telescope's star turn at schools', *Welwyn and Hatfield Times*, 10 September 1997; 'Pasta joke for students', *Welwyn and Hatfield Times*, 22 October 1997; 'Gawain's Triumph', *Horizon. News of the University of Hertfordshire*, 31 (2002), p. 3; University of Hertfordshire, *Annual Review 2002–03*, p. 32.

### Widening access:

'Director's Report', Hatfield Polytechnic, *Annual Report 1971–72, 1976–77, 1981–82, 1982–83*, pp. 12, 10, 38, 36; 'School of Humanities', Hatfield Polytechnic, *Annual Report 1978–79*, p. 20; 'Associate Students', Hatfield Polytechnic, *Annual Report 1975–76*, pp. 20–21; 'Combined Studies', Hatfield Polytechnic, *Annual Report 1980–81*, p. 41; 'Continuing Education', Hatfield Polytechnic, *Annual Report 1981–82*, p. 38; 'University of Hertfordshire', *Welwyn and Hatfield Times*, 10 January 2001; 'Professional Updating for Women', *Welwyn and Hatfield Times*, 5 May 1993 and 30 September 1992; 'Learning for the Locals', *Horizon. News of the University of Hertfordshire*, 18 (2000), p. 2; HL Deb 07 March 1984, vol 449 cc274–308 http://hansard.millbanksystems.com/lords/1984/mar/07/barriers-to-women-at-work-and-at-home#S5LV0449P0_19840307_ HOL_148; 'Stay on course', *Welwyn and Hatfield Times*, 12 February 1992; 'Career mums', *Hatfield and Welwyn Advertiser*, 2 February 1973; 'News from the University of Hertfordshire – Course puts women into business', *Welwyn and Hatfield Times*, 9 February 2000; 'University joins campaign to attract nurses', *Welwyn and Hatfield Times*, 29 March 2000; Ruth Michaels, 'A Custom Built Degree for Mature Students', *Studies in Higher Education*, 4, 1 (1979), pp.103–11.

### Examples of media appearances:

University of Hertfordshire, *Annual Review* 1998–99; 'University making the headlines – Students do battle for TV honours', *Welwyn and Hatfield Times*, 5 January 2000; 'BBC show prompts floods of calls', *Horizon. News of the University of Hertfordshire*, 61 (1993), p. 2; 'Blood Flow Research on Tomorrow's World', *Horizon. News of the University of Hertfordshire*, 58 (1993), p. 1; 'Seeking an answer that doesn't stare you in the face', *Horizon. News of the University of Hertfordshire*, 69 (1994), p. 4; 'Experiment for the people', *Horizon. News of the University of Hertfordshire*, 7 (1999), p. 2; 'Seen any ghosts lately?', *Welwyn Times and Hatfield Advertiser*, 28 January 1977; http://www.rockets.herts.ac.uk/index.html.

### On the buses:

'Transport Problem', *Hertfordshire Mercury*, 21 August 1953; 'Access to College', Hatfield Technical College, *Annual Report 1953–54*, p. 7; HCRO HCC21/29 'Signed Copies of Abstracts of Minutes of the Education Committee. Report of Further Education Sub-Committee', 9 November 1953, p. 31, Item 64; 'Poly's bus link stays', *Welwyn and Hatfield Times*, 13 March 1981; 'University*bus* goes public', *Horizon. News of the University of Hertfordshire*, 59 (1992), p. 1; *Horizon. News of the University of Hertfordshire*, 51 (2005), p. 1.

# Chapter 5: Student life and learning

'Principal's Report', Hatfield College of Technology, *Annual Report 1967–68*, p. 16; *Vocational Aspect* (Autumn 1954), p. 135.

### Student accommodation:

'Principal's Report', Hatfield College of Technology, *Annual Report 1964–65,1966–67*, pp. 6, 5; *Welwyn and Hatfield Times*, 4 January 1980; 'Desperate Poly bids to solve its digs crisis', *Welwyn and Hatfield Times*, 26 February 1982; 'Director's Report', Hatfield Polytechnic, *Annual Report 1982–83*, p. 4; 'Student Accommodation', Hatfield Polytechnic, *Annual Report 1985–86*, p. 40.

### On the gender balance:

'Student Numbers', Hatfield Polytechnic, *Annual Report 1970–71*; 'Director's Report', Hatfield Polytechnic, *Annual Report 1985–86*, p. 5; 'Library and Information Services', Hatfield Polytechnic, *Annual Report 1969–70*, p. 21; 'School of Engineering', Hatfield Polytechnic, *Annual Report 1979–80, 1980–81, 1981–82,* pp. 22, 19, 19; 'The bare facts spark a row' and 'No nudes is bad news, says Rag Mag', *Welwyn Times and Hatfield Advertiser*, 8 February 1974; 'A rag mag rumpus', *Welwyn Times and Hatfield Advertiser*, 27 January 1978; 'Student Accommodation', Hatfield Polytechnic, *Annual Report 1971–72*, p. 17; 'Halls of Residence', Hatfield Polytechnic, *Annual Report 1972–73*, p. 22.

### The Students' Union:

N. Thomas, 'Challenging Myths of the 1960s: The Case of Student Protest in Britain', *Twentieth Century British History*, 13, 3 (2002), pp. 277–97; 'Hatfield College students boycott lectures', *Welwyn and Hatfield Advertiser*, 11 October 1968; 'Poly students may get seat on "the board"', *Welwyn and Hatfield Advertiser*, 18 October 1968; 'Principal's Report', Hatfield College of Technology, *Annual Report 1967–68*, p. 3; 'Students' Union', Hatfield Polytechnic, *Annual Report 1974–75, 1978–79, 1980–81*, pp. 21, 16, 18; 'Director's Report', Hatfield Polytechnic, *Annual Report 1981–82*, p. 3; *Universe*, 16 June 1994.

### Student clubs and societies:

'Appreciation', Hatfield Technical College, *Annual Report 1954–55*, p. 7; 'The Students' Union', Hatfield Technical College, *Annual Report 1953–54* to *1958–59*; 'Physical Education', Hatfield Polytechnic, *Annual Report 1971–72*, p. 22.

### Student engineering projects:

'Aeronautical Engineering Department', Hatfield Technical College, *Annual Report 1957–58*, p. 8; 'Building a Turbi', *Flight*, 29 June 1956, p. 835; 'Air Race Disqualification Puts Civilian in Lead', *The Times*, 20 July 1959; Hatfield Technical College, *Annual Report 1958–59*, p. 6; 'Principal's Report' and 'Students' Union', Hatfield College of Technology, *Annual Report 1961–62*, pp. 11, 32; 'Six college students plan 1,000 mile go-kart trip', *Welwyn and Hatfield Advertiser*, 6 October 1961.

### Student stunts:

'Most-pushed pram in town', *Welwyn and Hatfield Advertiser*, 11 March 1960; 'Principal's Report', Hatfield College of Technology, *Annual Report 1961–62*, p. 6; 'They race 65miles to win 4½ gal. of beer', *Welwyn and Hatfield Advertiser*, 9 March 1962; 'Winners say: Now for the chariot hat trick', *Welwyn and Hatfield Advertiser*, 18 March 1966.

### Rag Week adventures:

'Ring Round the Moon', *Hertfordshire Mercury*, 1 May 1953; 'The Students' Union', Hatfield Technical College, *Annual Report 1953–54* to *1959–60*; 'What a Neck!', *Welwyn and Hatfield Advertiser*, 19 May 1961; 'World record is set up at Hatfield', *Welwyn and Hatfield Advertiser*, 25 March 1966; 'Students' Union', Hatfield College of Technology, *Annual Report 1965–66*, p. 39; 'Pretty Paula, 17, is chosen rag queen', *Welwyn and Hatfield Advertiser*, 24 May 1963; 'Rag raiding party kidnaps rival queen but gets no ransom', *Welwyn and Hatfield Advertiser*, 31 May 1963; 'College rag gets O.K. – and a warning', *Welwyn and Hatfield Advertiser*, 1 February 1963; 'Students' Union', Hatfield College of Technology, *Annual Report 1963–64*, p. 35; 'Students' Mock Bank Hold-Up', *The Times*, 22 April 1964; 'Audacious start to Rag Week', *Welwyn and Hatfield Advertiser*, 26 February 1971; 'Students' slogans anger 3 councils', *Welwyn and Hatfield Advertiser*, 4 February 1972; 'Firm comes to aid of students', *Welwyn and Hatfield* Advertiser, 18 February 1972; 'Bar up to student rag week romp', *Hatfield and Welwyn Advertiser*, 20 February 1976; 'Rag to Riches', *Welwyn Times and Hatfield Advertiser*, 2 March 1979; 'Hijackers stole trolley', *Welwyn and Hatfield Advertiser*, 5 February 1971; 'Bit of a drag – but everybody enjoyed themselves', *Welwyn and Hatfield Advertiser*, 29 January 1971; 'Oh boy! It's a girl –isn't it?', *Welwyn Times and Hatfield Advertiser*, 27 January 1978; 'Hijacked comet will be flying back soon', *Welwyn Times and Hatfield Advertiser*, 19 March 1971; 'Black march mob kidnap lecturers', *Welwyn Times and Hatfield Advertiser*, 27 March 1981; 'A stroll in the sun nets £200', *Welwyn and Hatfield Advertiser*, 14 March 1969; 'Pram pushers line up for the big race', *Welwyn Times and Hatfield Advertiser*, 19 February 1971; 'New records claimed for students', *Welwyn Times and Hatfield Advertiser*, 25 February 1972; 'Record Rag after ban on pranks', *Hatfield and Welwyn Advertiser*, 23 February 1973; 'Rag-time band out to make a new record', *Hatfield and Welwyn Advertiser*, 30 January 1976; 'Rag week makes silly progress', *Hatfield and Welwyn Advertiser*, 20 February 1976; 'Buy a slave for just 50p!', *Welwyn Times and Hatfield Advertiser*, 15 February 1980; 'Squaring up to pasta', *Welwyn Times and Hatfield Advertiser*, 22 February 1989.

### Crossing the Channel by bed:

'Sea-bed stunt was a winner – Rag week breaks all records', *Welwyn and Hatfield Advertiser*, 1 April 1966; 'Channel Crossing By Bed!' and 'Six boys and a girl set sail', *Welwyn and Hatfield Advertiser*, 11 March 1966; 'Hatfield water-babies made it – Six boys and a girl on the Seabed', *Welwyn and Hatfield Advertiser*, 18 March 1966; 'That bed is unsinkable', *Welwyn and Hatfield Advertiser*, 25 March 1966.

### Student protest:

'Students protest on overcrowding', *Welwyn and Hatfield Advertiser*, 6 February 1970; 'Telephone takeover by Poly students' and 'Switchboard pirates', *Hatfield and Welwyn Advertiser*, 8 March 1974; 'Students' Union', Hatfield Polytechnic, *Annual Report 1973–74*, p. 32; 'Thousand students in protest march', *Hatfield and Welwyn Advertiser*, 23 February 1976; 'Students' Union', Hatfield Polytechnic, *Annual Report 1981–82*, p. 15; 'Students' Union', Hatfield Polytechnic, *Annual Report 1981–82*, p. 15; 'Students' Union', Hatfield Polytechnic, *Annual Report 1985–86*, p. 13; 'New plans could destroy the Poly', *Welwyn Times and Hatfield Advertiser*, 10 December 1987; 'Poly song of protest', *Welwyn Times and Hatfield Advertiser*, 15 February 1989; 'Students' Union', Hatfield Polytechnic, *Annual Report 1984–85*, p. 18. For reference to rallies and demonstrations in support of the miners and anti-apartheid movements: 'Students' Union', Hatfield Polytechnic, *Annual Report 1985–86*, p. 14; 'Demonstrations, rallies and debates concerned with wider issues', 'Why David Evans felt sick when the Monsignor proposed a toast', *Welwyn Times and Hatfield Advertiser*, 31 December 1987; 'Student Ban on Team from South Africa', *The Times*, 8 December 1971; 'Review of 1974', *Hatfield and Welwyn Advertiser*, 3 January 1975; 'Students are facing increasing poverty', *Welwyn and Hatfield Times*, 19 February 1992.

**A global community:**

'Director's Report', Hatfield Polytechnic, *Annual Report 1978–79*, p. 11; 'Director's Report', Hatfield Polytechnic, *Annual Report 1979–80*, p. 7; 'School of Engineering', Hatfield Polytechnic, *Annual Report 1980–81*, p. 19; 'Overseas fees hit Poly', *Welwyn Times and Hatfield Advertiser*, 29 February 1980; 'Students' Union', Hatfield Polytechnic, *Annual Report 1979–80*, p. 20; 'Director's Report', Hatfield Polytechnic, *Annual Report 1985–86*, pp. 5, 10; 'Iran students sell up to stay at Poly', *Welwyn Times and Hatfield Advertiser*, 16 February 1979; 'Director's Report', Hatfield Polytechnic, *Annual Report 1982–83*, p. 40; 'Students to keep Babak at Poly', *Welwyn Times and Hatfield Advertiser*, 8 February 1980; 'Welcome news for Babak Kia', *Welwyn Times and Hatfield Advertiser*, 14 March 1980; 'Distance no object for reunion', *Welwyn and Hatfield Times*, 8 April 1992; 'Alan's shore a long way from home!', *Welwyn and Hatfield Times*, 29 April 1992.

# Index

## G

Gilbert Ash Ltd., building contractors 3

## H

Hatfield 1, 23–5, 45–6, 91–2, 178
> Hatfield Aerodrome Community Heritage Project 97–8
> relationship with students *see also* Students' Union: Rag Week 92–3, 134–5
> relationship with the institution 46–7, 52, 92, 96–8

Hatfield College of Technology xvi, 27–36, 44

Hatfield Philharmonic Orchestra and Chorus 94

Hatfield Polytechnic xvi, 32–8, 41, 43–7, 60, 81, 145
> Civil Emergency Management Centre 84

Hatfield Technical College xvi, 1–26, 120
> building of the college 3–10
> opening ceremony xvi, 1, 10–12

Hatfield Technical School 1–3, 60, 101, 127, 178, 181

Hepworth, Barbara 5, 8

Hertford Regional College 47, 167, 183

Hertfordshire College of Art and Design xvii, 47, 50–1, 53, 79, 111, 183

Hertfordshire College of Building 16

Hertfordshire College of Health Care and Nursing Studies xvii, 51, 77, 184

Hertfordshire College of Higher Education xvi, 39, 41, 74–5, 178, 182

Hertfordshire County Council xvi, 30, 41, 99–100, 178, 183–4
> councillors 14, 25, 33, 38, 181, 160–1, 163, 166, 183
> financing the institution xvi, 3, 9, 45, 57, 61, 117, 143, 178, 180,
> *see also* Ball's Park, Bayfordbury, Birklands, College Lane, Wall Hall

Hertfordshire Higher Education Consortium xvii, 186

Higher Education, the future of 147–51

Honorary awards 159–67

Horsfield, Dick 58

Hutton, Kenneth 181

## I

Industry, working with 12, 14, 16, 18, 29–30, 57 63–4, 66, 78, 128

International partnerships 73, 75, 83–5

## J

Jackson, Robert MP 142

Johnson, Alan MP 187

Joseph, Sir Keith MP 23, 25, 45, 141–2

## K

KASPAR 63

Kinnock, Neil MP 140

## L

Legislation and government reports
> Education Act 1944 1, 178, 181
> Education Reform Act 1988 45
> Further and Higher Education Act 1992 46, 147
> New Towns Act 1946 1, 178
> Robbins Report 1963 30–2
> Wilson Review of Higher Education 2011 151

Library and Information Services 21–2, 37, 80–4, 186
> HERTIS 113
> Higher Education Digitisation Service (HEDS) 115–16
> National Centre for Reprographic Documentation 82

## M

MacLaurin, Lord of Knebworth DL xvii, 52, 91, 157, 161, 184, 187

Mercer, T.G. 161, 183

Moore, Sir Patrick 65–6, 94, 163, 186

## N

Newsom, Sir John 8, 40, 111

Nicholson, Ben 5, 8

Nixon, W.E. 12

North Herts College 47, 106, 161, 183

North West Metropolitan Association for Management Development 67

# O

Oaklands College 47, 106, 167, 183
*Ode to a New University* 48–9
*Oracle, The see* Butler, Reg

# R

Research and consultancy 86–90, 98–100
    Adaptive Systems Research Group 63
    Automotive Engineering Centre 186
    Business Link 100, 184
    Centre for Astrophysics Research (CAR) 64
    Centre for Atmospheric and Instrumentation Research (CAIR) 64
    Centre for Research in Primary and Community Care (CRIPACC) 184
    Centre for Sustainable Communities 155
    Exemplas 100, 185
    Health and Human Sciences Research Institute (HHSRI) 90, 170
    Hertfordshire Intensive Care and Emergency Simulation Centre 186
    National Centre for Tactile Diagrams 69, 185
    Numerical Optimisation Centre 87
    Polyfield Services 99
    Science and Technology Research Institute (STRI) 90, 170
    Small Manufacturing Industries Development Association (SMIDA) 100
    Social Sciences Arts and Humanities Research Institute (SSAHRI) 90, 170
Research Assessment Exercise 89–90
Robinson, Rodney 58

# S

St Albans School of Art 50
Salisbury, 6th Marquess 98
Salisbury, 7th Marquess xiv, xvii, 158, 161, 187
Schofield, Julia MBE 101–2, 165, 182
Schools and children 58, 60–1, 96, 100–3, 181
Seear, Baroness 105
Sharman, Helen 65

Shipway, Frank 95
Shoemaker, Robert 111, 186, 188
Smith, Ralph Maynard 3
Snow, Lord C.P. *see also* Buildings: C.P. Snow Building xvi, 37, 56, 81–2, 160, 181
Sport *see also* Buildings: Hertfordshire Sports Village 96, 138–9, 182
    *Hertfordshire Hurricanes* 167, 185
Staff
    Appleton, Quentin 65
    Argles, Michael 21–2
    Bagley, David E. 81–2
    Barrett, Bob 182
    Bray, Bert 125
    Breese, D.I. 18
    Brown, Anna 121
    Burrell, Howard 79, 102, 111, 159, 185
    Burrows, W.G. 181
    Buxton, Neil *see also* Buildings: Learning Resources Centre xvi, 47, 162, 182, 186
        Polytechnic years 43, 117
        University years 46–7, 51, 76, 89
    Chapman, W.A.J. *see also* Student housing: Chapman Hall xvi, 13–14, 15, 22, 30, 32, 91, 98, 120, 140, 159, 178, 185
        Chapman Scholarship 14
        on the building and opening of the College 5, 10
        on the role of the College 12, 18–19, 27–8, 32–3, 66, 69
        on students 12, 17, 122, 127, 129–30, 132, 134
    Clark, Bryan 96
    Clark, Derek 84
    Cox, Mike 95, 159
    Crouch, George 125
    Dolling, Nellie 125
    Evans, Mike 182
    Fletcher, Ben 89
    Forster, Bill 113–14
    Gardner, Tony 113, 183
    Goldsworthy, Andy 186

# W